ICE *and* BONE

Tracking an Alaskan Serial Killer

MONTE FRANCIS

WILDBLUE
P R E S S

WildBluePress.com

ICE AND BONE published by:
WILDBLUE PRESS
1566 S. Pennsylvania St.
Denver, CO 80210

978-1-942266-39-6   Trade Paperback ISBN
978-1-942266-40-2   eBook ISBN

Cover Design/Interior Formatting by Elijah Toten
www.totencreative.com

CONTENTS

For the victims we know of, and those we do not.

John Michael Martin

Vera Hapoff

Annie Mann

Michelle Foster-Butler

Henry Ongtowasruk

Della Brown

John Doe

Mindy Schloss

INTRODUCTION

During the fall of 2014, while researching unsolved crimes, I came across a story in the *Anchorage Daily News* that piqued my interest. The article, dated September 28, 2000, had the headline: *"'THERE'S NOTHING WE'RE NOT DOING' — POLICE GIVE PRIORITY TO SOLVING SIX SLAYINGS."* The story recounted the killings of five Native Alaskan women and an African American woman who had been murdered within the span of sixteen months. There was no clear indication the slayings were linked, but fear was spreading among the residents of Anchorage that a serial killer was on the loose. The cases shared a number of similarities: most of the women were intoxicated at the time of their deaths and all of them were last seen alone and outside during early morning hours. However, the women had met their ends in different ways: three had been stabbed, one strangled, one drowned, and the sixth had her throat slit and her skull crushed by a rock.

Quoted in the article was a Native Alaskan activist named Desa Jacobsson, who had gone on a twenty-eight-day hunger strike to pressure federal authorities to investigate the cases, claiming that police were not taking the deaths seriously enough. Jacobsson, sixty-seven, intrigued me because she spoke to a larger systemic problem, namely, the victimization of Native Alaskan women and society's failure to protect them.

"If this was Chelsea Clinton this was happening to,

they'd be on it like white on rice," Jacobsson proclaimed to me over the phone, matter-of-factly. My call had taken her so off guard, she later told me, she initially couldn't speak.

"Are you still there?" I had asked, after several seconds of silence.

After a long pause, she said, "I didn't know it was going to affect me like this. Whoa."

Fourteen years had passed since the murders, and she said that my call, which came out of the blue, had caused all of her memories from that time to come rushing back.

"I thought everyone had forgotten," she told me. "Here I thought I was just going to retire, eat bonbons, and become a cougar," she told me during one of our many meetings that followed, making a joke about dating younger men, and letting out a hearty laugh. She then lowered her gaze, and a look of earnestness returned to her face. "But when you called, I realized, we have unfinished business."

In the months following the murders, Jacobsson had not only blamed the Anchorage police for failing to aggressively investigate the cases but also faulted the tribal leadership in Alaska for its apathy, saying as far as the six dead women were concerned, "The silence was deafening."

During our first conversation, Jacobsson was quick to point to crime statistics that showed Native women were far more likely to be sexually assaulted than white women in Alaska.

"We lead the nation in violence against women and children and sexual violence. And predators know the police here don't respond," she said.

According to figures compiled by the Justice Center at the University of Alaska Anchorage, just 18 percent of the rapes reported to the Anchorage police are prosecuted, a figure that is almost 20 percent below the national average.[1] It is a statistic that is all the more troubling given that Alaska has the highest number of rapes per capita of any U.S. state, and Native Alaskan women are more at risk than any other group. The Justice Department estimated in 2012 that one in three Native Alaskan women have been raped, and the reality is undoubtedly much more unsettling. At least one hundred of the 226 Native villages in Alaska don't have any kind of law enforcement—many of those same villages don't have road access or dependable phone service—making the reporting of such crimes impractical if not, impossible. The Alaska Federation of Natives has estimated the rate of sexual assault in many Alaskan villages to be twelve times the national average.

As for the larger cities such as Anchorage and Fairbanks, Jacobsson contended, a complacency on the part of public officials with regard to Native women leads to victim-blaming rather than pursuing the perpetrators. It's why, she conjectured, rapists and murderers have long been attracted to Alaska.

"I don't know what you know about predators, but these are the most practiced manipulators on earth. They know what they're doing, how they're doing it ... their radar is always on."

It was not the first time Anchorage had been gripped by fear a serial killer was lurking among its inhabitants. Robert Hansen, known as the "Butcher Baker," had kidnapped women and hunted them down in the Alaskan wilderness during a twelve-year period in the 1970s and 1980s. Prior to his death in 2014, he confessed to seventeen murders and

---

1 According to the UAA Justice Center, 18 percent of sexual assaults reported to the Anchorage Police Department from 2000 to 2003 were prosecuted, and 11 percent resulted in a conviction. As for the U.S., the National Violence Against Women Survey showed a prosecution rate of 37 percent and a conviction rate of 18 percent.

to raping at least thirty women. Chillingly, he lived among the residents of Anchorage, with his wife and two children, who, along with everyone else, were oblivious to his crimes.

That summer of 2000, however, no one knew who might perpetrate such butchery, and fifteen years later the mystery remained largely unexplained. At the writing of this account, three of the six murders remain unsolved and the other three cases are considered closed, each committed by a separate assailant.

When I reached the head of the Anchorage Police Department's Homicide Unit, Sergeant Slawomir Markiewicz said he could not share the files for the unsolved cases with me since they were still technically open. When I asked him if he believed if any of the unsolved cases from 1999-2000 were related, he engaged in a kind of meaningless doublespeak.

"I think I can safely say, there was no evidence to show that they were related," he told me. "And I think I can say vice versa ... that there was no evidence to show they were *not* related."

Suspicion often has swirled around a drug dealer named Joshua Wade, but there is little else to go on. Wade is serving a life sentence in connection with an unrelated murder and has confessed to others. As for the still-unsolved cases of the dead women, DNA evidence has not implicated Wade, and state prosecutors show little interest in pursuing new charges against a mass murderer already in custody, with no hope of release.

"In my personal evaluation, how many life sentences are you going to give a guy?" Assistant Attorney General John Novak said, as we sat in his office in downtown Anchorage. Novak told me he feels filing any new charges would be a misuse of state resources since Wade already would spend the rest of his life "in a cage."

"I think Joshua Wade is one of the inherently evil people that needs to be locked up for the rest of his life," Novak said. "And if ... did he kill others? Maybe. But it doesn't really matter to me."

It matters, however, to Desa Jacobsson and to the families of the victims. They continue to be incensed by what they perceive as a lack of motivation on the part of public officials to bring some closure to their wondering and grief. Jacobsson is equally troubled by what she described as a prevailing public sentiment that the women themselves were somehow complicit, or at least less sympathetic, because most of them were intoxicated at the time of their deaths.

"The message that was sent out, the victim blaming from the top down, from the police, to the Native leaders ... what it said to the perpetrators was that Native women are free game," she said. "That's the way it was then, and that's how it is now."

What has gone wrong in investigating and prosecuting these cases? Are authorities doing everything they can to bring relief to the victims' loved ones? Did Wade have anything to do with the three still-unsolved murders? This book was written in pursuit of those questions.

This is a true story. The quotes are taken from court transcripts, police interviews, secretly recorded police wires, and from dozens of interviews I personally conducted. There are instances where a quote is another person's recollection of what the speaker said. In those cases, if there was any disagreement about the statement, I have added footnotes to point this out.

I also feel it necessary, here, to say something about the killer portrayed in the following pages. I heard several times during the course of my reporting, both from law enforcement and from those close to Wade, that he would be thrilled to know he had been chosen as the subject of a book.

"He always wanted to be on CNN," one of Wade's confidants told me.

I have no interest in glorifying Joshua Wade, nor his evil deeds. Moreover, I do not consider him the true subject of this book. This narrative is about the havoc wreaked in the lives of victims, and those who loved them, all ordinary people going about their business, unsuspecting of the evil about to prematurely cut short, or to forever change the course of their personal histories. The edification of someone who spends twenty-three of a day's twenty-four hours alone in a prison cell, or whether he likes or dislikes the attention, is of little consequence to me.

Finally, the reader should know, that in the end, mysteries remain. Such is the stuff of true crime reporting; there are seldom satisfying resolutions. The story bears telling, however, if only so the victims, who can no longer speak for themselves, aren't forever lost to the night.

PART ONE: DELLA

ONE

Anchorage, Thursday, August 31, 2000

As Della Brown left the trailer park, the Northern Lights blazed across the sky in cosmic green streaks, and an inexplicable loneliness filled the air. The sun-filled Alaskan summer had, sadly, come to an end, and night soon would begin to intrude upon the landscape, descending upon the waters of Cook Inlet across the flat coastal lowland of the city, and east, to the white peaks of the Chugach Mountains. In Alaska, winter officially arrives in November, but it often snows in September. Before long, night would envelop the city, disorienting Anchorage's 260,000 inhabitants, forcing them to into a familiar but wholly unnatural quotidian existence. They would soon be drinking their coffee, going to work, dropping children off at bus stops, and shopping for groceries in a state of almost perpetual darkness.

The gathering of dilapidated mobile homes known as Idle Wheels Mobile Court was situated at the corner of two four-lane thoroughfares and the nearest liquor store was a half-mile away, on 36th Avenue. Della's recent DWI meant she couldn't risk driving, so she started walking north on Arctic Boulevard. She passed the very spot where she was pulled over by Anchorage police about a month earlier, just a few blocks from home. The taillights of her boyfriend's Jeep Cherokee were out, and when the officer came to the window, he said he could smell the alcohol on her breath even though she had a lit cigarette in her mouth. The officer wrote in his report that he noticed her "bloodshot, watery eyes" and when he asked her to step out of the vehicle, she faltered, stumbling onto the street. She told the officer she had consumed four or five Budweisers, but later, at the police station, she blew into a breathalyzer, which showed a .218 blood alcohol content, almost three times the legal limit.

Now, on her feet, she swayed only slightly. The alcohol and cocaine she had recently consumed should have numbed the humiliation of having her license taken away, but the high was just kicking in, and for a moment, she felt honest enough to accept the truth about her life. She glanced at her wrists, which bore the scars of her past desperation, and found herself at a pay phone, dialing her mother's number in Albuquerque.

"If you wouldn't have given me up ... I wouldn't be like this," she slurred to the woman on the other end of the line, not realizing the amount of guilt she was heaping upon her biological mother, nor how it would torture her for years to come. Daisy Piggott wasn't the mother she had grown up with, but her *real* mother, the one she had finally reconnected with in her late twenties, who gave her up when Della was an infant and Daisy was just eighteen, a victim of rape. Daisy was hoping to escape the shame from the violation she had suffered and to begin a new life in New Mexico, so she left her infant daughter behind, to be raised by her mother.

The white man Della knew as her father was, in reality, her adoptive step-grandfather. Along with his Anglo Saxon last name, Henry Brown had given Della a burden in life she struggled to bear: a secret that seemed forever lodged at the back of her throat, whose gnawing presence settled into her chest with such unease, she would find it difficult, as a grown woman, to allow her younger sister to be alone in the same room with him. Della finally had found the courage to tell Daisy why: she claimed that from the age of seven, she endured sexual abuse at the hands of the family's patriarch.[2]

How far back did this horror go? Della thought of the photo Daisy had shown her when they had reconnected, just four years earlier, the framed black and white image of an Inupiaq woman and a small child in the snow. The woman and toddler were in fur coats and both had the same blank expression.

"That little girl is my mother and your grandmother," Daisy had explained. Her people had come from the village of Shishmaref, a village of just 500 Inupiaq Eskimos that was rapidly eroding and disappearing into the sea. Della had heard about the effects of global warming on an Alaskan island off the Bering Strait and seen photos on the internet of weathered huts dangling off the sides of cliffs, about to topple into the water. This was where Daisy lived when her mother, Idella, had tuberculosis. Idella had a rib removed and spent the formative years of Daisy's childhood in a TB sanatorium. When Daisy was seven or eight, her mother returned home and married her first husband.

"He would beat her," Daisy had confessed. "We're not talking about just hitting and shoving. He would beat her until she was laying in her own blood."

Della glanced up and curtains of green light seemed to sway in the sky. She could see now, almost from outside her own body, how the pattern of abuse had repeated itself so precisely and unforgivingly in her life. When she met Rudy, she was sober and going to Alcoholics Anonymous, but now,

---

2 Three family members reported to me that Della Brown made these claims of sexual abuse against Henry Brown. Prosecutor Marcy McDannel also said in court, "There are several witnesses willing to testify that her father did, in fact, abuse her." At trial, defense attorney Jim McComas said Henry Brown, who died in 2006, denied the accusations. Charges were never filed. A close friend of Henry Brown's, Dwayne Anaruk, told me he was unaware of the allegations, saying, "I am surprised by that. That's not the Henry I knew."

they were both off the wagon and their alcohol-fueled fights were notorious in the neighborhood. She was thirty-three and he was almost twice her age, but he was strong, and Della, standing just five feet four, could do little to defend herself.

A month ago, Rudy had dragged her by her hair across the unpaved street of the trailer park, lifting Della off her feet as she kicked and screamed. A neighbor who lived in a trailer opposite theirs, Jacqueline Oglesby, saw the terrible scene play out. A showgirl at a stripclub called *Crazy Horse 2*, Jacqueline had called 911 more than once to report Rudy's abuse of Della; she had seen the bruises on Della's arms and heard the shouting coming from the trailer across the street late at night. One day, as they sat on the steps to Jacqueline's trailer, smoking cigarettes and watching children play, Della confided in Jacqueline that she wanted to leave Rudy but didn't know how.

"If anything ever happens to me, Rudy did it," Della told her.

Della had reason to fear for her life. In March of the previous year, Della and Rudy, on their second bottle of E&J Brandy, had argued after Della threw a bowl of soup at him. Rudy went into a rage, hitting and choking her. He covered her mouth and her nose with his hands so she couldn't breathe. After the attack, Rudy threatened to kill her if she reported him to the police. Della ended up in the hospital with a busted lip, bruises on her back, and red marks around her neck. In the emergency room, when an officer asked her who was responsible for her condition, she whispered Rudy's name. He spent the next two months in jail.[3]

Despite the abuse, she had to admit that there were

---

3 Although Rudy D'Apice acknowledged his conviction for assaulting Della on March 17, 1999, he testified that he didn't remember threatening to kill her if she reported him to the police.

moments when things did not seem so terrible at home. On this very August night, sober, she had cooked dinner and they ate together. Afterward, tired from a long day at Midas Auto Service, where he worked eleven-hour days, Rudy lay on the couch, as was his custom, to unwind and watch TV. Della sat on their second couch, crocheting a scarf for him. As he dozed off, Della asked if she could have some money.

"No, I don't want you drinking anymore," Rudy responded coldly, reminding her of her most recent attempt to take her own life, just a week earlier. When Rudy had picked her up from the emergency room, she had a bottle of prescription pills in her hands that were supposed to help her anxiety. She kept on crocheting. *Were they helping? Not enough.* She waited for Rudy to fall asleep, then took a credit card from his wallet, and slipped out of the trailer.

When Della was sober, she was reserved, but always quick to smile. Her dimples were girlish, and she had a way of endearing herself to others. She took joy in a part-time job calling numbers at a bingo hall, and despite her addictions, she managed to be a mother to her eighteen-year-old son, Robert. True, he had grown up watching her fend off violent boyfriends, but she hoped he would escape the cruel cycle of addiction and abuse.

She thought of her younger half-sister, Keenak, one of Daisy's other children. When they met, Della was in her late twenties and Keenak was just seven. The girl had welcomed Della into the family with open arms and instinctively gave her the nickname *Sissy*. At first, Della thought it was a joke or a game, but soon everyone in the family was calling Della *Sissy*, and it felt good, like she belonged. Keenak's hair was gloriously long, unlike Della's, which fell to her shoulders. They would watch TV together, as Della twisted the girl's long strands of hair into exact interwoven rows.

Keenak only occasionally visited from New Mexico,

so Della felt it was her duty as an older sister to introduce her to Alaska. They strolled the rolling hills and bluffs of Earthquake Park, a vestige of the 9.2 magnitude Good Friday temblor in 1964, where an entire neighborhood was swallowed by a landslide. In the spring, they went fishing in Ship Creek and picked berries in Arctic Valley. They also spent time in the kitchen. Della was a capable cook; Keenak loved the taste of her fish filets, her beef stew, the smell of her homemade cookies, and noticed how Della would never turn away a child in the trailer park who came to her door hungry. Back in New Mexico, as Keenak grew into a teenager, she would sneak to a pay phone and call her big Sissy in Alaska, to ask her advice on how to impress boys.

"Be yourself," Della would advise. "And don't stuff your bra."

****

Della had reached the liquor store. She handed over Rudy's credit card, and took the bagged bottle of E&J Brandy. Once outside, she screwed off the top, breaking the seal. As she swallowed, she felt the welcome, burning sensation in her throat, and then thought of Nora. The cruel irony did not escape Della that, at fifteen, she had given up her own daughter, just as her mother had given her up more than thirty years before. Della knew Nora had been adopted by a Native family and had returned to the village of her ancestors, more than 600 miles north. Nora had a real Native surname: *Nora Elizabeth Iyatunguk.* As a familiar fog descended upon her, Della felt somehow relieved; yet, like the village of Shishmaref, she felt weathered, as if she was eroding at her core, slowly fading into the sea.

TWO

A white Cadillac with a red top turned the corner in darkness and sped up Dorbrandt Street. Not even the looming broadcast tower of the Channel 11 studios, to the east, was clearly visible at this hour, but ahead, as the high beams flicked on, the driver and his three passengers could see something in the middle of the road. As the car pulled closer, the silhouette of a woman, lying on her side, came into view.

"I'm going to run her over," the driver said with a laugh, as the car rolled to a stop.[4] Joshua Wade was behind the wheel, an arrogant and troubled twenty-year-old with sandy-brown hair and piercing hazel eyes. Wade had borrowed the Seville with white leather seats from his father, an imposing drug dealer, and had decided to take two friends, Jesse Ackmann and Dwayne Clevenger, along with Dwayne's girlfriend, Anna Campbell, on a midnight joyride.

"Don't run her over," Dwayne urged from the backseat, not entirely sure if Wade was kidding.

"Then one of you move her out of the way," Wade snapped.

"Fuck that," Jesse replied.

If someone was going to do it, Dwayne decided it would have to be him. Dwayne was nineteen years old, fond of snowmobiles and monster trucks, with a low-sweeping brow that gave him a permanent look of concern. As he exited the

---

4 Wade denies making this comment, contradicting the accounts offered by Dwayne Clevenger and Jesse Ackmann.

car, he could see the woman was lying with her feet closest to the vehicle, in a fetal position. Dwayne could tell she was an Alaska Native; she was wearing a blue plaid jacket and he could see there was a wet spot on her blue jeans, near her crotch.

Dwayne let out a sigh and then cursed under his breath. It wasn't the first time he had seen a Native woman drunk and passed out in the street, especially in Spenard. Spenard was a once seedy part of Anchorage, dotted with pawn shops and strip clubs, a place where handwritten signs outside rundown double-wides advertised AMMO FOR SALE, where it was not uncommon to see homeless people passed out at bus stops or sleeping in the bushes along Spenard Road or near one of the city's cheapest liquor stores.

Dwayne glanced to his left at the trailer park across the street and then to his right at an abandoned green shed on the lot owned by the television station. The shed, which included a garage connected to a small room with a covered porch, was on the lot purchased by KTVA-TV years ago, but the shed had long since ceased having any official use. Now, with its walls coming apart and littered with large holes, it was a place for prostitutes to turn tricks and addicts to shoot up in the shadows.

Dwayne grabbed the woman's right foot and started to drag her toward the shed. She slumped from her side to her back, as he pulled her across the asphalt. This roused her slightly and she began to moan. Once she was fully out of the road, Dwayne let go of her foot and she collapsed with another moan, rolling back onto her side. He left her in the grass, next to the shed. He got back into the car, and the Cadillac sped off, into the darkness.

****

15

An hour later, Wade, Jesse, and Dwayne had returned to Dennis Whitmore's place in Spenard, about a block from where they had found the woman in the street. Dennis was a middle-aged neighbor and family friend Dwayne had known his entire life. Dennis ran an automotive repair shop out of his personal garage and had agreed to swap engines on Dwayne's Buick Riviera and Dwayne's girlfriend's car. Since the project was going to take a few days, Dwayne was helping out. Their work stretched from day into night and into day again, and they helped pass the time by drinking beer and R&R Whiskey. The garage soon became a hangout for Dwayne's friends, including Wade and Jesse, and a few others who had ties to a local street gang known as "GTS" or "Good Boys Trece Surenos."

Despite its Hispanic name, the members of GTS were all white and their impetuous twenty-year-old ringleader, Timothy Beckett, was known as *Romeo* and had the letters "GTS" tattooed on his neck. Romeo and his brother, Gabe Clark-Aigner, had aspirations of grandeur, but GTS was in its nascence and responsible for only a few petty crimes. As the gang grew, Romeo and his brother enacted initiations, requiring new members to commit a crime or random assault.

In court, a prosecutor would later characterize the gang as "short-lived" and "inept," a band of criminal wannabes. When the gang's activities escalated to include a series of armed robberies at the Spenard Motel later that year, a hotel clerk eventually shot and injured one of the young men, and once its members were placed under arrest, GTS, along with its grand ambitions, faded from existence.

Dwayne was not part of the gang, but he was dating Anna Campbell, a soft-spoken young woman whose brother, Danny Troxel, was Romeo's right-hand man. As for Wade, Dwayne had known him for a couple of years; they were acquaintances from school. Wade was not a member of GTS, but he had been in trouble with the law since arriving in Alaska at the age of thirteen to live with his father. He had racked up a long list of criminal offenses, mostly weapons and drug charges, and most recently an armed robbery, which Wade admitted to police was to retaliate against someone who had sold him some bad acid. In fact, Wade was wanted by police on a felony warrant in connection with a weapons charge.

Despite his rap sheet, Joshua Wade was different from his gangster friends. He aspired to be a tattoo artist and worked hard to refine his creative talent. He spent hours on macabre pencil drawings of naked women with overpowering breasts and demon horns. He also penned elaborate variations of a skull and crossbones. He was fastidious and obsessively neat; he kept his bedroom in a pristine state, CDs sorted in alphabetical order, his bed made military-style with tightly folded corners. He applied a similar meticulousness to his appearance; he almost exclusively wore crisp, white tank tops and took time every morning to style his hair with gel carefully on top, while keeping the sides and back trimmed short. He exuded a "tough guy" persona, spoke in a deep, gravelly voice, and had an unpredictable and explosive temper. One former neighbor described him as "a California boy, tan, and not bad looking." She paused, then added, "He gave me the creeps."

Wade liked to get high, which was why his eyes often were bloodshot; it might also have explained his extreme mood swings during those few days in Dennis Whitmore's garage. At times, he was buoyant, almost giddy, horsing around and drinking with the others. There were other moments, though, when he grew quiet and broody, pulling the hood of his sweatshirt up over his head and stared off into space. If the boredom overwhelmed him, he would lie down in the backseat of a classic car that was being restored

17

to take a nap.

When they returned from their midnight joyride, Dwayne and Jesse felt like kicking back with a beer, but Wade seemed distant and preoccupied.

"I'm going to see if that lady has any money on her," he announced abruptly.

As Jesse and Dwayne drank and continued to work on the cars, Wade disappeared into the shadows.

THREE

Lance Druba and his boyfriend Mark Rabbiosi were on their way back from an early morning alcohol run, with a twelve-pack of beer and a bottle of tequila, to their apartment on Dorbrandt Street, where they were having a party. As they passed the KTVA studios, their dog, a medium-sized terrier named Josie, started pulling at her leash with uncharacteristic force, in the direction of the run-down shed.

"That's odd. I wonder what's wrong with her," Lance remarked. Lance was gregarious and attractive, with a full head of wavy red hair. He was an animal trainer by profession—he had come to Alaska to train tigers at the Anchorage Zoo—but his addictions to drugs and alcohol had "taken over"; he had been fired, and had subsequently found a job at a pet food store.[5]

Josie's odd behavior had drawn Lance's attention to the shed, a place with which he was familiar. His addictions had brought him to some dark places—both literally and figuratively—and although he was ashamed to admit it, he had been inside the shed just a few months before, to do some cocaine with a prostitute. As they walked closer to the shed, it occurred to him that he and Mark could go inside and do a quick shot of tequila, and maybe some drugs, before returning home. That way, he reasoned, there would be more

---

5 Druba told me he has been sober and drug-free since April of 2010. He now lives in San Jose, California, and owns a pet store.

for them, and less to share with those at the party.

He handed the dog's leash to Mark, and with a small flashlight in one hand and the bag of alcohol in the other, he walked over to the small covered porch area of the shed. It was pitch dark but Lance could see the side door was already partially ajar, so he pushed it open a bit more with his right elbow. Before he could make his way through the doorway, he glanced down and saw the shadowy form of a person he thought was a homeless man, passed out on the floor.

"Oh my God, there's a bum in here," Lance said to Mark over his shoulder. Lance then directed his small flashlight toward the floor and realized he was mistaken. It was a woman, lying on her back, her naked legs spread apart and her pants around her ankles. As he directed the flashlight up the woman's torso, he could see smears of dark red, and when the light reached her head, he saw what he can only now recall as a "mangled mess" surrounded by a large pool of blood.

"Oh my God!" Lance exclaimed. In a state of panic, he turned around, pushed past Mark in the doorway, and with a crash, dropped the bag of beer and tequila, and took off running down the street. Mark was quick to gather the bag and its contents from the ground and follow with the dog. When Lance reached the bend where Dorbrandt Street turns onto 33rd Avenue, about a block down the road, he was hyperventilating. He bent forward, placed his head between his knees, and threw up.

"What the hell? What's the matter with you?" Mark asked, catching up.

"I think there's a dead body in there," Lance explained, catching his breath and wiping his mouth.

The news startled Mark and, after a moment or two of silence, a frightening thought occurred to him.

"Maybe the killer is still in there," he suggested. The

couple exchanged a wide-eyed look, and then both men took off running home with Josie scampering behind.

****

"Are you sure she was dead?"

Fifteen minutes later, Lance and Mark were back home and had described their gruesome discovery to some of the party guests. Lance was so disturbed recounting the scene, he went outside and started inhaling whippets, hoping to forget the image imprinted in his mind.[6] But Mark, who hadn't peered inside the shed, pressed Lance about what he had seen.

"How do we know she's *not* still alive?" he asked.

Given the amount of blood, Lance didn't think it was likely, but as time passed, he started doubting himself. As much as he didn't want to go back, he thought if there was even the smallest chance she was alive, he had to check.

"Maybe she needs our help," Lance said, his concern perhaps heightened by the nitrous oxide.

"I can drive," suggested a man at the party named Steve. Lance and Mark did not know him well, but they loaded up in his car, along with a prostitute named Casey.

****

When they arrived at the shed, they exited the car and approached the side door cautiously, flashlights in hand. Peering in through the open door, they could see the woman was not breathing and that her head had been partially crushed. They didn't need to check for a pulse; there was no doubt she was dead.

Steve was the only one to go inside. He entered the shed,

---

6 Whippets are small air-compressed containers that contain nitrous oxide.

circled the woman's body and instantly became hysterical. He ran outside and threw himself on the ground.

"What a horrible world!" he shrieked.

Annoyed by this display of histrionics, Lance drew his attention skyward. Maybe it was the nitrous oxide, he thought, but he could see the Northern Lights, with an unusual blue hue. The more he looked, the more it appeared the light was forming a large ring, like a halo, above the small shed.

"Are you guys seeing this?" Lance remarked to Mark and Casey. They were all high, and they claimed that they, too, saw the cosmic shape in the sky. They agreed that it seemed *so weird, so spiritual.* For a moment, they stood in awe, gazing up, wondering if the heavens had opened up to welcome home a lost soul.

FOUR

When the prostitute known as Casey called police at about 3:00 a.m. to report the discovery of a woman's body in a run-down shed in Spenard, she told the operator she had been led there by "mystical forces" and that there was a "Northern Lights-like aura" surrounding the shed, which prompted her to investigate.[7] Once actually pressed on this point by an officer, Casey admitted that her friends had seen the woman's body first and had taken her there later to confirm the woman was dead.

Officer Mark Rein, who worked the night shift in Spenard, was the first officer to respond to the scene. He was initially directed to 36th Avenue and C Street, where he found Casey, whom he recognized as a prostitute and crack addict from the neighborhood. She told him the crime scene was elsewhere, so he asked her to get inside his squad car. Her sudden jerks and darting eyes suggested to Officer Rein she was high at the time, which accounted for her overall sense of confusion. She initially directed him to 36th Avenue and Dorbrandt Street, but eventually settled on the correct location, four blocks away.

The squad car pulled up to Dorbrandt Street and 32nd Avenue, along a small wooded area separating the shed from the road. Officer Rein was giving updates on his radio as he drove, and soon, other squad cars arrived at the scene.

---

7 These quotes are taken from the criminal complaint filed by the State of Alaska in its case against Joshua Wade.

"That's it," Casey said nervously, pointing. Officer Rein was familiar with the shed; it was a short distance from the Hells Angels Clubhouse and it had been the subject of complaints from several concerned citizens who wanted it knocked down because of the unsavory activities it attracted to the neighborhood.

"You stay here," Officer Rein told Casey, exiting his car.

Sergeant Bill Richardson pulled up in his squad car and retrieved a spotlight from the trunk. From the road, Sergeant Richardson pointed the spotlight at the shed. A beam of yellow light reflected off the trees, casting shadows on the building's faded green panels. With a flashlight, Officer Rein went around the rear of the shed, approaching cautiously, uncertain if anyone, especially the alleged attacker, remained inside. The garage door had fallen off its hinges and sat slightly askew. The rotting wood panels had separated, forming several spaces through which Officer Rein shone his flashlight. Shadows danced off the opposite wall, but he detected no movement inside.

He made his way around the shed and met Sergeant Richardson near the covered porch. Under the blazing, yellow glare of Sergeant Richardson's spotlight, they could see a woman's body through the open doorway. She was on her back, and her blue jeans had been pulled down to her ankles. A shoe was still on her right foot, and crime scene analysts would later find the left shoe inside her left pant leg, which had been turned inside out. Her left arm rested on her abdomen, her right arm was above her head and her bra and blue tank top had been pushed up over her breasts. She was not wearing underwear, and her genitals were exposed. The left sleeve of a blue plaid shirt remained on her forearm, but the rest had been pulled from her body.

It was a chilly morning, and there were no puffs of breath, no rise and fall of the abdomen, no signs of life. Officer Rein and Sergeant Richardson could see the woman's head had been badly beaten and her blood had pooled on the wooden slats beneath her and was partially dry. Without even stepping inside the shed, they concluded her death had not occurred within the past few hours and that she had been the victim of a most brutal sexual assault.

FIVE

In charge of processing the crime scene was John Daily, a seasoned homicide detective who had been with the department's Crime Scene Investigation unit since its inception in the 1980s. He was bald, with a thick brown mustache, a matter-of-fact demeanor, and spoke in swift, monotone utterances. He immediately recognized the conditions in the shed were less than ideal; it was filthy and he knew the lack of clean surfaces would make collecting trace evidence difficult. The entranceway was dirt and gravel and the floor in the shed, which at one time was linoleum, had been covered with plywood. Between the slats, there were open spaces where trash had collected—old beer cans, cigarette butts, and discarded papers, some of which were old files from the TV station dating back to the 1950s.

The shed had no electricity, so police set up a number of large halogen lights to illuminate the interior and exterior, taking care not to contaminate the crime scene. Detective Daily assigned Officer Derrick Hsieh the task of photographing the scene; it was Hsieh's first homicide case, and he appeared eager to do a thorough job. He photographed blood spatter near the door and took several photographs of the victim before she was touched or moved by the forensic team. One close-up of the victim's face showed three partially burnt matches in her hair, near her eyes. Detectives later would conclude the matches were used after the victim's death by someone showing "disrespect" to the woman's body by throwing lit matches onto her face.[8]

Officer Hsieh also photographed the fatal injury to the woman's skull both at the scene and later during the autopsy. The medical examiner permitted him to touch the back of the woman's skull. He later described it as having lost all integrity, that the bones were completely crushed, and that the back of her head felt like a bag of melting ice.

What was noticeably absent from the shed was any kind of weapon that could cause such destruction to bone and flesh. Detective Daily could tell just by looking at the head injuries that a large blunt object, such as a rock, had caused the fatal blows. He dispatched an eighteen-member auxiliary search team in an effort to recover a weapon. The team searched the surrounding lots and a nearby trailer park but retrieved nothing that appeared connected to the woman's death.

Still, Detective Daily found dozens of items he considered significant; crime scene analysts seized forty-four pieces of evidence from the shed. The items included: a clump of black hair appearing to match the victim's found on the ground, a couple of feet from the side door of the shed; the victim's blue tank top; her bra; her blue plaid shirt; her shoes; a blue plaid coat found in the doorway west of where the body was discovered; and a red tank top covered in blood that appeared not to belong to the victim, found a few feet east of the body. A small branch found on the victim's abdomen was determined to have no evidentiary value and was discarded. A crushed beer can was found sitting on the bloody floorboards a few feet east of the body, and although it was covered in dust and its contents did not appear to have been recently consumed, there was some blood on it, so detectives bagged it as evidence. The shed was strewn

---

8 Detective John Daily made this conclusion and related it from the witness stand.

with old papers, having been used as a storage space for the television station, and detectives collected several loose papers with bloody shoe prints on them, and one piece of paper with a bloody fingerprint.

A considerable amount of blood was on the blue plaid coat, both inside and out, and forensic experts reasoned the woman had been beaten first while wearing it, and that the coat was then tossed aside, near the doorway, sometime during the attack.

Dr. Michael Propst from the medical examiner's office administered DNA swabs of the victim's mouth and vagina. Detective Daily then assisted Dr. Propst with removing the woman's clothing as the doctor looked for trace evidence on the body, using a cotton swab to collect any such evidence around the woman's breasts and abdomen. They noticed one of the woman's hands was stiff and curled, signifying that rigor mortis had set in, and that she had been dead for more than a few hours. Carefully, the two men rolled the victim over, looking for any other significant evidence.

Knowing that retrieving viable fingerprints from anywhere inside the shed would be a challenge, and reasoning that the attacker had certainly touched the victim's exposed skin, Detective Daily attempted to lift fingerprints from the body with a procedure known as the cyanoacrylate fuming method. He considered it a longshot but had successfully performed the same procedure at another homicide scene a couple of years prior, so he thought it was worth a try. He erected a plastic tent over the body and introduced fumes from cyanoacrylate, the chemical found in superglue, to the skin. The reaction of the fumes can produce a white outline of fingerprints that can then be photographed, and processed; however, to his dismay, the effort this time was to no avail. Dr. Propst then wrapped the body in a sheet, and the still-unidentified woman was loaded into a coroner's van and taken to the morgue.

SIX

September 2, 2000, 11:34 a.m.

Police continued their work at the crime scene well into daylight, and the neighborhood was soon filled with murmurs of speculation as to who the dead woman was and how exactly her life had come to an end. The auto repair work at Dennis Whitmore's garage was still underway when the crime scene tape went up just a block away and crime scene analysts dressed head to toe in protective gear started taking impressions of shoeprints in the soil outside of the shed.

Romeo, the GTS gang leader, was with Jesse in front of Dennis Whitmore's garage, siphoning gasoline out of a car that was headed for the junkyard. Jesse recalled it was a particularly sunny day as they saw police cruisers passing by on Dorbrandt Street. Wade had been asleep inside the garage, and when he awakened, he seemed rattled by the presence of the police so nearby. When an officer stopped by the garage with news someone had been murdered, his sense of unrest escalated. Wade felt a pang of dread when he saw Romeo and his girlfriend, Sabrina, walking down the street in the direction of the crime scene.

Once near the shed, Romeo stopped at the yellow police tape and waved over an officer. He introduced himself with his proper name, Timothy, and said he had information that might be helpful to their investigation. Officer Eric Hamre made an audio recording of their conversation.

"I am currently at 32nd and Dorbrandt," Officer Hamre

began. "And with me is Timothy Beckett. Date of birth is 10-9-79. It is September 2nd, and the current time is 11:34. Okay, Timothy, basically what did you see?"

"I was driving and going to get dropped off to work on my friend's car, and basically I saw a Native girl about yay high," Beckett explained, holding his hand eye level. "Maybe a little taller ... with some big black guy walking down the street."

"About what time was this?"

"At about eleven o'clock."

"Have you ever seen either one of them before?"

"Nah."

"What was she wearing?"

"A T-shirt and jeans."

"What color T-shirt?"

"I couldn't tell, it was too dark. We were just driving by, I just got a glance."

"How tall do you think she was?"

"Shorter than me. And I am about five-ten so probably about five-seven."

"How much do you think she weighed?"

"Your guess would be as good as mine," Romeo responded with a laugh.

"Did she seem to be heavy-set or medium build?"

"Medium, about 130."

"Okay. Did she have anything else that you can remember like glasses or anything, like a ponytail or ...?"

"No I don't think she had a ponytail. I think her hair was down."

"Okay, how long do you think her hair was?"

"Past her shoulders."

"If you were shown a picture of her, would you be able to identify her?"

"Nah."

"What about the black male? How tall was he?"

"About as tall as you," Romeo said, referring to the officer's six-foot stature. "Or bigger than you."

"Weight wise?"

"He was heavy build. Heavy. You got 'extra heavy' in there?" smirking and gesturing to the officer's notebook. "Nah, just kidding. He was heavy build."

"How old do you think he was?"

"About thirty."

"What was he wearing?"

"Black shirt and blue jeans. And some white shoes."

"White shoes?"

"Yeah, white shoes. Those white shoes. That's the only thing I'm positive about, he had white shoes."

"If you saw the picture of him would you be able to identify him?"

"Not as good as I would a gorilla," Romeo said chuckling. "I didn't get a good glimpse of his face."

"Where were they walking when you saw them?"

"Right here on this corner."

"Did they appeared to be arguing?"

"They were talking. Driving by, it didn't look like they were fighting."

"Okay, anything else that you can remember about them?"

"The girl had another shirt under her arm," Romeo added.

"She had a shirt under her arm?" the officer responded, a bit perplexed.

"Yeah, she was carrying a shirt under her arm."

"What color was that shirt?"

"I couldn't tell."

"Anything else you can tell me?"

"They were standing pretty close to each other, so I know when I am fighting with my girl we're not standing shoulder to shoulder or in this case shoulder to rib cage. So ..."

"And you couldn't identify them again if you saw them?"

"No, it was too dark."

"Okay, I appreciate your help, thank you."

Romeo and Sabrina lingered for a while, watching police work the crime scene, then they walked away, back in the direction of Dennis Whitmore's garage.

SEVEN

"Who are you and what happened to you?"

Dr. Franc Fallico liked to ask this question of any victim who came across his examination table at the morgue, confident their injuries would tell him the story of his or her demise. Dr. Fallico was a peculiar yet kind man with greying hair who would eventually become Alaska's Chief Medical Examiner. He spoke eloquently and from the back of his throat in a pitch higher than most men. He examined the woman's body carefully, inspecting it for any signs of trace evidence that might have been missed at the crime scene. He measured and weighed the victim's body, noting she was sixty-four inches tall and 122 pounds and then explored her most visible injuries.

He noted a laceration above the right eyebrow, measuring three inches by one inch, an irregular wound with two to three "funny shaped" holes, which he concluded had been caused by a blunt force wound, and by an object that was not sharp.[9] He also noted a laceration on the left scalp and a black left eye. There were two wounds on the victim's neck—one under the right ear and another extending from the front of the neck to the right side—that Dr. Fallico considered "peculiar" because of a redness that indicated

---

9 This quote is from Dr. Fallico's testimony at trial.

they were older than the fatal injury to the head.[10] He posited the cuts on the neck had been caused by a dull knife. He noted bruising and cuts on the right leg: a large linear cut above the knee and a smaller one on the lower part of the leg. The cuts were similar to the wounds on the neck in that they appeared to be older injuries, leading Dr. Fallico to conclude they were likely caused by a blunt force object with a sharp edge, perhaps by the same dull knife.

Dr. Fallico washed the body and carefully shaved the victim's head, in an effort to more accurately categorize the wounds. On the right side of the head, a laceration stretched from the right eyebrow to the forehead, and Dr. Fallico also noted bruising on the right eyelid. He noted small hemorrhages, or red dots known as petechiae, on the lower portion of the victim's neck, consistent with the striking of a blunt object. He reasoned these wounds had been caused at least six hours before the woman's death because the dilated blood vessels were evidence the body had time to react to the injuries.

"The point here," Dr. Fallico would later explain, "is there was life present, a heartbeat, for a period of several hours, in my opinion, after the wound was made on the living body."

On the scalp, there were three distinct wounds. One was so deep he could see fragments of bone; he noted the overlaying tissue had been pounded away as if a hammer had come down on an anvil, compressing the scalp against the skull, splitting the tissue with what he reasoned were powerful thrusts of energy. The back of the skull was so badly damaged that as he moved the victim's head,

---

10 Dr. Fallico explained during his testimony that the redness had come from dilated blood vessels, which indicated the body was trying to heal the wounds, leading to his conclusion the cuts on the neck occurred before the blunt force wounds to the head.

fragments of bone fell onto the examination table. He noted the injuries seemed consistent with being struck repeatedly by a blunt object, such as a rock. As he examined more closely, he could see that pieces of the woman's broken skull had penetrated a membrane surrounding the brain, and had caused bruising and bleeding, and hemorrhages on the brain itself. Dr. Fallico concluded the blows to the head were what caused the woman's death and that she had died within an hour of suffering such massive trauma.

Dr. Fallico also noted the victim had no defensive wounds, no broken nails or signs of a struggle, but her blood-alcohol level was .248, which would have put a woman of her weight on the edge of unconsciousness and may have explained why she didn't resist her attacker. In addition to the alcohol, analysis of her urine showed she had consumed a large amount of cocaine not long before her death. Dr. Fallico recovered a man's pubic hair from her vagina, and found semen in her vagina and anus; there were no signs of recent injury to either area, but he later would explain that this did not mean she had not been raped.

Based on the state of rigor mortis, Dr. Fallico concluded the woman had been killed approximately twenty-four to thirty-six hours before the police arrived at the crime scene Saturday morning. He also ascertained, based on the presence of white blood cells, the small cuts to the woman's neck and legs had occurred from one to twelve hours before her death. Dr. Fallico also concluded, based on the lividity of the woman's blood, she had died facedown but had been found by police on her back, meaning someone had moved her after her death.[11] In fact, crime scene investigators had

---

11 Dr. Fallico explained in court that after the heart stops beating, gravity takes over, and the blood remaining in the body will settle in one place, enabling him to determine what position the body was in at the time of death.

concluded that the victim had been rolled onto her back away from the pool of blood, and closer to the door, where her body may have blocked the door, preventing it from opening fully. They also noted the door itself had blood stains on it, and reasoned it had banged against the woman's face or head several times.

Some of the same CSI technicians who were at the crime scene attended the autopsy, to take photos and to collect any trace evidence found on the body. They also took fingerprints of the cadaver, which registered a positive match for a thirty-three-year-old woman who had multiple interactions with police, mostly as a victim of domestic violence. Her name was Della Marie Brown.

EIGHT

It was about 1:00 a.m. in Albuquerque, New Mexico, when James Britten was awakened by a phone call from his mother's sister, Mary, who had some terrible news. She had spent the past few hours at the morgue in Anchorage and had identified the body of James's half-sister, Della, as the victim of a gruesome homicide. Mary wanted to reach her sister, Daisy, but thought it was not the kind of traumatizing revelation any mother should receive over the phone. James, himself trying to process the unexpected and horrible news, got out of bed, dressed, and he and his wife made the eight-mile drive to his mother's apartment.

Daisy had done her best to make a life for herself in New Mexico, having fled Anchorage after being raped at the age of eighteen, but she lived with a persistent feeling of guilt for leaving her oldest daughter behind. When Della, in her twenties, had reached out to Daisy, Daisy welcomed her into her extended family. Della became acquainted with Daisy's other four children, James, Gloria, Keenak, and Kenny, by visiting with them on the phone and exchanging home movies by mail.[12] Della would talk to her half-siblings at length about her love of the outdoors; she told James she wished she could introduce him to the Last Frontier and she quizzed Gloria about her interests, her life in Arizona, and her sons. When it came to her own life, however, Della

---

12 James and Gloria were a result of Daisy's first marriage, and Keenak and Kenny, a girl and boy in their teens, resulted from Daisy's second marriage to Kenneth Piggott.

remained guarded.

"I knew she loved me and cared about me," Gloria said, lamenting the physical distance that separated them. "But if we would've been able to be together … we could've had a better relationship."

Of all Daisy's children, Keenak knew Della the best, because as a girl, she would visit Anchorage, and Della was thrilled to take her under her wing. It was Keenak who had given Della the nickname *Sissy*, and she saw Della idealistically, through a child's eyes.

"She had a really big heart. She smiled about everything. She made sure that everything was okay," Keenak remembered.

Della encouraged Keenak to love poetry, and when, as a pre-teen, Keenak asked Della to teach her how to apply makeup, Della told her she was beautiful without any makeup, and plus, it wasn't good for her skin.

"We would watch scary movies together. We would go on walks and hikes. We would even drive. She would even drive me around Alaska, you know … she would bring me to her favorite spots. We would go and sit there and escape from reality and enjoy nature."

****

By the time James and his wife arrived at his mother's apartment, it was 2:00 a.m., and James had worked himself into quite a state. He pounded on the door with such force, Keenak, who was eleven at the time, was startled awake by the commotion, and she thought everyone in the entire apartment complex must also have heard and, like her, had sprung up from their beds. Daisy was a small woman, standing less than five feet tall, and when she jumped up from a sound sleep on the sofa bed she shared with her husband, she so quickly swung open the door that she was still trying to gain her balance as she fumbled for the light switch. When she saw her son's face, flushed and distraught, she instinctively knew something had happened to one of her children.

"Is it Gloria?" she asked, referring to James's younger sister.

"No, it's Della," he replied, shaking his head. "Sissy is dead!" he exclaimed, falling to his knees.

What followed was a scene sure to have awakened the neighbors, if the pounding on the door had not; a cacophony of wailing and crying, as Daisy fell to the floor. A sinking, desperate feeling of guilt took root inside Daisy, from which she would never fully recover. She replayed in her mind, over and over again, a recent phone conversation during which Della claimed her life would have turned out differently had Daisy not left her behind in Anchorage.

"You have four other kids, and they're okay," Della had pointed out, drunk, and therefore bold enough to make such a declaration. "If you hadn't left me behind, I wouldn't be like this."

The words had pierced Daisy at her core. Since reconnecting with Della, she had blamed herself for all of her daughter's failings—her alcohol and drug problems, her violent boyfriends, the abuse she endured—and now, Daisy blamed herself, in part, for her daughter's death.

"The guilt of me giving her up ... I live with that," Daisy said, years later. "I forever carry that guilt."

Most of Della's family in New Mexico could not bear the immediate expense to travel to Alaska, but James felt strongly his mother deserved, at the very least, to be in Anchorage to attend Della's memorial service. He bought her an airline ticket and the following day Daisy was on her way back to the city she had fled, more than thirty years before.

NINE

Lieutenant Nick Vanderveur, a 20-year veteran of the police force only a few months from retirement, was named lead detective on the case. Officer Tim Landeis, who was new to the homicide unit, was named the "second," with the intention he would learn from Vanderveur's vast experience and eventually take over the investigation. Vanderveur ordered officers to canvass the neighborhood surrounding the shed, to ask if neighbors had spotted a woman fitting Della's description in the area during the preceding few days. Knowing that Della was extremely intoxicated at the time of her death, detectives also contacted several nearby bars. A waitress at Pancho's Villa, a restaurant and bar Della frequented just a block from the shed, confirmed Della was a familiar face. She reported that Della liked to drink margaritas there and that she had seen Della with a man at the bar, but the timing of her observation was unclear, and ultimately, investigators did not pursue the lead.[13]

With Della identified, investigators next had to track down the people who were last to see her alive. Detective Vanderveur dispatched homicide investigators to Della's

---

13 At the trial, Detective Landeis testified that the waitress had pointed officers to a man by the name of Charles Jacobsson, who allegedly had information about the sighting of Della and a man at Pancho's Villa. Landeis said he had previous contact with Jacobsson on another case, and due to his demeanor and level of intoxication, he considered the information he provided "unreliable." When asked on cross examination why a follow-up interview was not conducted with the waitress, Landeis replied, "I don't know exactly."

address at Idle Wheels Mobile Court, where they found and interviewed Della's father,[14] son, a few neighbors, and Della's boyfriend, Rudy D'Apice.

Henry Brown explained that he and his wife lived in the same trailer park as Della, and Della's eighteen-year-old son, Robert, had a separate trailer that he occasionally shared with his mother. Henry said, however, that Della lived more permanently at Space 64 with her boyfriend, Rudy. He said the couple was having trouble; in fact, he reported he had last seen his daughter on Wednesday night when she stopped by to announce she was leaving Rudy for good and that she wanted Henry to use his key to let her into Robert's trailer, because she was locked out. Henry said he obliged. He added that he suspected his daughter was using cocaine and had been seeing other men.

Police found Robert at Space 69, five trailers down from the one his mother and Rudy shared. Robert knew they had a violent relationship, and his mother would occasionally stay with him when the couple fought. He assumed that's why she was there when he returned home from work on Wednesday night. They did not speak, and when he awoke the next morning, she was gone and the trailer in a sorry state, with cigarettes, an empty bottle of brandy, and cake crumbs strewn across the floor. Robert told police that he did not know his mother well, because she had a serious drinking problem, and that his grandparents had raised him.

A neighbor, Steven Lupien, told police he had last seen Della Thursday, around 9:30 p.m. Lupien was certain about the time, because he remembered he was watching the TV show *ER* when Della came by his trailer to ask if she could borrow ten dollars. Lupien said he knew that Della drank but that she appeared, at the time, to be sober and in

---

14 Although Henry Brown legally adopted Della, he was technically her step-grandfather.

a good mood. He gave her the money, recounting that Della was always good about paying him back. Lupien was a former paramedic, and he considered Della a friend; he told detectives she would confide in him that she and Rudy were having problems, but Lupien added that Della seemed very devoted to Rudy.

When officers pulled up to Space 64, to the trailer Rudy and Della shared, they found a pile of women's clothes in a garbage bag on the steps and a bottle of pills on the railing. Inside, they found Rudy, drunk and distraught. Rudy was a white man, slight in stature, an alcoholic with slicked-back hair, whom one observer described as a "mousy, weaselly kind of guy ... like a greasy car salesman."[15] Rudy explained that Della had left him three nights ago, and when she didn't return after a couple of days, he had packed up her things in a rage and left them out front. He later realized she had left behind her anxiety medication, prescribed to her after a suicide attempt just ten days prior, so he had left the bottle of pills on the railing. He said he had periodically checked the number of pills inside, thinking that Della might have come back to take her medicine, but he said the number of pills remained the same.

It did not take long for officers to discover that Rudy and Della had a history of domestic abuse during their tumultuous, three-year relationship. In fact, just eighteen months earlier, Rudy had assaulted Della so violently she was hospitalized. According to a police report, Rudy punched and choked Della after the two had argued, and Della had thrown a bowl of soup at him. Della offered the following account to an officer from her hospital bed:

---

15 This is a quote from Anne Gore, who was an alternate juror at the murder trial.

Della: He kept putting his hands over my mouth and I couldn't breathe. I couldn't scream … and I couldn't breathe. I tried. (sobbing) He said if I didn't shut up … he was going to …

Officer: He was going to what?

Della: He was going to kill me.

Rudy served two months in jail for the attack, but the couple's turbulent relationship continued after his release.[16]

Rudy told police he and Della had argued on Thursday night when he refused to give her money for liquor. According to Rudy, she told him she was leaving him and he figured she had run off with another man. Police broke news to Rudy that they had found Della dead, in a shed about thirteen blocks from home.

"How did she die?" he asked.

"Blunt force trauma, to some degree," an officer replied.

"Where? The head?" Rudy asked.

"Yeah, uh-huh," the officer responded.

Rudy had no outward reaction to this news. He paused, seeming to be deep in thought.

"Hold on a second," Rudy paused. "I'm thinking back. Wednesday night, some guy crawled through the window of her trailer.[17] That's what Henry told me. A guy crawled into her trailer, and we haven't seen her since. Wednesday night I was sleeping on the couch and she kept trying to wake me up … she said, 'Rudy, Rudy, wake up.' I said, 'No, I want to sleep.' I was taking a nap. It was before the news come on. Cause I woke up at ten—'til ten. And she was gone. And she

---

16 Though the sentence was four months, Rudy testified that he served sixty days in jail.

17 Here, Rudy is referring to the trailer occupied by Della's son Robert. The report of a strange man crawling into the trailer was never confirmed by police.

was sitting here knitting. But Henry was telling me ... and I don't where the hell he got this ... but he told me that he seen somebody crawl through the damn window."[18]

"Robert had discovered that someone had come into the house," the officer said, offering an explanation. "He just figured it was Della, that she had locked herself out."

"Heck, no," Rudy protested. "I asked Robert today, I said, 'Where the heck is Della?' I said, 'She's been gone for a couple days.' He says, 'All I seen was a full bottle of brandy and a full pack of Merits on the floor. The whole trailer was trashed. Cakes all over the place.'"

"Did Della know anybody down there by the 32nd and Dorbrandt area?"

"I know exactly where you're talking about. That's down by Hells Angels."[19]

"Uh-huh."

"Not that I know of."

Rudy told detectives that Della didn't work regularly, and that she received about $700 a month from one of Alaska's Native corporations.[20] He said she had left behind all of her belongings when she left their trailer on Wednesday night. At some point during the interview, the subject of money came up, and Rudy grew animated and angry.

"I found out Thursday that I have a hundred-dollar withdrawal!" Rudy exclaimed. "Taken out of my Visa account! And I didn't take no hundred-dollar withdrawal! I call Visa and said, 'What the hell you doing, charging me an

---

18 This and other statements attributed to Rudy D'Apice in this chapter are verbatim quotes from taped interviews with police.

19 The shed was located about a block from the Hells Angels clubhouse in Anchorage.

20 The U.S. Congress passed the Alaska Native Claims Settlement Act in 1971, as a response to widespread poverty among the indigenous people of Alaska. The Act effectively created a number of Native corporations, which pay out dividends to their shareholders on a monthly basis.

extra hundred dollars? I have a hundred-dollar withdrawal on Thursday, so you find out where that hundred-dollar draw came, what branch, or whatever!'"

"We'd like to have that credit card," the officer interjected.

"You can have it," Rudy replied, pulling it out of his wallet and handing him the card.

"Did they happen to tell you when on Wednesday the withdrawal took place?" the officer asked.

"I called up yesterday, and they said it was charged on the 31st. And I keep all of my receipts right here," he said, gesturing to his wallet.

"Are you missing a credit card?" the officer asked.

"No. I am not missing a credit card." Rudy replied.

"So how can someone take a withdrawal without a credit card?"

"Here's the one I took today," Rudy explained, showing his ATM receipt. "A hundred dollars. And now I'll show you the last one I took. This is what I was bitching at Henry about. I said, "God dammit there's one hundred dollars out of my God damn account!' See, I keep all my goddamn things, everything," Rudy said, displaying another ATM receipt.

"If you're not missing a card ..." the officer said.

"I'm not!" Rudy interrupted.

"So how did she take the money out?"

"The only thing I can think is as I was sleeping she got my wallet, took the card, went down in, got the money, and then put the card back. That's the only thing I can ... I can't figure it out either! That fucking pisses me off! How the hell did she get my God damn card?"

Rudy's agitated response over one hundred dollars, coupled with his lack of any apparent grief or shock having just learned of Della's murder, appeared suspicious. Not only did he have a violent past with Della, he had never searched for her after she disappeared, or even asked around the trailer park, quizzing friends or acquaintances on her whereabouts. Moreover, if he was truly concerned about her well-being, he had certainly never called police.

Officers pressed Rudy to think back, to concentrate on what could have happened to Della. Rudy was silent for a moment, then something came to his mind.

"I come back from work on Thursday night," Rudy recalled. "I came in and poured myself a drink and looked out the window and could have swore that I saw Della. She was standing there on the porch talking to someone. But the person wasn't outside, they were inside the trailer, I couldn't see who it was. I looked out that window right there. And she was there for about five minutes, talking to this person. Then I did something, I turned around and she was gone. Either she went into the trailer, or she was gone, walked down the steps. Now, when this happened it was a little after six o'clock. Thursday night, 6:15 or 6:20 something like that. I could have swore it was Della because the side view. ... I seen the side view and it was her hair, the way she fixed her hair. She had it all nice and thick, I could tell from looking out the window."

In addition to the stolen money, the impression that Della was primped for a date with another man appeared to only reinforce Rudy's motive for wanting Della dead. In fact, during his second interview with police, Rudy admitted he was aware that Della was having an affair with an African American man by the name of Monty Dugan, and that she had admitted this during one of their notorious fights. Monty stayed three to four nights a week at the trailer of one of Della's friends, Jesse Choi. Rudy suggested to police that perhaps Monty was the source of the semen the coroner had found inside Della.[21]

Even though he had discarded all of Della's clothes, stuffing them into a garbage bag left on the front step, Rudy at first was reluctant to turn over all the items to police.

"I didn't want them to have her clothes," Rudy later recalled. "I thought maybe her mother or someone would want them."

Rudy finally agreed, however, and also helped them identify the blue coat found covered in blood in the shed, as belonging to Della.

He also would emphatically answer the question officers had in mind from the moment they pulled up to Space 64.

"Did you kill Della?"

"No way. Absolutely not."

---

21 Police would later track down Monty Dugan in Texas, who admitted to having an intimate relationship with Della. They took DNA sample from him, which excluded him as the source of semen found in Della at the time of her death.

TEN

In Alaska, the ground freezes in early October, rendering the soil as hard as granite; digging graves the next six months is nearly impossible. For this reason, funeral homes are known to store dozens of bodies in cool containers, delaying burials until spring. This meant many families of the deceased would have to wait months to experience the finality of having their loved ones lowered to their final resting places. Della's family, however, was fortunate in this one respect: the ground had not yet succumbed to the snow and ice.

Just as Della was being laid to rest, officers arrested a man named Kevin Ayers on unrelated charges. Wanted on several outstanding warrants, including charges of assault and stalking, Ayers said he had information about the woman who had been killed in a shed, and he insisted on speaking with a Detective David Parker, whom he knew from one of his previous cases.[22]

Once in an interrogation room with Detective Parker, Ayers explained that his brother, Carl, was a tattoo artist who also helped clean and maintain a small auto garage owned by Dennis Whitmore in Spenard. While at his brother's apartment, Kevin Ayers said, two young men, Dwyane Clevenger and someone named Romeo, had come to Carl to inquire about tattoos. Kevin Ayers told Detective Parker that during that visit, Dwayne had recounted a horrific story

---

22 According to police records, Kevin Ayers had a long criminal record, including convictions for drug offenses, assault, making a false report, and driving without a license.

about someone named Josh who had shown up at Dennis Whitmore's garage the previous week with blood all over him. Clevenger told Ayers Josh had confessed to beating a woman to death in a nearby shed, first with a rock and then a shovel. During return visits, he allegedly had continued to beat the woman and had slit her throat. Ayers said, according to the story, Josh was motivated by a hatred of Native Alaskans, and that he had sexually assaulted the woman, after she was dead.[23]

****

On September 13, a few days after Kevin Ayer's arrest, police received an anonymous call to Crime Stoppers. The caller, who received a $1,000 reward for the information he provided, was later revealed to be Timothy "Romeo" Beckett, the same man who had approached an officer at the crime scene with information about a Native woman and a black man who he had seen walking near the shed. Romeo told Crime Stoppers that someone named Josh had confessed to killing the woman who had been identified as Della Brown. Romeo said Josh told him, "Man, I just got done killing this girl," admitting that he had "bashed her face in" with what the caller believed was a rock. Romeo echoed details Ayers had already provided to police, saying Josh had sexually assaulted the woman. He added that he saw blood on Josh's clothing and that he believed that Josh had burned his clothes and had disposed of evidence.

Romeo told police that Josh (he did not provide a last name) lived with his father at Manoogs Isle trailer park, and drove a white Cadillac with a red top. The Anchorage office of the FBI offered its assistance following up on that tip, sending field agent Lou Ann Henderson to the trailer park,

---

23 Details of Kevin Ayer's account to Detective Parker appear in the affidavit in support of the criminal complaint against Joshua Wade.

where she quickly spotted the car, parked outside a trailer. The license plate came back to a Gregory Alan Wade, and records from the Alaska Public Safety Information Network showed his son, Joshua Alan Wade, also lived there. Agent Henderson ran a criminal background check on Josh and discovered he was wanted on a $5,000 felony arrest warrant on a petition to revoke his probation; the original charge related to misconduct involving a weapon.

Romeo claimed to have split his Crime Stoppers reward money with Danny Troxel, and they both remained anonymous until someone else called Crime Stoppers on September 25, naming Danny Troxel as someone with crucial information about the case.[24] Della was just one of six women who had been murdered recently in Anchorage, and the caller said that Danny Troxel knew "who [was] doing all the murders of the Native females."

Shortly after that call, police arrived at Danny's mother's house, where they found Danny and Romeo, and officers promptly brought both of them to police headquarters for questioning. They were separated and interviewed in different rooms.

Detective Vanderveur and Sergeant Ken Spadafora first spoke to Romeo.

"Here's what the deal is ... um, we got word that your buddy here may have heard something about a homicide," Sergeant Spadafora explained.

"Uh huh," Romeo acknowledged.

"Okay, so we want to ask him some questions about that, and that's why we're down here."

"Right," Romeo replied.

"Has he told you anything?"

"No."

---

24 The second person to call Crime Stoppers and receive a reward was identified in court as the uncle of Danny Troxel's girlfriend.

"Well, we're going to see what he's got to say, and we'll go from there, okay?"

"Uh huh."

"And of course if he tells us he told you something, we'll come back in and ask you some questions."

"Yeah, of course."

"I understand he's your buddy, you know ... and you want to wait to see what he says first you know. ..."

"We'll I don't know nuttin' about nuttin'," Romeo interrupted. "We been campin' for the last, like, month-and-a-half, two months. We got receipts and everything."

****

Ten minutes later, two police officers entered the room, Detective Chris Jones and Detective Eric Hamre; Hamre was the officer Romeo had spoken to at the crime scene.

"Ain't nobody 'round here got a cigarette, do they?"

"No," Detective Jones replied. "You can't smoke in here. Let's talk about your camping trip. Who went on this trip?"

"Me, Danny, his sister, my girlfriend Sabrina, and my friend Tim."

"When did you guys go?"

"I don't remember the exact date. ... I remember it was ... uh, they were camping during that ... when that murder happened because I was working on a car. I heard it on TV. I was there and talked to a detective the day everybody was there ... all the police and shit were there."

"Okay, when did you guys get back to Anchorage?"

"Oh, it's been about a couple weeks."

"You've been back in Anchorage for a couple of weeks?"

"Yeah."

"Okay, well again, more the point of why we're here is what you guys have been hearing ... I mean, you guys are out on the street."

"Somebody starts talkin' about somethin' and that's when I walk outta the room," Romeo said. "I've been shot because somebody thought I was a snitch."[25]

"Well, we're not asking you to snitch," Detective Jones assured.

"Being that you guys are friends," Detective Jones continued, referring to Danny, "This is kind of an important deal, okay? This involves a homicide, so we've gotta ask these questions. Has there been anything you have seen or heard ..."

"Just what's been on the news," Romeo interrupted.

"Anything Danny has told you?"

"No."

"Anything about a body?"

"Nope." Romeo paused. "Well, I seen the body the day the cops were there. I caught a glimpse of her shoe. That's about it. And there was the big black guy walking down the street with a small Native lady. I told the detective about that."

"Yeah, you told me." Officer Hamre interjected.

"Oh, that was you?" Romeo asked, turning to Officer Hamre.

"Yes."

"I'm just kind of confused," Detective Jones said. "Maybe I'm getting the time frame all screwed up, but I thought you said you were out of town."

Romeo explained that he had gone camping but returned to Anchorage to work on a car at Dennis Whitmore's garage. "Danny was outta town, I wasn't."

"Okay, you came back to town," Detective Jones asserted.

"Yeah, I came back to town," Romeo said.

"Okay, and again, I'm not asking you to be a snitch,"

---

25 Romeo claimed he had been shot on February 2, 1998.

Detective Jones said. "I'm just trying to figure out what's going on."

"Well, a crime is a crime," Romeo replied. "And a murder's a murder. That's two different things."

"That's the way I look at it too," Detective Jones said.

"Yeah, you know, if it was my family dead, you know …" Romeo's voice trailed off.

"You'd want someone to step up," Detective Jones said, completing the thought.

"Exactly."

"So if I knew anything, I wouldn't be afraid to say," Romeo said. "Especially when I heard there's a $15,000 reward."[26]

"Would anyone you know do something like this?" Detective Jones asked.

"Oh I know some hard asses," Romeo said. "But not enough to do something like that."

"You don't think?"

"No."

"Okay."

"They got to have a reason. But for some shit like what happened to that poor old lady in the shack, no, I don't know anybody who'd do something like that. That's just fucking pointless and ruthless. There's no reason to kill anybody to me personally. Money ain't worth it."

Detective Jones and Detective Hamre exited the room, and eight minutes later, they returned. Detectives were getting nowhere with Danny, but Romeo had no idea what he was saying in the other interview room, and Romeo was growing concerned.

---

26 Police were unaware, at this point, that Romeo had already called Crime Stoppers and received a $1,000 reward for his tip about Wade. The figure of reward money was grossly exaggerated by members of the GTS street gang; at one point a rumor circulated that the reward had grown to $1 million.

"Back again, huh?" Romeo asked.

"Have you ever been in that shack?" Detective Hamre asked.

"No, never," Romeo replied.

"So there's no way we'd find your hair or DNA or anything like that in the shack?"

"No."

"No? Okay, well it just seems like a real coincidence that we're getting information that you might know something, or Danny might know something about this homicide, and then we find you two together. You were there at the scene the morning of, and you were there the night before ... so that all seems kind of unusual. You understand how that could be strange?"

"Yeah, well it's like, that morning I walked over there, you know ..." Romeo explained, seeming slightly rattled. "My little friend Peaches[27] comes up to me and tells me, 'Hey man, there's a whole bunch of cops down the road.'"

"Uh huh," Detective Hamre said attentively.

"You know then I told the cop, I mean I told you, what I knew, and then I went back home, and you know, I've known Danny since he was a kid so there's no big deal there."

Romeo acknowledged he was at Dennis Whitmore's garage on the night before police discovered Della's body, but he denied knowing anything about a homicide.

"If you saw something, or gone into that shack, we just need to know that. It ain't that big a deal, but we gotta know," Detective Jones said.

"Well, I'll give you every pair of shoes I own, I will give you every piece of clothing I own. I let you do fiber samples of anywhere around my house, and you will not find one

---

27 "Peaches" is a nickname for Jonathan McCune, one of the people associated with the GTS street gang; he was also present in Dennis Whitmore's garage at the time of Della Brown's murder.

trace of evidence of me in that yard or that shack. Cuz I never stepped foot in that place."

ELEVEN

The next morning Lieutenant Vanderveur arrived at work to find a voicemail from Romeo indicating he and Danny did indeed have information about the case and that they were ready to talk. The voicemail system showed Romeo had placed the call within thirty minutes of leaving the police station the previous day, but Lieutenant Vanderveur had already gone home. Danny had previously denied any knowledge of a homicide, and police warned the two friends that withholding information was a serious crime, especially in a murder case, and that they had "a window of opportunity" to come clean and tell the truth.[28] Romeo and Danny both would later claim a police sergeant had told them they could go to jail for the rest of their lives for withholding information about a murder.[29]

Danny and Romeo again were interviewed separately by Anchorage police.

"See, we went back to the house last night," Romeo explained, "and I didn't know that he knew nothing about nothing."

"You mean Danny?" the detective asked.

"Yeah, we went back to his house and started talking. And he knew the same shit I know. We were both in the

---

28 The quote is from an affidavit written by Lieutenant Vanderveur in support of the criminal complaint against Josh Wade.
29 Danny, Romeo, and Wade's attorneys alleged such a threat was made by police, but such a statement is not contained on any of the police recordings entered into evidence.

shop, we were both there. Other people, too, but I'm not putting in their names because they don't know shit. We're all there in the shop working on my car. This guy Josh comes in. His name is like Wade or Ward or some shit."

"Josh Wade?"

"Yeah. He comes into the shop, and he's covered from his fucking neck down with blood. And he's like, 'I need to wash this off.' He was trying to say it was spaghetti sauce, and I was like, 'Yeah whatever, I'm working on this car.' I guess then, fucking, I overheard him saying it to someone standing right next to me that he killed the Native girl."

Romeo said that, at some point, Wade convinced him to walk up to Sicily's Pizza to use the pay phone and suggested they take the long way around, up Dorbrandt Street. As they neared 32nd Avenue, Wade asked Romeo if he wanted to see something. Wade motioned to Romeo to follow, and he approached the side door of the shed. At first, the door wouldn't budge, but with one big push Wade forced it open. There were no streetlights nearby, but an angled ray of moonlight streamed in through the open door. Romeo said he could see the body of a woman, partially clothed and on her back, her legs spread apart. He also could see the woman's badly beaten face; it appeared one side her head had been crushed. Romeo explained he had been exposed to carnage before, but he had never seen so much blood. He said his eyes were still focusing in the darkness, but he could see that Wade was pointing to some object near the woman's body. "And he's like, 'Help me move this rock. ... My dad says I need to move this rock.'"

"Did he point to a rock?" the officer asked.

"Yeah, he pointed to a rock. It was black, I couldn't really see. ... I stood there for a second, thinking in my mind, 'Is this fucking real or is this a joke?' You know, he's like, 'I need you to help me move it.' I was like, 'I am fucking gone.

Fuck this.'"

"How do you know Josh?" the detective asked.

"I don't know Josh. I just met him."

"And he just started talking to you?"

"Yeah, bragging."

"Had you talked to this kid before? Before these days?"

"No, never before in my life."

"He just comes up to you and starts spilling all of this?" the detective asked, with a doubtful tone. "So what did he say?"

"He was like, 'I killed this bitch.' I thought it was a joke."

Romeo told police that Wade had spent two nights cruising around in his father's Cadillac, and, at some point, Wade's father, known to everyone as "Bubba," had put his foot down. He ordered Wade to return the car, so Wade enlisted a small group of people at the garage to come with him on the errand: Jesse, Romeo, and Romeo's girlfriend, Sabrina Loomis. They all rode in the Cadillac to Bubba's trailer, where Jesse had parked his Ford Bronco earlier that evening.

Romeo said Wade stopped near the shed on Dorbrandt Street along the way. The others watched as Wade got out of the car and walked into the shed. He immediately returned carrying something long, with a handle. He opened the back door of the Cadillac, where Romeo was sitting with Sabrina, and tossed the object onto Romeo's lap.

Romeo at first had told detectives he had been driving, but when he got to this point in the story, he claimed he was in the backseat and that Wade was behind the wheel.

"I thought you were driving," the detective interrupted.

"Oh, I'm mistaken. I'm mistaken," Romeo replied. "We picked up the car. We came back ... we took the car back, the Cadillac back to his dad's house ... and that's when the shovel happened. So a couple days later he's still talking about stuff, so the body's been dead for a while now."

"Josh is the only one allowed to drive his dad's Cadillac," Romeo added.

Romeo claimed that Wade did not say anything as he tossed the object on his lap, and it took a moment for Romeo to recognize it as a red snow shovel with a wooden handle. Wade got back into the car and continued driving.

"I was like, 'What's up with the shovel?'" Romeo said. "And he said, 'I just killed this cat with it.'" Romeo said he paused, unsure of what Wade meant.

"I was like, 'You mean a real cat, as in a feline?'"

Romeo said that Wade let out a laugh but didn't answer. A few minutes later, Wade pulled the car into the parking lot of the Club at Eagle Point Apartments, just across the street from the trailer park where his father lived. The car came to a stop, and, according to Romeo, Wade told him to toss the shovel out of the car. Romeo complied, he said, tossing it out of the window and into some bushes.

Romeo claimed that later, when he saw the woman's body, he was overcome with a sense of panic. He would later reveal, under oath, what was going on in his mind: *I'm going to go to jail 'cause my fingerprints are going to be on that damn thing*, he thought. *Why did he throw that shit on my lap? When it's going to be my fingerprints on there?*

Romeo's insistence to police that the incident with the shovel happened before he ever saw the woman's body is a detail he hoped would save him from being prosecuted as an accessory to the murder. However, it was clear Romeo had not clearly thought through his version of events. His initial account to police was so jumbled and contained so many gaps and contradictions, detectives weren't sure what to think. Even simple facts such as whether Romeo was driving the Cadillac or sitting in the backseat, seemed inexplicably fuzzy.

"Were you doing dope that night?" the detective asked.

"No, I don't do drugs but I was drinking, I was a bit hammered. We were drinking R&R.[30] But I know Josh was 100 percent sober."

As for why Romeo had come to Officer Hamre at the crime scene on the day Della Brown's body had been found, police could only speculate. Was he trying to send them down the wrong path? Divert their attention from Wade? The fact he had mentioned the woman was carrying another shirt appeared suspicious, given that a red shirt had been recovered near the woman's body, a detail that had not been released to the public. Whether Romeo had actually seen a Native woman walking with a black man was equally unclear, but when he returned to the garage and related to Wade that detectives were taking impressions of shoe prints in and around the shed, he recalled that Wade had reacted with anxiety and paranoia. Romeo also said that Wade had promised retribution if he told anyone about Wade's connection to the dead woman in the shed.

"He said if I started talking I would be next," Romeo recalled. "He said, 'I'm going to fucking kill you and your girlfriend if you say anything.'"[31]

In constructing a timeline, detectives were trying to pinpoint the day Della had been killed. Romeo alleged several days had passed between the woman's death and the day on which police discovered her body.

"A couple of days," Romeo said. "Like four days. The second day she was dead he went back to fuck with her. He smashed her face in some more with a rock, and he slept with [her]."

"You mean he had sex with her?" the detective asked.

---

30 R&R is a brand of Canadian whiskey.
31 This quote is from one of Timothy Beckett's interviews with police. He repeated this claim on the witness stand.

"Yeah," Romeo replied, adding that Wade had premeditated the woman's murder.

"The second he'd seen her, he planned on killing her."

"He told you that?" the detective asked.

"Yeah he said, 'I was going to kill the bitch anyway, it didn't matter to me.' But he was probably going to do it in a different way. He probably was just going to slice her throat rather than beating her."

Romeo would modify his timeline several times during the interview, saying later, "I'm not too sure exactly what day he killed her. It could've been Monday. It could've been Wednesday." The glaring problem with this assertion was that Della's family and at least one neighbor reported seeing her as late as Thursday night. The police knew Romeo was either lying or severely confused, and they were trying to figure out why.

"Now I got a big question I have to ask you," the detective said. "I'm glad you're telling us the truth here, about this thing with the shovel. Now I'm going to ask you straight up. And one question is, did you have anything to do with this girl's death?"

"No, never, nothing. Like I said I just met this cat that day."

"Now, if I'm hearing you right, you helped him get rid of the shovel."

"Yeah, but I didn't know what it was about. I didn't know nothing about the shovel."

"I'm having a little trouble with your times here," the detective said, shaking his head.

"I'm having trouble with my times, too," Romeo replied.

"I want to make sure you're not filling in times here because you're reluctant to tell us about your moment with the shovel. I don't want you to be."

"I will tell you anything you want to know about that

shovel."

"Did you know, did you know, had you already seen him with a blood on him prior to you being involved with that shovel?"

"I couldn't tell if it was blood or what it was. But he had stuff, like red stuff on his shirt."

"So he had red stuff on his shirt, and the shovel came afterwards, right?"

"I believe it came afterwards, yeah."

"Let's just pause here. Now you say you're sitting in the backseat and he tosses this shovel in your lap. And now you're worried … you're getting upset at him …"

"That was the next day when I found out he used the shovel to kill the girl. And he never said he used the shovel to kill their girl, to me."

"I'm having a hard time understanding because you're saying …"

"Wednesday he throws the shovel on my lap," Romeo interrupted. "Then on Thursday he comes up to me and says, 'I killed this girl, yada, yada, yada,' and then I go berserk on him because I had the shovel on my lap from yesterday. I start flipping out on him."

"You've been very clear up until this point that on the first day when you were working on the car you heard Jesse and Josh talking," the detective said. "You may not have known everything, but you have a clue. You have a clue. And again, it does not matter, I need to know the truth now. I understand you didn't know details … but it seems like you had a clue."

Romeo paused. "Yeah, I had an idea," he replied.

****

Down the hall, Danny told police a similar story.

Detectives were still trying to sort out the timeline given Romeo's inconsistent statements about the sequence of events, but the gruesome details of how Wade reportedly tortured, killed, and sexually assaulted Della Brown were basically alike.

"[Josh said] that he seen her lying on the side of the road, just all passed out and drunk and he was going to check her to see if she had any money or jewelry," Danny said. "And when he stuck his hand into her pocket that she wet herself and it got onto his hand and he just got really mad and he flipped out and he started beating her."

"Did he tell you what he was beating her with?" the detective asked.

"He said he started smashing her head with a rock. He just grabbed a rock and started beating her with it."

Danny explained that Dennis had banned his visitors from using the phone at the house, so occasionally members of the group would walk to the pizza place up the road to use a pay phone. Danny had hoped to learn something about fixing cars, but it proved to be a more boring task than he had anticipated, so when Wade asked him to walk up the street with him to use the pay phone, he welcomed the chance to get some fresh air. When they passed the shed on Dorbrandt Street, Wade waved him over and made him promise he wouldn't tell anyone what he was about to show him. Danny agreed. He said that Wade handed him a cigarette lighter and asked him to light it so he could see inside the shed. As Wade entered the shed, Danny stood on the small porch area in complete darkness. He approached slowly and could hear a rustling inside. Danny said he extended his arm through the open doorway. He flicked the lighter with his thumb and an orange glow illuminated the room. Below him, just a few feet from where he was standing, he saw the silhouette of a woman, lying on her back, in a pool of blood. Danny said he did not cry out or gasp, rather, he felt quite unable to speak. The woman's head was right in the doorway, and she was on her back. Wade was standing at the other end of the body, near the woman's feet.

"He said, 'The door won't shut, so I need you to help me move her,'" Danny said. Danny said he stood motionless for a moment and then began to shake. Danny said he watched as Wade pulled the woman more fully into the shed. Danny felt paralyzed by fear but eventually managed to turn around and walk away, heading back in the direction of the garage. Wade came running after him.

"He said, 'We can't go back right now. We have to make it seem like we went to use the pay phone.'"

Danny hesitated but finally he agreed to walk to the pay phone with Wade before returning to the garage.

"And he was saying, 'Don't tell anybody.' And I was like, 'I am not going to, I'm not going to say anything.' I don't remember his exact words, but he said something like, 'Remember, I know where your mother lives. I'll kill her if you say anything.'"

Danny said when they eventually returned to the garage, his sister, Anna, could tell something was wrong with him. He told her not to worry, that he wasn't feeling well because he had been drinking too much. He was shaking, partly from the cold, but also because of what he had just seen. Danny told police that Wade offered him his hooded sweatshirt and that he had accepted the gesture without much thought. A little while later, Anna came up to Danny with a quizzical look on her face.

"She pointed to the sweater and said, 'What's that on your sweater?' And so I looked down and there was a stain. It was a red stain."

One could convincingly argue that Danny and Romeo had coordinated their accounts to police, given Romeo's concern about the shovel possibly containing his fingerprints and Danny's concern about wearing a blood-stained sweatshirt. It may also partially explain why they were both willing to wear a wire and have their conversations with Wade recorded by police.

TWELVE

Just two days after their second interview with police, Romeo and Danny were strapped with recording devices and given an unmarked police vehicle, which, unbeknownst to them, also was equipped with a recording device. Detective Tim Landeis was in charge of dealing with the young informants and, it was fair to say, he had his hands full. Landeis was a self-assured cop with the look of a wrestler, a round face, cleft chin, and a receding hairline; it was his first real involvement in a homicide case and also his first time dealing with informants. The FBI also provided assistance; Agent LouAnn Henderson made sure the recording devices were working and appropriately discrete.

"Okay, we're on right now," Agent Henderson said, facing Romeo and Danny.

"You don't have to yell, remember," Detective Landeis advised.

"Hey this thing ain't gonna break down I hope," Romeo said, referring to the unmarked car, which was an old Chevy. "This is a piece of fuckin' shit. Hey, thanks for giving us a nice car guys, really."

Danny laughed.

"This really builds up my self-esteem," Romeo added. "Seriously, this thing isn't going to break down, is it?"

"No," Detective Landeis replied.

"So we just drive straight up to his house from here, right?" Romeo asked.

"Straight to his house," Lieutenant Vanderveur affirmed.

"Can you hear me?" Romeo said, moving his chin to his chest and closer to the hidden microphone. "Tim's gay," Romeo said, referring to Detective Landeis, who was out of earshot. Danny burst out laughing.

Police had concocted a plan to spark a conversation about Della Brown's murder between the informants and Josh Wade, by placing a copy of the *Anchorage Daily News* on the dashboard of the car. A front-page article had just been published that morning displaying photos of six women, including Della Brown, whom had been murdered within a sixteen-month period. Quoted in the article was Captain Bill Miller, who said the department had deployed its full resources to finding a killer or killers.

"If it turns out to be one person or six, we're going to get them," he told the paper.

Before leaving the station, Detective Landeis gave Romeo and Danny a cell phone so he could reach them before and after they made contact with Wade. Romeo and Danny got into the car and began to drive to Wade's dad's house, on the other side of town.

"I gotta roll the window down, I wanna smoke. Hold my soda for a second," Romeo said as he drove, handing his can of soda to Danny.

"Motherfucker, I only got two hands," Danny replied.

"Shut up," Romeo said, still struggling to roll the window down, without success. The car swerved as Romeo took his attention off the road.

"Hey look, mine rolls down," Danny said. "Now, steer straight. Keep swerving and they're going to think you're drunk."

Romeo and Danny pulled up to Wade's trailer, and saw his father, Bubba, standing outside. Romeo leaned over Danny, and spoke to Bubba through the passenger side window.

"Hey, is Josh here?" Romeo asked.

Bubba nodded.

"Can you tell him to come out?" Romeo asked.

"Go ahead," Bubba replied.

"Oh, is he in the front room?" Romeo asked. Just as he said this, Wade exited the trailer and walked over to the car. They noticed right away Wade had shaved his head. "Hey Josh! What's up boy? What's up dawg?"

"Who's riding with you?" Wade asked.

"It's me and Danny," Romeo replied.

"What's up?" Wade asked, seeming a bit distant.

"What's up? What you paranoid for, man? It's me and Danny."

"Hey, what's up over there," Wade said, acknowledging Danny.

Romeo explained they were going to the pawn shop and asked Wade if he wanted to come along.

"Yeah, okay," Wade said, getting into the backseat.

"What you so 'noid about, man?" Romeo asked.

"About what?" Wade asked.

"I don't know, you just seem kinda 'noid to me." Romeo replied, as he drove. Romeo and Danny hadn't seen or talked to Wade for almost a month, since he had taken them to see Della Brown's body in the shed.

"Where the fuck you been at, man?" Romeo asked.

"Mountain View," Wade replied. "Fuckin' hos, makin' money."[32]

"Shit, go make me some money!" Romeo said, playfully.

"Fuck you, bitch!" Wade replied.

"Shit, nigga," Romeo said.

"Where's Dwayne at?" Wade asked. "He walked right past me in Carrs[33] and I was about to bomb his little faggot-

---

32 Mountain View is a part of Anchorage, north of the airport.
33 Carrs is an Anchorage-based supermarket chain.

ass white boy ... why you tryin' to avoid me, man?"

"He probably didn't recognize you, man," Romeo offered. "You shaved your head, dawg."

"That and fuckin' Jesse's little bitch ass," Wade said. "I can't wait to see that motherfucker."

"Why, what's up with that?" Romeo asked.

"Whoop his ass," Wade replied. "He hasn't called me, said shit to me, nothin'."

"Where'd you get this car?" Wade asked, changing the subject.

"Oh, that's my partner's car," Romeo explained. "He's fuckin' letting me borrow it for a few days, man."

"What pawn shop we going to?" Romeo asked.

"Spenard," Wade replied.

"Spenard Pawn?"

"Yeah."

"I just need to get some more money so I can re-up man, then I can go get my shit back," Wade explained.

Wade said he was trying to convince his girlfriend to give him money and wished she hadn't discovered that he was in town.

"Where'd you go?" Romeo asked.

"California," Wade replied. "Just got back two days ago. My homeboy went down there to see his cousin."[34]

"Well, the cops are lookin' for my ass," Romeo said. "Yo, mine and Danny's for some shit ..."

"In this?" Wade asked, referring to the car.

"No," Romeo replied. "That's why I'm driving this..."

"Well, I'm not going to jail," Wade replied.

"Look," Romeo said, gesturing to the newspaper on the dashboard. "Look at this shit, dawg."

"Uh, I ain't fuckin' touching it," Wade replied.

---

34 Wade did not go to California as he claimed; police had been surveilling him in Anchorage for more than a week before this encounter.

"That shit right there's got me 'noid, dawg" Romeo said. "I'm dippin' state.[35] Me and Danny, we're dippin', bro. We got our tickets and everything. We out. We gone. Next Friday, we gonna be out. I just gotta pick up my tickets, man." Romeo glanced at the newspaper. "Yo, that bitch look like it, there? She look familiar?"

"That ain't her," Wade replied, scanning the faces of the dead women in the paper. "Where's the lady at? She ain't in here."

"She ain't in there?"

"Wait a minute," Wade paused. "That's her ... that's her ..."

"Who?" Romeo asked.

"Right there," Wade said, pointing to the photo of Della Brown. "Right there, on September 2nd."

"That bitch?" Romeo asked.

"That's that other bitch," Wade said, referring to another woman pictured in the article.

"Man, you makin' the papers, dawg," Romeo said.

"That's that other bitch from a long time ago," Wade said, still staring at the paper. "I was still in jail."

Wade appeared engrossed by the article and, at this point, was ignoring Romeo, who seemed to be having a completely separate conversation.

"Where's the nearest Cash America?" Romeo asked.[36]

"That's the bitch! That's the bitch!" Wade said excitedly, as if the news was just setting in.

"Hey, you goin' to Cali ... I wanna go with you when you go ... yo, I'm dippin' Friday, wanna go with us?" Romeo asked.

"Hold on a minute," Wade said, carefully studying the

---

35 "Dippin'" is a slang term, meaning to leave suddenly or abruptly.
36 Cash America is a chain of pawn shops with several locations in Anchorage.

women's faces. "There's only three on here, man. They ain't got shit on me! Motherfuckers trying to put extra shit on me!"

"Them niggers ain't got nuttin' on nobody," Romeo said, without missing a beat. "Man, you know the police are too stupid up here to know anything."

"Yeah right," Wade replied. "If they were smart, they'd find my condom wrapper."

"Hoooo, right," Romeo replied. "All right, yo."

"I fuckin' never told anybody that I raped that lady," Wade said.

"Hey, I don't want to know shit," Romeo replied.

"I never raped nobody, dude," Wade said.

"I ain't trying to hear that man," Romeo said. "Don't tell me shit."

"That's really sick, I threw up afterwards, man," Wade said. "I threw up all over. Then I was like, 'Fuck that.'"

"Hey, you wanna kick it at our telly[37] if we get one?" Romeo asked.

"Yeah," Wade replied.

"Kick it with us a little bit," Romeo said.

"Have to man," Wade said. "That'd be cool … fuck … I was staying in Mountain View but the spot got hot, and shit man, I had to leave. Fuckin' undercover sittin' there behind garbage cans, writin' shit down about the apartment."

"Are you for real?" Romeo asked.

"I mean, there was just way too much shit going on there," Wade said. "There was a Bronco parked all the way at the end of the street and shit. We ran up on it and they all ducked down in the car whenever we walked up to it. Fuck that, man."

"So yeah, let's kick it soon," Romeo said. "Give me your number and shit."

---

37 Slang word for hotel.

"2-6-8 …" Wade began.

"Write it down on that," Romeo replied, referring to the newspaper.

"Hell no," Wade replied. "I want to keep this."

"Well, rip a piece off then man and shit. Rip a piece off," Romeo said. "What are you gonna do? Hang it on your fuckin' wall?"

"I got plenty of newspaper clippings," Wade replied. "I got this bitch's newspaper clippings and this bitch's newspapers," he said, pointing to two of the women pictured in the newspaper article.[38]

"What?" Romeo asked.

"No, not that bitch," Wade said.

"All those bitches?" Romeo asked. "You did all those bitches?" referring to all six women pictured on the front page.

"These bitches and those bitch," Wade replied.

"Those are all you, right there?" Romeo asked. "Man, what's up with you and Native women?"

"She was black, man," Wade replied, referring to Michelle Foster-Butler, the only victim who was African American.

"Ah, you couldn't a done that black bitch," Romeo replied. "She's too fine … that bitch look too good."

"Not that good naked," Wade replied.

"Anyway, I'm going to hit you up when I get this telly, man," Romeo said. "You come kickin' with us and shit."

They arrived at the pawn shop but discovered it was closed.

"You want me to drop you off somewhere?" Romeo asked Wade. "Or do you wanna go to your crib?"

"No," Wade replied. "Back to my house."

---

38 Here, Wade is referring to two different women but their identities are not made clear on the audio recording or in the transcript.

As they made their way back to Wade's trailer, Danny interjected, "She's gettin' pretty in the face," pointing to one of the women in the newspaper.

"I don't know," Romeo said. "Some of these bitches in here are pretty ugly, dawg."

"Oh, that ain't shit," Wade said.

"You raped that ugly ass bitch," Romeo said, referring to Della Brown.

"It didn't have nothin' to do with that," Wade said. "I don't know, my adrenaline was goin'. My dick got hard."

"Your adrenaline got goin', your dick got hard," Romeo said. "My shit usually shrivels up and hides, man."

"Fuck that," Wade said. Danny laughed.

"Teach you a lesson to stick your hand in somebody's pocket again, won't it?" Romeo asked.

"Oh no, I didn't do that," Wade replied. "It was all a lie."

"Oh, was it?" Romeo asked.

"See, that's some sick shit," Wade replied.

"So you didn't get piss on your hand?" Romeo asked.

"No, bullshit man," Wade said. A flash of anger came over his face. "Who told you that?"

"D," Romeo replied.

"Who?"

"D."

"All right," Wade said. "You see Dwayne, you tell him when he fuckin' sees me, he better run."

"No, not Dwayne," Romeo said. "Jesse."

"All right, well, tell that motherfucker ..." Wade said. "Where you goin' now?" he added, abruptly changing subjects. They had just pulled up to Wade's trailer.

"Eagle River," Romeo replied. "Might spend the night there. Keep your pager on you, man. If I don't hit you up tonight, I'm going to hit you up tomorrow ... come kick it with me and Danny."

"I'm calling this bitch up now," Wade said, opening the car door. "I got to get some weed."

"All right," Romeo said.

"Stay out of trouble," Danny added.

The car door slammed shut.

****

As soon as Wade was out of sight and back inside his trailer, Romeo and Danny stared at each other in disbelief.

"Motherfucker!" Danny said. "Shit, he's willing to talk. Damn. Well, we did our dirty work. That shit was pretty smooth."

"Man, that was easy," Romeo remarked. "You guys like that?" he said excitedly, knowing that police were listening in. "Hey, the motherfucker admitted to three of 'em man! If you don't like that, you can kiss my ass!"

THIRTEEN

Police considered that Joshua Wade may have killed several of the women pictured in the newspaper, but, at least initially, they were not focused on him as their only suspect. Investigators also considered a serial rapist, Gregory Poindexter, who targeted Native women. Poindexter had assaulted and raped no fewer than five women, all of whom were intoxicated and alone at the time; in fact, one of his victims had been attacked the night before Della Brown was killed. In 1995, Poindexter lived just a block away from the abandoned shed where Della's body had been found, and he knew the neighborhood well. Also, Poindexter was large in stature and African American, and police wondered if he was the tall black man Romeo had described, seen walking with a Native woman near the shed near the time of the murder.

A man named Raymond Gordon also briefly came under suspicion. Investigators had questioned him in connection with the death of a 13-year-old girl, Delaney Zutz, who had been stabbed to death and found in a wooded area near her home.[39] Gordon had admitted, during questioning by Anchorage police, that he knew Della Brown. When pressed on the nature of their connection, Gordon divulged that he had known her intimately. This information was passed on to Detective Landeis, who conducted a follow-up interview with Gordon and collected a saliva sample from him, so his

---

39 In August of 2004, a jury convicted eighteen-year-old Branden Ling of first degree murder for killing Delaney Zutz.

DNA could be tested.

Also briefly scrutinized was the man known as Steve, who had driven Lance Druba and his boyfriend to the shed after they had initially stumbled upon Della's body. Steve, whose real name was Kenneth Cassidy, had not only entered the shed and circled the body; he also had a large bloodstain on his jeans. He told detectives that he had cut his finger and wiped the blood on his clothing. Police collected a sample of the blood but almost immediately determined, after questioning Cassidy, that he had nothing to do with Della's death.

Della's boyfriend, Rudy D'Apice, was perhaps the most obvious suspect given his history of violence with her, along with the appearance of a motive, not to mention that police had failed to establish his alibi on the night of her death. By the end of September, however, the investigation had shifted and was almost entirely focused on Joshua Wade. Police were convinced of his guilt since they had him on tape, ostensibly confessing to the murders of three women. Undercover officers began staking out Wade's trailer park and trailing his every move.

It didn't take long for Jesse Ackmann to get word that Romeo and Danny had gone to the police, and he knew officers would soon come knocking on his door. Jesse, twenty-two years old, with long, curly black hair and a mustache, was a close friend of Wade's and had been reticent about going to the police. He later testified that he had been extremely drunk during the days spent at Dennis Whitmore's garage and had blacked out many of the details. Given that Romeo and Danny had fessed up, however, Jesse felt he didn't have a choice; he decided to go to the Anchorage police station and tell detectives what he knew.

He told police about finding a Native woman passed out in the street during a late-night joy ride in Wade's father's

Cadillac. He said Dwayne had dragged the woman to the side of the road, near an abandoned shed. Several hours later, after returning to Dennis Whitmore's garage, he and Wade had argued when Jesse refused to come with Wade to "see something." Wade had later confessed to Jesse that he slit the woman's throat but that she was "tough" and "didn't want to die." Wade ultimately killed her with a rock, which, he told Jesse, he later threw into a lake.

One of the reasons Jesse was concerned about going to police was that he had run into some legal trouble of his own. On the day police found Della Brown's body, he had resisted arrest while refusing to leave Dennis Whitmore's property, and after being involved in a drunken brawl with one of Dennis' friends earlier in the day. Responding to a call to police from Dennis' girlfriend, an officer found Jesse passed out in his car, parked in the driveway. The officer had trouble rousting Jesse, and when he did wake, Jesse apparently became aggressive and attacked the officer, who returned his drunken swings with a generous dose of pepper spray.

The attempted assault of a police officer was a serious charge, and perhaps it's why, after divulging what he knew about Della Brown's murder, Jesse agreed to wear a police wire to help authorities build their case against Wade. He must also have wondered whether he could be indirectly implicated in the homicide, having admitted that although Wade had returned to the garage to complain that the woman "wouldn't die," no one, including Jesse, had intervened, called for help, or made any effort to save the woman's life.

Detectives instructed Jesse to call Wade and set up a meeting. The two friends hadn't talked in weeks, and Jesse was nervous, given what he knew and how Wade would react to hearing from him out of the blue. Jesse decided to keep the request simple, telling Wade just that he "needed to talk to him."

"Good," Wade replied. "Because I need to talk to you, too." They made plans to meet later that day.

Jesse was fitted with a recording device hidden under his shirt and was concerned that Wade would try to pat him down. Detective Jones suggested that Jesse wait for Wade to come to him, so he wouldn't have to get out of the car, but Jesse thought that would only raise Wade's suspicions.

"I'd feel better if I got out and went up to the door, man," Jesse said.

"Why?" Detective Jones asked.

"Just so ... so he's easy with it," Jesse replied.

"He's got people there, man?"

"No, he's got his dad."

"I thought I heard people in the background," Detective Jones said, referring to the call Jesse had made earlier to Wade's trailer.

"That was the TV," Jesse said.

"Well, you're talking to me about being worried about being patted down," Detective Jones explained. "That's the way to avoid it. Okay? I want to alleviate as many fears as possible."

As with Romeo and Danny, police insisted on providing an unmarked vehicle owned by the police department, equipped with a recording device. Jesse was resistant to this, especially when he saw the rundown Toyota pickup police wanted him to drive.

"Can I go in my own truck?" Jesse asked.

"No," Detective Jones replied. "This is the car we got, man."

"Phhhhhh, man. Never gonna ... he's never gonna believe that's mine."

"It's not yours. It's not yours," Detective Jones said. "You borrowed it. Your rig is busted again."

"Who'd I borrow it from?" Jesse asked.

"You tell me," Detective Jones said. "You work on cars all the time. Got a friend he doesn't know?"

"Just be cool man, you're gonna be fine," another officer said.

"Yeah, you're gonna be fine," Detective Jones reassured.

"Just be yourself," the other officer said.

****

There is no talking for several minutes on the recording, only the sounds of traffic, the clicking of a turn signal, a sneeze, and at least one belch. As Jesse pulled up to Wade's trailer, Jesse cleared his throat. Wade was standing outside, where he had apparently been waiting.

"What up, fool?" Wade asked. "Fuckin' traded, man?" he asked, glancing at the pickup truck.

"Turned my IROC the fuck in," Jesse said, referring to his Camaro.

"Uh huh," Wade paused and then laughed. "Man!"

"What did you need to talk to me about, man?" Jesse asked.

"There's some fucked up shit goin' on," Wade replied.

"I know," Jesse said. "They've been coming around. They, they even come by my house man, the cops."

"About what?" Wade asked, seeming concerned.

"I talked to Dwayne the other day. He said that, fuckin' everybody's fuckin' talkin' shit dude, about that whole fuckin' scene."

"Talking shit like what?"

"I don't know. He won't fuckin' say. He called me up. He's like, 'Oh, have you heard?' He's like, 'Somebody's been talkin' and saying your name. They been sayin' that somebody's been fuckin' talkin'.' I don't ... I don't know

79

man, but I know I wasn't fuckin'… I wasn't home, like two days ago, man. Fuckin' cops came by and was asking Jamie[40] this and that and where I was. Man, I was stayin' away from my house ever since, man."

"What kind of questions?" Wade asked.

"I just told you, man," Jesse replied. "Where I was, this and that. I'm fuckin' spooked about that shit, man. Cuz fuckin' Dwayne paged me up, right? I call him back and he's actin' all fuckin' shiesty shady over the fuckin' phone, sayin' that uh … fuckin' they been uhm … asking questions about uhm … you know, what they've been askin' questions about, man. That's why I started wonderin', 'What the fuck?'"

Jesse's nerves were getting the best of him.

"Well, you want to roll somewhere?" Jesse asked.

"Yeah," Wade replied. He got into the car.

"See, that's what I'm sayin'," Jesse continued as he drove out of the trailer park. "I'm telling you, some fucked up shit's goin' on dude. Shit ain't fuckin' cool."

"I'm not trippin'," Wade said.

"Well, I'm trippin, man," Jesse admitted. "I'm trippin' cuz they're fuckin' askin' for me. Know what I'm sayin'? I don't know shit, only I got to go to court on the fuckin' second over that bullshit at fuckin' Dennis's house."[41]

"You got nothing to worry about," Wade interrupted. "Especially you and Dwayne. There's nothin' that they can … there's nothin' anybody can say to put you in that." Wade paused, then added, "There's nothing that anybody can say to put *me* in that."

"Well, I been thinkin' about it, man," Jesse said. "I mean, I was there when the shovel was fuckin' ditched, and, and, if

---

40 Jamie was Jesse's wife at the time.
41 Jesse is referring to his altercation with police and subsequent arrest at Dennis Whitmore's house on the day Della Brown's body was found by police.

Romeo's fuckin' talking shit, that's the only way they could even know about that shit, you know what I'm sayin'?"

"Well, Romeo told me he wouldn't tell 'em shit, cuz Romeo came to me with some shit that I ain't ever told nobody. I said, 'Who the fuck told you that?' And he said you."

"Said me?" Jesse asked incredulously.

"Yes sir," Wade replied.

"I ain't even, I ain't even talked to fuckin' Romeo, man." Jesse said, his heart beginning to race.

"I thought it was funny that he came to find me yesterday," Wade said. "That was really weird."

"Well, I wanna know why Dwayne's calling me up, says there's cops lookin' for me," Jesse said. "I know he's still kickin' it with Romeo. Romeo's fuckin' gone to the cops." Jesse let out a loud belch.

"Well," Wade said, starting to reflect on his encounter with Romeo and Danny the previous day. "If he woulda handed me that newspaper yesterday, and it wasn't yesterday's paper, I woulda flipped out. But it was yesterday's paper with all those bitches mentioned in the paper."[42]

"Have you seen it already?" Jesse asked.

"Yeah, I seen it."

"All I know man, I've been spooked, man." Jesse said with a tinge of panic in his voice. "I don't know how it actually works, know what I'm sayin'?"

"Jesse," Wade said, raising his voice. "There is *nothin'*, there is *nothin'*, that can be said or done that would put you in that. Really."

"Danny was talkin' shit, telling me that you didn't trust

---

42 Wade is referring to the newspaper article shown to him by Romeo and Danny. The front page article featuring photos of all six murdered women appeared in the *Anchorage Daily News* on September 28, 2000, the same day Romeo and Danny took part in the police wire.

me," Wade said.

"That I didn't trust you?"

"I said I didn't trust anybody, man," Jesse said. "I'm just fuckin' spooked."

"I understand what you're sayin', but I'm telling you, if anything was fuckin' poppin' off, I'd be the first to know," Wade said. "My address is known. Prints are in the fuckin' computer. They know me by the book. Ain't gonna see my face on *America's Most Wanted*."

"Shit man, I thought you were fuckin' mad at me for some reason," Jesse said.

"I wasn't mad," Wade explained. "I was just wonderin', man. 'What, damn, where the fuck is Jesse? He ain't comin' around.'"

"After that shit man, I was like, 'What the fuck, dude.'"

"Well, that's just it. You don't understand. You gotta understand my situation with that shit. Oh, what, oh fuck, I ain't even gonna say shit," Wade said, catching himself. "With everything goin' on, man, someone quit comin' around me is givin' me a bad feeling, that's all."

They had arrived back at Wade's trailer and were parked in the driveway.

"Let's go in here," Wade said, getting out of the car. Jesse followed and entered the trailer knowing that he was more vulnerable out of the car if Wade wanted to pat him down. Jesse saw Wade's dad, Bubba, watching TV in the living room.

Jesse and Wade went into another room, and they talked for several minutes with the television blaring in the background. It soon became evident that Jesse was growing antsy.

"I gotta get the fuck outta here, give somebody a ride real quick," Jesse said abruptly.

"You do?" Wade asked.

"Yeah."

"Who?"

"Fuckin'... my friend Jamie and one of his friends," Jesse stammered. "I'm just gonna give 'em a ride real quick, and I'll be right back."

"Do me a favor," Wade said, pointing at Jesse's shirt. "Give me a shot of that, man."

Jesse realized Wade wanted to see if there was anything under his shirt. "I ain't got nothing on me, man," Jesse replied.

"You can't say I'm not paranoid, man," Wade said. He was becoming agitated. "Can't say ..." Wade stepped closer to Jesse.

"Come on man," Jesse said, feeling a sense of panic sweep over him. "Fuck this shit, man. Fuck you, man. Fuck you, man. Fuck that shit, man."

"I'm fuckin' paranoid," Wade said, worried by how defensive Jesse was acting.

"That's bullshit, being paranoid," Jesse said.

"Listen, listen, you tell me ..." Wade said, looking directly into Jesse's eyes.

"Paranoid ass," Jesse interrupted.

"Stop. Stop. You listen. You tell me ... you give ... you feel ..." Wade was now convinced something wasn't right. "You think it's weird that Romeo pops outta nowhere?"

"Let them fuckin' pop outta nowhere," Jesse shot back. "I ain't fuckin' tried to ask you nothin', man. I ain't tried askin' nothin' fuckin' incriminatin', nothing, man."

"Hey come 'ere, come 'ere," Wade said, reaching out for Jesse's shirt.

"This ain't fuckin' cool man," Jesse said, raising his voice.

"How is it not cool?" Wade shouted.

"Cuz man, fuckin' trying to ask me to fuckin' do that

shit, man," Jesse shouted back. "How long have I fuckin' known you, man?"

"Why you trippin' so bad, then?" Wade asked.

"Cuz, you know, that's fucked up, you even asking me to do some shit like that, man. When, when have I ever been a fuckin' snitch, dude?"

"That ain't got shit to do with it."

"Well, fuckin' quit, quit your fuckin' trippin', man," Jesse said, walking toward the front door.

Wade was trailing close behind. "Jesse, this shit ain't no mother fuckin' joke, man! This is a life! This is somethin' that someone could go to jail for life! Fuckin' life! Did you see how many other things are being connected to this one?"

"No man," Jesse replied.

"There's six fuckin' life sentences!" Wade said. "Fuck that, I don't give a fuck who it is, man. I don't care if it's my mother fuckin' mom! I'm coming at her sideways!"

"Well that's fuckin' cool man," Jesse said letting out a sigh. He walked outside and to the pickup truck, and Wade followed. "Chill out, man. Damn. You ain't got no reason to trip, dude. Come on, man."

"No one comes, dude, no one comes around me ... and then all of a sudden, pow!" Wade exclaimed. "Romeo pops up. Pow! You pop up outta nowhere. Now you're making me feel fucked up or fuckin' shakey, cuz you're actin' funny as shit when I said pull your shirt up!"

"Why should ... why the fuck would you even ask me somethin' like that, man?"

"Because I ain't trustin' nobody."

"That's just foul, man. That's just foul," Jesse said.

"That ain't foul. And this shit's funny to me," Wade said, referring to the pickup truck. "I never seen this shit before."

"I told you, man. I fuckin' traded it in, man. It's a fuckin' trade-in." Jesse could tell Wade didn't believe him.

"Whatever man, just fuck it, man. I'm cool, man."

"Man, I can be all fuckin' shiesty-shady all I want to," Wade said. "What's the big deal about you just …" Wade reached for Jesse's shirt again, and Jesse backed away.

"Why ain't you pullin' up your shirt, man? What the fuck is the big deal? You're really making me scary about this shit right now."

"I ain't being scary, man."

"Then why ain't you pullin' your shirt up?"

"There ain't nothin' to fuckin' pull up, man. There ain't nothin' to see, dude. Just let me … look, dude. I'll call you back in a fuckin' minute, man, all right? I'll call you back in a fuckin' minute. Let me go fuckin' give this dude a ride. Just called 'em, I said I'd give 'em a fuckin' ride, dude. I'll be right back, all right? Quit trippin', man. Come on, man. Who the fuck am I? I mean, how long you known me, man? Come on. All right man, chill out, man. Damn."

Jesse got in the car. He shut the door, started the engine, and pulled away from Wade, who was still standing in the driveway, fuming.

As Jesse drove, he let out a large belch and a sigh. The cell phone the police had given him rang.

"Hello? Yeah, all right." Detective Jones said they would debrief as soon as Jesse arrived back at the police station. Jesse drove there in silence, and when he arrived, he turned off the engine and got out of the pickup truck.

"You okay?" Detective Jones asked.

"Whew!" Jesse replied.

"Have a little bit of tension there?" Detective Jones asked.

"I knew he was gonna do that, man," Jesse said, shaking his head.

"What'd he end up doin', friskin' ya?"

"No, he didn't, he didn't. I didn't let him. Even still, puts me in a bad situation right there."

"Well you got outta there. That's the important thing. How did the conversation go?"

"Well, I didn't get anything out of him," Jesse said. "Whew. Unbelievable."

"Yeah, I know," a female officer said. "But you did a good job."

****

Within minutes of Jesse's visit, officers moved in to arrest Josh Wade. Detective David Parker was sitting in an unmarked police vehicle, in the parking lot of a shopping center, when he heard on the radio that the suspect had left his home on a bicycle. Detective Parker began patrolling the area near Wade's trailer park, and as he drove southbound on Lake Otis Parkway, he saw a young man he thought could be Wade, riding a bicycle on the sidewalk, traveling in the opposite direction. Parker quickly made a U-turn but by the time he turned the car around, the young man on the bike had disappeared.

Police set up a perimeter in the area, and the neighborhood was soon swarmed with patrol cars. Detective Parker took a position near Campbell Creek, near a small park, where the creek turns north, not far from the spot he had last seen the young man he thought was Wade. It was after midnight, and Detective Parker sat there for a while, staring into the darkness. Then, off in the distance, the opaque form of someone walking into the creek came into focus. It was dark and the area was unlit, but it appeared to Detective Parker that the person was carrying a bicycle on his shoulders. At that moment, a marked patrol car pulled up beside Detective Parker's unmarked car, and he saw the figure abruptly change direction, and take off, disappearing into the woods. Officers spent a few hours scouring the area, but called off the search about 3:00 a.m.

****

Later that same afternoon, police got a tip that Josh Wade had been spotted at a home on a back road, just off Boniface Parkway. It was about 5:00 p.m. and the change of shifts was just taking place, so more than thirty patrol cars descended upon the neighborhood, as police set up a perimeter around the house. After about twenty minutes, Wade realized he could not escape, and he surrendered.

The owner of the house, a woman police would only describe as a friend of the suspect, gave police permission to search the premises, and they seized several items of clothing along with a pair of black, high-top Nike sneakers, gloves, and a pack of cigarettes, all of which were soaking wet. Police learned that after crossing Campbell Creek, Wade had called this friend, and she had picked him up in her car. Detectives discovered that when she arrived, Wade was cold and wet, and he quickly got into the backseat of the car, ducking down so no one could see.[43]

****

Once at the jail, Detective Parker was given the task of collecting physical evidence from Wade, and was preparing to take him to a hospital, where blood samples would be taken. Wade was in a small interview room; the door was open and there were officers posted outside, as Detective Parker fastened a waist chain to Wade, alongside Officer Tyler Chevers, who also was inside the small room. Detective Parker asked Wade to lift his arms as he slipped the chain around his waist, then secured it to his handcuffs.

---

43 Police interviewed a passenger in the car, who relayed this information.

Wade took the opportunity to taunt the officers for taking so long to catch him, despite coming close several times.

"You guys need to teach your people how to do surveillance," Wade said, after a long pause. "Not just cut someone off and stare at them."[44]

Wade's bail was set at $1 million, and he was arraigned on charges of first-degree murder. Sergeant Ken Spadafora told members of the local media that police had information "that may link [Wade] to some of the other unsolved homicides." Police refused, however, to elaborate.

---

44 These are quotes taken from a police report written by Officer Tyler Chevers.

FOURTEEN

After Wade's arrest, patrol cars surrounded the trailer owned by Greg "Bubba" Wade at Manoog's Isle Trailer Park, about four miles north of Dennis Whitmore's garage. Bubba was aware that authorities had staked out his home and, in anticipation, had removed his drug stash and other potentially incriminating items. Police had prepared for the raid by obtaining a search warrant permitting them to seize "any newspaper or other type of articals (sic) relating to the deaths of [Ms. Brown and several other homicide victims]." The warrant was amended twice, first adding authority to seize "trace evidence" and then adding authority to seize "clothing or other items containing biological matter and footwear."

They also eventually seized Bubba's Cadillac, which they scoured for traces of blood or DNA. They hauled Bubba down to the police headquarters where they accused him of concealing evidence of his son's misdoings, an accusation he vehemently denied.

Bubba was a sociable yet intimidating drug dealer with a protruding belly and graying beard, who, despite his gruff demeanor, was considered by his closest friends to be a "big Teddy Bear" with a keen sense of humor.[45] His prized possessions included a 1984 Harley Davidson motorcycle and the white 1990 Cadillac Seville, which explained why

---

45 The reference to a "big Teddy Bear" is from an essay written by Greg Wade which recounts major events of his life.

he was so upset police had seized the car and why he reacted with such distress when they returned it with damaged upholstery.

"They cut my fuckin Cadillac to pieces," he complained. "There was nothing left in it."[46]

An excommunicated Mormon who once was ordained as an elder in the Melchizedek priesthood, Bubba had since lived his life by the credo set forth by Ralph "Sonny" Barger, the founder of the Oakland chapter of the Hells Angels: "Treat me good, I'll treat you better; treat me bad, I'll treat you worse."

Such a life philosophy suited his role as a drug dealer, but as a parent, it had proved disastrous. Bubba claimed he had tried and failed to go legit in 1993, when his ex-wife sent their troubled and delinquent son to Anchorage to live with him. He was working late hours as a nightclub bouncer and had saved enough money to buy three tow trucks. State records showed Bubba and his son co-owned the "Red Baron" towing company. Bubba had hoped that when his son became old enough to drive, he would take part in the family business.

"I just wanted him to do something, not lie around all day and steal from people or smoke pot," Bubba recalled. "So I bought him his own tow truck and instead of using it to make money, he cost me money by running into a city vehicle with it."

Bubba eventually decided that lawful entrepreneurship required too much effort, and it wasn't long before he returned to his more lucrative vocation of selling drugs. He had discovered, though, that the towing business was a good cover for drug dealing because it gave him the ability

---

46 All of the quotes from Greg "Bubba" Wade in this chapter are from my interview with him on December 6, 2014. Police recovered nothing of significant forensic value from the car.

to be out at all times of the day and night, without raising suspicion with the police.

The younger Wade began stealing from his father's stash and selling the drugs to his father's customers, unbeknownst to Bubba, and pocketing the proceeds for himself.

"Or he'd steal my stuff and put some of it back, and I had complaints about my drugs," Bubba recalled. "He didn't give a shit. I was the one paying the bills."

Josh also was getting high. He had been smoking pot since the age of twelve, and his father had given up trying to get him to stop.

"You couldn't keep him from doing it," Bubba recalled with a shrug.

The younger Wade's criminal exploits soon became more brazen. Two months after his sixteenth birthday, he was caught by police behind the wheel of a stolen car, in possession of cocaine and a loaded, stolen 9 mm semiautomatic handgun. As always, Bubba was there to bail him out of jail and to offer false assurances to a judge that he was able to control his delinquent son.

He was not the kind of teenager who heeded the advice of adults, but there was one lesson from his father Wade had taken to heart: *If you're going to break the law, don't be stupid enough to get caught.* So when the younger Wade showed up that night in September with his sweatshirt covered in blood and with a fantastic story about how he had killed someone in a shed, Bubba was drunk and not entirely sure if his son was lying, but his response was simple.

"Don't tell anyone what you did," he told his son. "And if there was anything to prove that you were there … get rid of it."

During his interview with police, Bubba denied that he had offered such advice to his son. He also worried his drug business would be exposed, so he invoked his

Fifth Amendment right to not incriminate himself. He did, however, file an affidavit on July 31, 2001, objecting to the way in which police officers had searched his trailer. In the document, Bubba explained that his "personal habits" differed from his son's: "Josh is neat, and I am a slob." Bubba also said Josh considered his bedroom his personal space. In the document, Bubba claimed that detectives had accused him of "hiding evidence" for his son. "I did no such thing," Bubba wrote. Bubba said he spent the next few days at a friend's house because he was prevented from returning to his trailer by police:

> At some point, it seems like several days later, a detective called me on my cell phone while I was at work. The detective said he wanted to take some items from Josh's room. I don't really remember if he even told me what he wanted to take. The detective told me that if I didn't agree, he would have to return to court and get another search warrant. He said that it would take a while to do this, and that I would have to stay out of the home for at least another day. I had no clean clothes to wear and needed to return to the house, so I agreed. The detective made it sound like he was positive he could get the warrant and it was just a formality. He also made it clear that I could not go home if I did not agree to let them take what they wanted.

What police wanted, among other things, was a small utility knife and a folding pocket knife found on a shelf in the northwest bedroom of the trailer, Josh's room. The police report that details the earlier search and seizure of items in the trailer ends with the following note:

In the northwest bedroom, there is a small utility knife with a key chain on it and a folding pocket knife that has black and white markings its handles. They're on a shelf on the south wall of the bedroom. These items are not on the search warrant and we cannot take them.

In spite of this declaration, police called Bubba and, without obtaining further permission from the court, seized the two knives.

Although it had been wiped, one of the knives had on it a substance that appeared to be blood. That knife would prove to be a key and much disputed piece of evidence in the murder trial of Joshua Wade.

FIFTEEN

It would take more than two years for the case of *State of Alaska v. Joshua Wade* to go to trial. The defendant remained in jail during that time and, on December 30, 2002, the Nesbitt courthouse in downtown Anchorage welcomed 235 prospective jurors who were summoned and asked to fill out a twelve-page questionnaire. The document, designed to detect certain biases, included such questions as: "What TV shows or movies dealing with police, lawyers or courts do you watch regularly or have seen recently? Have you taken courses or received training in psychology, domestic relations or domestic violence?"

Based on their answers, the jury pool was whittled down, and the remaining potential jurors returned to the courthouse a week later for *voir dire*, a process by which attorneys from both sides and Superior Court Judge Michael Wolverton quizzed members of the jury pool in person. When it was all over, twelve jurors and two alternates were selected.

While the jury was well-balanced with regard to gender, with seven men and five women, there was a glaring detail concerning the ethnic makeup of the jury: there was not one Alaska Native on the panel. There were ten Caucasians, one Latino, and one African American. The panelists included: a fifty-year-old woman who did clerical and accounting work for her husband, a marine surveyor; an older African American man who rode the bus every day to the courthouse; the jury foreman, Mike Rodriguez, who worked for an oil company on the North Slope; a young woman who was a caregiver for people with disabilities; an older man who had recently retired from a job in state government; a young woman who worked for a bank, and was described by a fellow juror as being a "techie type"; a Fish and Game Department employee who was described as being "very smart and sure of himself"; and a man who worked for a commuter airline.[47]

Most of the attorneys on the case were well known throughout Alaska. The prosecutor, Mary Anne Henry, was the first woman to prosecute homicide cases in the state and had been doing so since the late 1970s. She was a Harvard graduate and widely considered a very capable and experienced litigator. One juror, who recalled Ms. Henry from the five years she spent as the District Attorney in Ketchikan, Alaska, regarded her as "an institution." She was assisted by Marcy McDannel, an inexperienced yet capable attorney who later would earn the nickname "Maximum Marcy" for her zeal in prosecuting defendants.

The defense had put together a "dream team" of sorts, headed by a well-known criminal defense attorney, Jim McComas, widely considered one of the best defense attorneys in the state. McComas was sizable in stature and in personality, and when asked to describe him or his oratory skills, colleagues would not hesitate to use the word "brilliant." Fond of bolo ties and suspenders, his courtroom attire once was described by a newspaper reporter as that of a "strip mall preacher."[48] Physically he resembled Santa Claus with his long gray hair, bushy white beard and rosy cheeks. Yet in court, he was fierce and unforgiving and commanded such a presence other trial attorneys would frequently show

---

47 The descriptions of the jurors came from a juror whom I interviewed and who wanted to remain anonymous.

48 Reporter Mike Doogan used this description in an article in the *Anchorage Daily News* on April 11, 2003.

up in the gallery just to watch him cross-examine a witness. One juror observed, "Mr. McComas could be compared to Matlock, but he was [a] little less folksy. He was absolutely the most capable attorney in the room. I remember thinking how lucky Wade was."[49]

Cindy Strout had successfully defended two previous murder cases with McComas. She had long, straight brown hair without bangs, which often was pulled back. Her fashion was ordinary—long skirts and comfortable shoes—but she had a flair for the dramatic and lit up when in front of a jury. In describing McComas and Strout to its readers, the *Anchorage Daily News* said the pair "[had] emerged as a formidable criminal defense duo."[50]

By the time the trial had finally started in January of 2003, Daisy and Kenneth Piggott had made the difficult decision to relocate their family from Albuquerque to Anchorage. Daisy's adult children stayed behind in New Mexico, but her son Kenneth Jr. and daughter Keenak, who were both teenagers, were uprooted from their schools and friends in the Southwest and soon arrived in Anchorage with little more than the clothes on their backs.

"We took what we could, and that was about it. We had to literally start all over again," Daisy recalled. "I had to go to court. I had to see."

Daisy's sister had offered the family her trailer, and so they moved in, the children enrolled in school, and Daisy made it her mission to be in court for every hearing in the case, no matter how insignificant.

Daisy was among those in the packed gallery, along with members of the local media, when opening statements got

---

49 The quote is taken from an e-mail written to me by the juror mentioned previously who wished to remain anonymous.
50 Quote from an article in the *Anchorage Daily News* dated December 31, 2002.

underway. Native activist Desa Jacobsson, who had taken a great interest in the case, also had vowed to be present for every hearing. She and a woman from the court's victim advocate office sat on either side of Daisy and followed her in and out of the courtroom in what Jacobsson described as a "goose formation," to protect Daisy from the onslaught of questioning reporters, and to quietly usher her out of the courtroom, if the testimony became too gruesome or autopsy photos were shown.

Such was the case when, in her opening statement, Mary Anne Henry showed some of the gruesome photos of Della's body, taken the morning she was found in the shed.

"She was dragged into that shed ... she was beaten on the head, and cut on the legs and neck, and left to die."

A photo of Della's beaten face flashed on an overhead screen.

"Joshua Wade told Dwayne Clevenger that he used matches to look at Della's body, and this is an awful picture. Matches were found on her eyelids and in her hair. The defendant told Jonathan Walker that he wanted to cut Della's throat but he had a dull knife so he practiced, and cut her legs to see if the knife worked."

The next photos, of Della's bloodied legs and then her throat, flashed on the screen.

"There's a cut on her thigh, another cut above her knee. Wade told Dwayne and Jesse he tried killing Della by cutting her throat. You'll notice there are cuts on her throat. Wade told Jonathan Walker that he cut Della's throat multiple times. He told Dwayne and Jesse, 'The bitch is tough she just won't die.' There are multiple cuts on her throat. They are not fatal wounds. They are not easy to see but, once again, we find the injuries on her are consistent with exactly how Wade described it."

Henry admitted many of the state's witnesses had

criminal pasts but asserted they had all reported basically similar accounts that pointed to Joshua Wade as the murderer.

"Joshua told at least four people that he killed Della Brown by beating her skull in with the rock, multiple blows to the head. The medical examiner will testify that Della died from multiple blunt force trauma to the head. And according to the medical examiner, these multiple blunt force injuries are consistent with using a rock. Wade told Jonathan Walker that he raped Della Brown. He repeated this on the wire with Beckett and Troxler. Della was found with her pants pulled down to her ankles. Wade told his friends that he raped her after she had been beaten because he said the adrenaline got going and that's when he got excited. He also told his friends that he used a condom, and that is why there is no semen from Joshua Wade in the body of Della Brown.

"In summary, the evidence that the state expects to present and this case will show that only Wade, and no other person that you will hear about in this trial, meets all of these facts. Joshua Wade had come upon Della Brown lying in the street and knew she was unconscious and vulnerable, and was in close proximity to the crime scene at the time of her death, and decided to visit the filthy shed multiple times, after spotting Della on the street. He was seen with blood on him at the time of Della's death. He described Della's nonfatal injuries with much accuracy in multiple locations that could not have been easily seen with the condition of the body in a dark shed. And he knew of the large cut on Della's throat, which did not kill her, even though she died face down in a pool of blood. And he described exactly the kind of blows that actually killed Della Brown. He later brought people to see the body, admitted to killing Della Brown and ran from the police and tried to hide out. After you've heard the evidence in this case, we're going to stand before you again and we're going to ask you to render the only true and just verdict in this case: Joshua Wade is guilty of murder in the first degree. He's guilty of robbery, he's guilty of sexual assault, he's guilty of tampering with witnesses, and he's guilty of tampering with evidence. Thank you."

It was clear from Ms. Henry's opening statement that the state was going to rely on witness testimony rather than physical evidence to tie Joshua Wade to Della Brown's murder. The defense had decided to exploit this obvious shortcoming in the prosecution's case.

"What happened to Della Brown is a horror, it is an inexcusable crime," Cindy Strout told the jury. "It needs to be solved. But my client Joshua Wade is the wrong man. This case shouldn't even be in trial because of the state has not solved the case."

Strout went on to explain that the semen found inside Della Brown's vagina and anus was tested by the state, and that the DNA results excluded her client. She said a fingerprint found in blood as well as a hair found on the victim's body did not belong to Joshua Wade, nor did they belong to Della Brown.

"The police searched Josh's home thoroughly and found nothing connecting him to the homicide. They searched his car thoroughly and again, found nothing connecting him to the crime. No hairs, no fibers, nothing from his house, nothing from his car. This case shouldn't be in trial. They haven't solved it yet. They haven't found the killer."

Strout said Wade's admissions to several people that he had committed the murder amounted to "false bragging" meant to impress members of the GTS gang; she argued that Wade had simply stumbled upon Della's body after someone else had killed her.

"Josh became the easy suspect, and I guess you can see how the police fell for that," Strout told the jury. "It was the easy solution to this horrible crime."

The defense could have ended its argument there, relying simply on a lack of evidence and thus, reasonable doubt that Wade had committed the murder. But Strout went a step further, claiming the defense had developed several theories based on evidence its own investigator had uncovered, which pointed to other suspects. She singled out Della's boyfriend, Rudy D'Apice, pointing out that police had never established an alibi for him on the night Della was believed to have been murdered. Strout suggested Timothy "Romeo" Beckett, the GTS gang leader, may have been the murderer, calling his actions "suspicious," asserting that he blatantly attempted to manipulate the police investigation. The third suspect the defense examined, Strout said, was the serial rapist, Gregory Poindexter.

"He targeted Alaska Native women, women just like Della Brown," Strout told the jury. "An angry, violent man attacking women in Anchorage at exactly the same timeframe that Della Brown was killed."

Strout finished by pointing to a final possible suspect, who had left his DNA in Della Brown, and who may have been the source of the bloody fingerprint found on a loose piece of paper in the shed.

"We can't ignore the good possibility another suspect exists. The man who may have left his DNA. The man who may have left his fingerprint in her blood. And a pubic hair in her vagina. One has to wonder if this may be a younger man, a juvenile, his prints are not on file. Maybe another gangbanger. Maybe someone else entirely. There is no reliable evidence that Joshua Wade committed the charges the state has charged. And there is substantial evidence that these other men, known and unknown, are most likely responsible for her death. It only takes one drop of reasonable doubt."

SIXTEEN

The state began its case by calling to the witness stand a number of people who had observed Wade's behavior during those few days spent at Dennis Whitmore's garage, including Whitmore himself. Whitmore described an atmosphere fueled by beer, whiskey, and a lack of sleep. He said that visitors were given strict instructions not to come to the front door or to disturb his girlfriend, who was trying to sleep inside the house. He had even disconnected the noisy electric garage door opener so as not to wake her but, even so, the racket inside the garage almost drowned out a loud knock on the garage door.

"I was busy working on the Buick. So I hollered, 'Come in! Just lift the door!'" Dennis testified. As the garage door came up, he said he saw Wade, out of breath and trying to hide something on his hands. As he came closer, Dennis said he could tell it was blood.

"What did you think?" Mary Anne Henry asked.

"Just another night in Spenard," Whitmore replied, assuming that Wade had been in a fight.

"He asked to see Dirty," Dennis continued, explaining that "Dirty" was Dwayne's nickname.[51] "So I told him, 'Yeah, he's at the front of the shop.'" Whitmore said Wade grabbed one of the old, greasy T-shirts laying on the front of one of the cars, wiped off his hands, and walked to the front

---

51 Clevenger said the nickname "Dirty" was a reference to his lack of cleanliness at home.

of the shop. Whitmore couldn't hear over the sound of the impact wrench what Wade was saying to Dwayne and Jesse, but Wade continued to pace back and forth, acting "hyped up" as he talked, as if he was experiencing an adrenaline rush, or was high on something.[52] Wade was so agitated, Whitmore recalled, that he eventually allowed him to go into the house, to wash his hands. When Wade returned, his hands were clean, but he was still acting strange, pacing back and forth.

"I finally told him to get out," Whitmore testified, explaining that Wade's incessant pacing was unnerving. "I said, 'You're driving me nuts, and I'm trying to work here.'"

Detectives were anxious to locate the rag Wade had used to wipe off his bloody hands, but Dennis explained that he paid a young man to maintain and clean the garage and that many of the old, greasy rags had been thrown away. Whitmore permitted officers to search the garage anyway, and they seized several rags, none of which appeared to contain any blood.

****

More disturbing details of what Wade was alleged to have done to Della Brown came from Dwayne Clevenger, who testified that Wade left and returned to the garage several times. Each time he came back, he pulled Dwayne and Jesse aside, and his confessions became more graphic.

"He had told me he kicked her and she was farting and he thought it was funny so he kept kicking her," Dwayne recalled. "And he had beat her up pretty bad, and he was going to try to kill her. That he was going to kill her."

Under direct examination by Mary Anne Henry, Dwayne also described initially finding Della Brown passed out in the

---

52 Dwayne Clevenger and another witness, Patrick McCune, also described Wade as being "hyped up."

road, while riding in the car with Wade, Jesse, and Dwayne's girlfriend, Anna Campbell:

Clevenger: [Josh] told me to get out of her car and pull her off of the street. So I got out of the car, I grabbed her and pulled her off the street by her leg. Or by her foot. Yeah, by her foot.

Henry: When you pulled her off the road where did you actually leave her?

Clevenger: Right on the side of the road.

Henry: Did she wake up or say anything?

Clevenger: I could tell she was still alive, she moved. Like she was kind of moaning or whatever.

As for what Wade had later confessed, it was no secret that Wade liked to brag, and at first, Dwayne said, he thought Wade was joking, or at least grossly exaggerating the truth; but there was a look in Wade's eyes, an excitement with which he made the claims, that suggested otherwise. It was believable enough, he thought, when Wade claimed he had pulled the woman into the shed and checked her pockets for money, but when he later admitted slitting the woman's throat with a carpet knife and trying to strangle her with a twisted up T-shirt, Dwayne and Jesse had both reached for another shot of whiskey.

As for why he went into such a rage, Wade had allegedly offered the explanation that when he checked the woman's pockets and got urine on his hands, that he had lost control. He also expressed a disdain for Native Alaskans, telling Dwayne and Jesse both that Natives were worthless and he was doing a favor for any Native he killed.[53]

According to Dwayne, during one of his frantic return visits to the garage, Wade was asking around for a condom. He later admitted that as he was beating the woman in the head with a rock, he had become aroused and that he had raped her.

In spite of this ostensibly damning testimony, Clevenger was far from a convincing witness. Details of his account changed from day to day, and from what he had initially told the grand jury, and before that, the police. Jurors also had trouble hearing what Clevenger had to say; reporter Sheila Toomey, who covered the trial for the *Anchorage Daily News,* observed that "[Clevenger] mumbled so badly that the judge had to repeat many of his answers."

Dwayne had also surprised both the prosecution and defense when he testified to an event he had never previously mentioned to authorities. He said that at about 6:00 a.m. on September 1, 2000, Wade insisted on giving him and his girlfriend, Anna Campbell, a ride back to her mom's trailer at Diamond Estates. Anna was unaware of Wade's disturbing admissions even though she was in the garage when Wade had initially shown up, out of breath. Dwayne told the court he was hesitant to accept the offer of a ride from Wade, given what he had divulged to them earlier, but Dwayne was still drunk, and he eventually agreed. They got into the Cadillac; Dwayne was in the passenger seat and Anna was in the backseat. They had traveled no farther than a block, when Wade pulled the car over at Dorbrandt Street and 32nd Avenue. Dwayne said he watched as Wade got out of the car and entered the shed. The sun still wasn't up and there were no streetlights, so he couldn't see what Wade was doing.

---

53 Wade strongly disputes he made such statements, despite reports to the contrary from multiple sources.

Dwayne said he heard about ten loud thumps and Wade returned minutes later.

"He was like, 'Did you hear that?'" Dwayne recalled. "And I said, 'Yeah, what was it?' And he hit her in the head with a rock ten times."

Dwayne had never before claimed to have heard the fatal blows that killed Della Brown until testifying at trial, and McComas took him to task on cross-examination:

McComas: We heard yesterday the tapes in which you said it was Jesse and Danny and Romeo, or some combination of them, who had told you that Joshua had hit the woman in the head with a rock. But you testified to this jury that not only Joshua told you directly, but that you were an *ear witness* to him hitting the woman in the head with a rock. That's what you told them yesterday, correct?

Clevenger: That's correct.

McComas: According to you, Jesse was in the car with you, right?

Clevenger: No, I don't think so.

McComas: When the car stopped in there on 32nd near the shed and Josh went to the shed before you heard crashing, you and Jessie were in the car together, right?

Clevenger: No sir, I don't think he was in the car with me.

McComas: Well, you told the police on October 2nd that Jesse was with you.

Clevenger: I'm sorry, I was confused about that.

McComas: Jessie is not going to back up the story, is he Mr. Clevenger?

Clevenger: No, he is not going to say he was in the car, because he wasn't.

McComas: Well, why were you saying that he was?

Clevenger: I was confused.

McComas: You were confused about who was in the car with you when you supposedly hurt somebody getting their head bashed in with a rock?

Clevenger: Yes.

McComas: When did you realize Jesse wasn't in the car with you?

Clevenger: Just now, when I thought about it.

McComas: Just now? You didn't talk to Jessie last night? Or last week?

Clevenger: No sir. I talked to him about a month ago.

McComas: So is it your testimony that you were by yourself in the car when Mr. Wade went to the shed?

Clevenger: No sir, I wasn't by myself. My girlfriend was there. Anna Campbell.

McComas: So Anna Campbell is also an ear witness to this crashing sound, is that right?

Clevenger: Yes sir.

McComas: Were the windows up or down?

Clevenger: They were up.

McComas: And you heard at least ten crashes, is that right?

Clevenger: Correct.

Dwayne's assertions were problematic on several fronts. In his grand jury testimony Dwayne claimed that he was in the car with Jesse and Wade, and there was no mention of Anna Campbell. What's more, Anna Campbell would testify that she was in the car but had not heard any kind of thumping sounds coming from the shed. Dwayne's credibility further deteriorated during an exchange with McComas in which he admitted to providing false testimony about hearing firsthand from Wade that he had sexually assaulted Della Brown:

McComas: So your sworn testimony that Josh confessed to sexually assaulting this woman and asked all around the garage for a condom was false?

Henry: Your Honor, may we approach? Objection.

Judge: Perhaps you can rephrase the question.

McComas: So when you testify that Joshua had confessed to you directly, out of his own mouth, that he had sex with this woman and asked all around the garage to try to get a condom, that was false testimony, right?

Clevenger: No, he was asking people for a condom. But he wasn't the one who told me about having sex with her.

McComas: Alright, so that part, claiming that Josh had sex, that was false testimony.

Clevenger: Yes.

McComas: And you got confused in your mind between what Josh had said and what someone else said he had said, right?

Clevenger: Yes sir.

McComas: Now, about this asking around for a condom business. That appears nowhere in your September 30th statement, nowhere in your October 2nd statement, and nowhere in your grand jury testimony. When you're describing what you know and what you've heard, you don't claim that anywhere. Where did that come from?

Clevenger: I don't know. I can't explain that, sir.

McComas: That seems like it would be something pretty hard to forget, doesn't it?

Clevenger: There's a lot of things in my head going around about this, and I'm confusing stuff, but I'm just trying to tell you everything that I remember.

SEVENTEEN

In contrast to the other witnesses, Jesse Ackmann had been close friends with Joshua Wade for seven or eight years. Jesse told the grand jury, "[Josh has] always been someone who likes attention, to be the center of attention. He's even gotten mad when other people have gotten more attention than him."

On the witness stand, Jesse recalled that Wade admitted to beating the woman with his fists, kicking her in the face, and using a small Stanley pocket knife to slit the woman's throat. He also recalled seeing a small knife with a retractable razor blade on Wade's keychain, with blood on it.

"He was trying different things to kill her, I guess," Jesse recalled. "I heard him say many times, repeatedly, 'The bitch is tough, and she doesn't want to die.'"

Jesse repeated claims that he had made to police, namely that Wade had killed the woman by crushing her head with a rock and that he had disposed of the bloody rock by throwing it into a lake. He also recalled the incident in the car when Wade retrieved a shovel from the shed and threw it into the backseat of the car, onto Romeo's lap.

"I remember he said he had to get rid of the shovel because it was used to beat the woman," Jesse told the jury.

Jesse said he had later argued with Wade because he refused to go with him to see the woman's body.

"I was kind of enraged at the idea that he would even ask me. I got mad, and I was like, 'No.' He actually got angry at me and Dwayne because we didn't want to go with him, and we got into an argument about it."

"So I take it you never went to go look at the body?" the prosecutor asked.

"No," Jesse replied.

The defense went to great lengths to show that Jesse was an alcoholic who had blacked out several crucial events, which he later filled in, after talking to other witnesses. McComas even went so far as to pull Jesse's juvenile record to demonstrate that he began abusing alcohol and drugs at the age of twelve or thirteen. At that point, Jesse became angry and asked the judge if he was the one on trial.

"I'm sure we're all interested in your questions, Mr. Ackmann," McComas retorted. "Suppose you answer mine! Mr. Ackmann, you have a substance abuse problem?"

"I don't think you ever stop having a substance abuse problem," Ackmann responded.

****

Dwayne and Jesse had heard the gruesome details of what Wade claimed he had done to the woman in the shed, so they refused to go when he insisted on taking them to see her body the next night. After repeated refusals, and an argument, Wade set his sights on those who were less suspecting of what they would see. One such person was Danny Troxel's sister, Anna Campbell. Anna was dating Dwayne Clevenger, and so Dwayne was quick to step in and let Wade know he was not taking his girlfriend anywhere. Instead, Dwayne suggested to Wade that he should take Anna's friend, Jonathan McCune, who had been hanging out at the garage. McCune was known as "Peaches," a somewhat naive but sincere seventeen-year-old, whose nickname had resulted from an unfortunate incident at a friend's tanning salon, when he unknowingly slathered himself with self-tanning lotion, rendering his skin a bright peach color.

Under direct examination by Marcy McDannel, Peaches told the jury he thought he and Wade were going somewhere to smoke weed, since Dennis didn't allow marijuana in the shop. He said as they approached the shed, he could sense that something was wrong:

McCune: When we were walking up to the shed I was kind of like itchy, you know. And I kind of started falling behind. [Josh] walked into the shed, and he was in there for a few seconds. And then I walked up to the doorjamb, and he lit up a lighter and I looked down and I seen a lady and I automatically presumed she was dead.

McDannel: Why was that?

McCune: It was my first instinct. I just looked down and saw her, I later found out it was Della Brown, that was her name. Her body laying there … and it took me a second to realize what I was looking at. Then I turned around and walked away.

McDannel: During that second were you able to see injuries to Della Brown?

McCune: I didn't see any specific injuries. I realized I was looking at a person. Instinct told me it was probably a dead person, and I just closed my eyes [and] turned around.

McDannel: Did you see any blood?

McCune: I didn't see blood. I want to say it was kind of a traumatic experience, you know, I tried as hard as I could to block it out. I want to say I saw streaks, but I can't physically picture her face anymore. I've blocked it out so much. I freaked out in my mind, you know. Just kind of instantly shot. I turned around and started walking away.

McDannel: And what did Mr. Wade do?

McCune: He followed me and started asking me, "Why are you running away? You're a pussy. You're a bitch," this and that. Telling me, "You can't handle it," stuff like that. Then he started asking me, "Who do you think did that?" And I had so many thoughts running through my mind so I turned around and I said, "I think you did that!" Then I caught what I said and I was just like, you know, "Don't worry, I won't tell anybody. If anybody asks me." And I just kept walking. And he kept talking to me still and I don't know exactly what he was saying I was just too shocked.

****

A twenty-six-year-old landscaper named Danny Knue testified he had known Josh Wade for about four or five years and that he had been living with Dwayne's parents, across the street from Dennis Whitmore's place. Questioned by prosecutor Keri Brady, Knue told the court he had been working on a Chevy Astro van in the driveway of the Clevenger's house during the first week of September and that Wade had come by periodically to talk to him while he worked:

Brady: What did he tell you?

Knue: He had told me he had done things to a person … and it's kind of hard to explain … it's kind of like he was using me as a psychiatrist or something.

Brady: What specifically did he say that he did to the person?

Knue: There were comments about sex. He had asked me at one point why he had had sex with her. He brought up hitting her in the head with a rock.

Brady: Did he tell you he had sex with her before or after he hit her in the head with a rock?

Knue: Neither.

Brady: What was his demeanor like when he was describing these things to you?

Knue: He was Josh. He was kind of upset at one point, I don't know if that was because of the situation at hand. … There was one point we were discussing it, and he seemed pretty bent out of shape. Distraught and troubled.

Knue told police Wade was "bawling," during one of their encounters, though on the witness stand he clarified that Wade was "really upset [but] wasn't physically crying."

Brady: Did you want him to discuss any of this with you?

Knue: No.

Brady: How did you react?

Knue: I was basically ignoring him as best as I could.

I told him quite a few times to stop talking about it.

Brady: Did Mr. Wade say anything to you about her wetting her pants?

Knue: He had said that she had peed or something, and I don't know in detail how it happened ... but somehow he had gotten it on him.

Brady: Did he ever take you to the shed to see the body?

Knue: The topic came up once, but I ignored it and kept going about what I was doing. I wasn't interested.

Brady: Did he do everything at once? Or was he going back and forth?

Knue: It was back and forth.

Brady: Does Mr. Wade dislike Native people?

Knue: Yes.

****

Jonathan Walker was a twenty-one-year-old friend of Jesse's, the only African American in the group at the garage during those few days, and he was giving Wade a ride back to his father's house when Wade confessed to him that he had beaten, raped, and eventually killed a woman in the shed on Dorbrandt Street. Jonathan was surprised to hear Wade speak so candidly and with such detail about the killing; they were not close, but had been acquaintances for about four years, and would see each other now and then in the neighborhood.

At some point between the time Wade had confessed his deeds to Jonathan and the trial, Jonathan had been involved in a car accident, and his injuries had affected his memory. Worried about Jonathan's ability to recall specific details, the state played for the jury a taped interview police had conducted with him on September 30, 2000.

"[Josh] said he tried to cut her throat but he thought the razor was dull so he cut her leg a few times to see if it wasn't," Jonathan told the police. "He said he cut her throat several times. Then he said he threw the condom and the condom wrapper on top of the shed."

"I could see in his eyes that he was like, kind of bragging about it, but you can see in his eyes he was kind of hurt and scared, you know?" Jonathan continued. "And I was like, 'Why did you do that?' And he was like, 'I don't know, I don't know what's wrong with me.' He said, 'I didn't come from a bad home or nothing like that.' He's like, 'I just don't like Natives.'"

Jonathan said he had seen the woman's body the night before, when he left the garage to walk over to a friend's house, and Wade insisted on tagging along.

"He was like, 'Do you want to see a dead body?' And I was like, 'No, not really.' And he was like, 'Well, just come over here.'"

Jonathan reluctantly followed and watched as Wade turned the knob of the side door and then kicked it partially open, against the force of something in the doorway. Wade slid through the doorway sideways. Through the partially open doorway, Jonathan saw the naked hip and buttocks of a woman, who was laying face down, her head close to the door.

"I saw that, and I didn't want to see anymore. I started walking away, and he was like, 'Wait, wait up, man.' And I said, 'That's not cool man.'"

"Did you touch the door at all?" the officer asked.

"No sir."

"And you never went in the shed?"

"No sir. I'm not stupid."

When Jonathan later challenged Wade's claims of brutality, Wade had shown him a blue cotton FUBU hoodie with smears of blood on the white lettering. When officers asked Jonathan if he knew what had happened to the sweatshirt he said, "[Josh] kept saying he was going to dispose of it. He said he was going to throw it away, burn it or something. I told him, 'You're stupid because that stuff will come back on you. They have all kinds of stuff under her fingernails, blood on her body, you know … and that's just got to come back on you, you know, if you did that shit.' And I was saying, 'You are a sick white boy. Straight up.'"

EIGHTEEN

It was evident from the start that the state's case was tenuous. Despite the fact Josh Wade had confessed his murderous crime to no fewer than seven people, there was not one shred of physical evidence, no smoking gun, that singled him out as the perpetrator.

The hooded sweatshirt with blood on its white embroidered letters had apparently been burned. Police had combed the shed and the neighborhood surrounding it, but the alleged murder weapon, a bloody rock, was nowhere to be found. Also, despite Wade's statement to Jonathan Walker that he had thrown a condom wrapper on the roof of the shed, detectives had not recovered a condom nor a condom wrapper. The bloody carpet knife that police had seized from Wade's bedroom wasn't used as evidence in the trial because Mary Anne Henry apparently was worried it had been illegally seized by police. Besides, the knife had been wiped mostly clean and the small amount of blood remaining on it had been tested for DNA and the results were inconclusive. (Marcy McDannel later characterized the knife as "suggestive" rather than "conclusive" evidence.)

Without the knife, there was no physical or forensic evidence that pointed to Joshua Wade; the semen found inside Della's vagina and anus as well as the male pubic hair found on her body did not match Josh Wade's DNA. The bloody fingerprint found on a piece of paper inside the shed near the body also was not his.

The prosecution took its biggest hit when, about a month into the trial, District Attorney Susan Parkes delivered a bombshell: Mary Anne Henry was stepping down from the case due to "health reasons." The DA's office said Henry suffered from severe asthma, among other ailments, and that she would continue on in an advisory role. Henry's unexpected departure left the prosecution with the considerable challenge of finding an attorney capable enough of getting up to speed on the case and someone who could also square off with Wade's high-profile defense team. The announcement came as a shock to everyone and, perhaps most of all, to Della's mother.

"That was a real heart-stopping moment for me," Daisy Piggott recalled. "Before she quit ... I asked her, 'Mary Anne, how do you think the trial is going? Do you think we're going to get guilty?' And she said, 'I don't know.' I knew we were in trouble."

Marcy McDannel, who joined the team a few weeks before the trial began hoping to learn from Henry's two decades of trial experience, was thrust into the primary role. She was joined by Keri Brady, who was coming off of maternity leave and had no prior knowledge of the case. The pair was eager but inexperienced; not only were the two novice attorneys struggling to get up to speed, neither one of them had ever prosecuted a homicide before.

To its detriment, the new prosecution team had a demeanor in court that many court spectators, including the victim's family, found unprofessional. The pair frequently joked in open court within earshot of reporters and others in the gallery. The joking between McDannel and Brady had even bothered the defendant, who exploded during a recess when the jury was not in the courtroom. *Anchorage Daily News* reporter Sheila Toomey recounted the outburst in an article that appeared in the paper on April 10, 2003:

"What the f--- do you guys think is so funny?" [Wade] screamed at assistant district attorneys McDannel and Keri Brady, who had been laughing and joking at the prosecution table, as was their habit during recesses throughout the trial.

The judge and Wade's lawyers hastened to calm him down, and he didn't say anything else. However, on the way out, his hands manacled, he managed to throw his used tissues at the television cameras.

McDannel said later that she and Brady weren't talking about the case.

Another setback had come to the prosecution months prior, when the two gang members on whose testimony the state had based its case were arrested for a string of armed robberies at a local hotel. The state decided to cut deals with Romeo and Danny, providing the promise of more lenient sentences in their robbery cases in exchange for their testimony against Joshua Wade. Jurors were made aware of these arrangements, and both Romeo and Danny would testify in their prison jumpsuits, which only served to further deteriorate their credibility on the witness stand.

At least the prosecution could be confident jurors would hear the Beckett-Troxel police wire, although not in its entirety. The court had ordered any reference to other victims that Wade might have killed be edited out. Wade's statements about recognizing the photo of Della Brown in the newspaper would stay in, as well as his apparent description of the sexual assault.

****

As the state's star witness, Timothy "Romeo" Beckett

proved to be problematic for a number of reasons, but mainly because, on cross examination by Jim McComas, Romeo admitted to telling police a number of lies.

The lies included: Romeo's claim that Danny knew nothing of the murder because he was out of town at the time; Romeo's assertion he had never been involved in a home invasion robbery; and his initial claim to police that he had not seen Della Brown's body, but just the tip of her shoe when he was at the crime scene.

"It's obvious, ain't it? That would be a lie," Romeo testified of the last untruth. "I never claimed to be a saint."

McComas also grilled Romeo about why he had approached an officer at the crime scene claiming that he saw a Native woman walking with an African American man near the shed in the days before the murder:

McComas: What were you doing telling this to the police? What were you trying to accomplish?

Beckett: I wasn't trying to lead them to Josh.

McComas: Were you trying to lead them to someone else?

Beckett: I don't know, but I wasn't trying to lead them to Josh.

McComas: Were you trying to protect Josh?

Beckett: Not trying to protect him, so to speak. But not put it in his direction.

McComas: Not only put it not in his direction but the effect of doing this is to get the police start thinking they need to start looking for a large black guy, right?

That's misleading them, isn't it?

Beckett: It's not misleading them. They just asked me if I seen anybody walking, and I told him that I saw some people walking.

McComas: Even though, according to you, that Josh had made a confession to you.

Beckett: They didn't ask me that. They just asked me if I saw someone walking. So I told them what I seen.

McComas: The native female you were describing, it was that based on the woman you saw in the shed?

Beckett: No, it was based on the woman I saw walking.

McComas: The woman in the shed had a couple of shirts, did you know that?

Beckett: No, I didn't know that.

McComas: And the height is off, but the weight is right on time.

Beckett: What can I say?

McComas: Just a coincidence.

Beckett: I don't know.

McComas pulled out a photo of Gregory Poindexter, the serial rapist.

"Does that look like the black man you're talking about?" McComas asked. Even though Romeo told police that he had not observed the black man's face, he insisted

Poindexter was not the man he had seen, claiming the man he recognized as Poindexter from the TV news was much fatter than the man he had seen on the street.

When Romeo said from the witness stand that Wade had threatened him while they both were in jail, the defense objected and the judge quickly ordered the jury to file out of the courtroom. The two sides had stipulated that none of Wade's other alleged criminal activity would be mentioned in court, and that included the allegation of threats made against another inmate. After the jury was gone, McComas and Romeo got into a heated exchange.

"You're claiming that Mr. Wade has made threats to you since September 2nd?"

"Yeah, I am," Romeo replied. "I'm also telling you that because of that punk asshole over there, no matter what prison I go to, I got to stay in a hole, like the last year and a half, like I've been doing, sitting in a hole. So what else do you want to know?"

"Go ahead, Mr. Beckett. Get it all off your chest," McComas said.

"Let's proceed, Mr. McComas," Judge Wolverton chided.

"Yes, Your Honor. Who have you reported these threats to?"

"DOC[54] knows about it," Romeo answered.

"DOC knows that Mr. Wade threatened you?" McComas asked with skepticism in his voice.

"Oh, or how about I'm sitting there, and your man come over and kick my door? Or how about the time the U.S. marshals sat there and said, 'Snitches get stitches.' He said, 'Yeah, there are people waiting for you.'"

"Good, then there should be reports about this, and the prosecutor knows all about it. Because why would that be kept from her?"

---

54 Department of Corrections.

"Because that's between him and me," Romeo said, staring with disdain at Wade.

"Do you remember that Judge Wolverton ..." McComas began, but Romeo interrupted him mid-sentence, and the two men began shouting over each other, until McComas's voice boomed the loudest.

"Excuse me Mr. Beckett! You will wait until I have asked my question!" McComas shouted.

"Well, I'll give you your damn answer if you just ask it!" Romeo shouted back.

"Go ahead and ask your question," Judge Wolverton instructed, maintaining a sense of calm.

"Do you remember the judge telling you not to refer to any other crimes that Mr. Wade may have committed?"

"I remember the rules that I read said I could talk about the newspapers where he pointed out [the victim] ... but I couldn't talk about all the fights he got into ... or the time he's done. But nobody ever said I couldn't talk about the threats he did against me."

"Well, you know that threats are criminal acts, don't you sir?"

"I don't live in your world, dude," Romeo replied. "Your man killed someone and raped them, and I've got to sit in a hole ..."

"Mr. Beckett, I think *you're* the one who killed her," McComas said.

"I know you do," Romeo replied, seeming unfazed.

"And I think you sent your buddy Danny out on a hunting trip after it happened."

After a ten-minute recess the jury was back in the courtroom and McComas questioned Romeo about the shovel. Romeo testified that he directed police to where he said he had thrown it out of the car. Although it was not in the bushes where Romeo claimed he had left it, they found it nearby, conspicuously, leaning against an apartment building. Forensic tests on the shovel would later show it was completely clean—no traces of blood, human tissue, or hair:

McComas: You told the police that a few days after you had thrown the shovel that you became concerned that your fingerprints could be on it and that was the only evidence that could tie you to this crime, isn't that correct?

Beckett: Yes. Well, yeah.

McComas: So did you go back then and move that shovel from where other people hadn't had known you had thrown it, to some different location so it would never be found with your fingerprints?

Beckett: If I were to do that I wouldn't have kept it in the same general area.

McComas: Exactly.

Beckett: No, I mean in the same vicinity.

McComas: And that's why you told Peaches McCune that you ditched that shovel off Old Seward Highway and Lake Otis, right?

Beckett: No, I didn't say that. I don't recall saying that, at least.

McComas: So if Peaches McCune testifies under oath that you told them that you ditched the shovel off of Old Seward, are you going to say that is not correct?

Beckett: I'm going to say I don't recall.

124

NINETEEN

Wade's defense team had spent months preparing for trial and developing its own leads as to who the "real killer" was. Jim McComas and Cindy Strout went to great lengths to introduce their alternate theories of the case and brought other suspects before the jury, one by one.

One notable exception was Gregory Poindexter, who already was in jail serving time for multiple rapes. The defense petitioned the court to force him to testify; the judge held a hearing outside the presence of the jury, and Poindexter attended by way of a conference call. The hearing did not last long, however; the judge ruled that Poindexter had a clear Fifth Amendment right to not incriminate himself and would not have to testify.

"Okay, at this point Mr. Poindexter we'll let you hang up," Judge Wolverton said. "If you have any questions you should discuss them privately at another time with your attorney."

"Yes. Okay," Poindexter replied. Then, on the line, there was a loud sound. "WOOOOO!"

"Well, that sounded like someone getting away with murder,"

McComas remarked. "Actually judge, I want the record to reflect as Mr. Poindexter hung up the telephone, in case it wasn't clear on the recording, that he made a sound that I would describe as extremely joyful and triumphant to the effect of 'WOOOOO!'"

"It sounded like a squeaking chair to me," the prosecutor

interjected.

"It went right over my head, I didn't hear anything like it," the judge admitted. Wolverton later reviewed the recording of the hearing and determined that he had created the sound himself, when he bumped his microphone.

The defense hired an FBI expert, Gregg McCrary, who reviewed Poindexter's profile and those of his victims and concluded that Poindexter should have been considered a suspect in Della Brown's murder. However, the physical evidence did not appear to support the theory; Poindexter had been eliminated as the source of the semen found inside Della Brown at the time of her death, and DNA testing also excluded him as the source of the male pubic hair found on her body.

In addition to telling jurors about the prevalence of false confessions as they might relate to Wade, McCrary also provided testimony about the kind of people who offer false tips to police in an effort to appear helpful, but who are, in truth, the real perpetrators. He spoke in generalities but the implications were clearly meant to bolster the theory that Timothy "Romeo" Beckett was Della's killer.

The most obvious theory was Della's angry, abusive boyfriend, Rudy D'Apice, had killed her in a jealous rage. Cindy Strout spent hours cross-examining Rudy in pursuit of that theory:

Strout: Do you have an alibi for the night Della was killed?

D'Apice: No.

Strout: It's just your word that you were home on the Thursday she was killed?

D'Apice: Uh-huh.

Strout: And you have no immunity for murder, do you?

D'Apice: No.

Strout: So if you admitted to this jury that you killed Ms. Brown in an angry jealous rage, you could be prosecuted for her murder couldn't you?

D'Apice: I imagine so.

Strout referenced Rudy's assault of Della eighteen months prior to her death, for which he had served jail time:

Strout: You had tried to prevent her from breathing by covering both her mouth and her nose.

D'Apice: I don't remember that.

Strout: But you don't think she was lying about that, do you?

D'Apice: No.

Strout: And before the police got there, you made her wash the blood off her body and told her you would kill her if she reported this, didn't you?

D'Apice: I don't remember that.

Strout asked Rudy about an incident in 1998 in which Della had accused him of rape. Della told a police officer that Rudy thought she was sleeping with another man and that he had attacked her in a fit of rage. Della said Rudy was drunk and couldn't get an erection, so he forced a yellow broom handle between her legs. According to the police report, Della claimed that when she told him it hurt and that she wanted to leave the trailer, he smacked her on the head with a piece of wood he had laying around from a home improvement project. She claimed that Rudy had blocked the door and refused to let her go until she calmed down. The officer said in his report that Della, once at the hospital, attempted to leave the emergency room three times, that she couldn't go through with the sexual assault exam. The officer also noted that he could smell the stench of alcohol on her breath.[55]

When asked about the incident in court, Rudy became agitated. "No way! Ludicrous. It's a lie!" he said.

Under oath, Rudy admitted he was angry with Della when she disappeared. He also admitted that he had put all of her personal belongings in a garbage bag, which he left outside on the front step:

> **Strout:** And when the police came and wanted to take that bag you wouldn't let them have it, would you?
>
> **D'Apice:** No.
>
> **Strout:** Were you worried that the police might inspect some of the belongings in there? And that there might be some kind of blood on some of the items? Were you worried about that?
>
> **D'Apice:** No.
>
> **Strout:** Maybe you packed up all her belongings because you knew that she wasn't coming back.
>
> **D'Apice:** No, no way.

---

55 Although a police report was written, charges were never filed. D'Apice died in 2007.

TWENTY

After two-and-a-half months of testimony, both sides had rested their cases, and the prosecution began its closing argument.

"What is the evidence that Joshua Wade killed Della Brown? Well, we have Joshua Wade's words," Keri Brady told the jury. "He told at least seven people what he was doing, while he was doing it.

"Joshua Wade made statements on the wire consistent with those confessions, saying, 'There's that bitch,' and 'My adrenaline got it going, and my dick got hard.' You know that he said that. Those are on the wire.

"All the witnesses testified that Joshua Wade was seen coming and going from the garage alone. Several of the witnesses saw him with blood on his hands and described him on his return as agitated, breathing heavy, and pacing.

"Why do you think Wade asked for help moving the body? Because he is evidence conscious. What do you think he was trying to do? He was trying to get people in there pacing. He was trying to get other people's footprints and other evidence mixed around because Wade understood what evidence is all about.

"Wade told people his dick got hard during the beating. Wade confessed to rape to Jonathan Walker and Danny Knue. Wade asked for a condom. In fact, Dwayne told people he was running around asking everyone for [a] condom."

Brady pointed out that while there was no conclusive

physical evidence that Della had been raped, experts say injuries are less likely to occur when a victim is unconscious. "And the condition of Della's clothing suggests rape. Her pants were pulled down and left inside out, her jacket was discarded, her plaid shirt was left half off."

As far as the charge of tampering with evidence, Brady said it was clear from witness testimony that Wade had disposed of the bloody rock and the shovel.

"Wade never told anyone that he beat Della with a shovel. All Wade said is that he used the shovel. He didn't use the shovel to beat Della. What Wade used the shovel for was he used the shovel to get rid of the rock that was sitting on the papers. After he left, he returned to the garage, washed his hands, came back to the shed and didn't want to touch the bloody rock."

Brady also said Wade had tampered with evidence by moving Della's body. "Witnesses agree that when they were taken to see the body that the body was originally blocking the door. The body was moved away from the door, deeper into the shed to prevent it from being seen. In fact, Wade told [Danny] Troxel that he wanted to move the body so he could shut the door.

"The defense is going to assert that even though Joshua Wade confessed in detail to seven people and although he was seen with blood on his hands and shirt that night, and although he took people to see the body, and asked for help moving the body, he spoke consistently about the crime on the wire, and that he ran from the police, that anybody except Joshua Wade killed Della Brown. It's the 'anybody but me' defense."

Brady then made an unexpected assertion about Della, saying that she likely was in the shed prostituting herself to get drugs. Brady referenced the ten dollars Della had borrowed from her friend and neighbor, Steven Lupien, the night she was killed.

"We know there was cocaine in her system, and ten dollars is not enough to pay for a large amount of alcohol and cocaine. Della clearly met someone who gave her alcohol and cocaine in exchange for sex." Under the prosecution's theory, this explained the source of the semen found inside Della and the pubic hair found on her body.

Brady concluded her closing argument by addressing the credibility problems of many of the state's witnesses. "The state's case is not dependent upon the credibility of any one witness. I can imagine that you're going to hear a lot in the defense's closing argument about the witnesses' credibility and why you should not believe the witnesses. When you're looking at that you need to keep in mind that all the witnesses agree about all of the major things and the wires match up to what the witnesses said. The state's case has corroborating evidence from independent witnesses, and it all points to one place. All of that evidence points to Joshua Wade. What's the state's case? Well, we have the confessions where he told all of these people that he killed Della and then we have admissions on the wire that correspond to the confessions, so when people are telling you he called Della 'that bitch' and when people are telling you he talked about strangling her with a white T-shirt and cutting her legs with a knife, all of that matches the physical evidence that was later found in the case. All of those things match up, and they all mean one thing: he's guilty."

****

The defense tag-teamed its closing argument, with Cindy Strout going first, addressing the lack of physical evidence against Wade. She criticized both the police and the DA's office for failing to adequately investigate the case.

131

"It appears that they're now beginning to understand the crime scene evidence and the forensic science but there's a huge problem. It has not dawned on them yet. Because they don't understand the time-of-death evidence and other forensic evidence. That the timing of Ms. Brown's death and the condition of her body revealed the exaggerations and lies from their witnesses about what Wade supposedly said and when he said it. And when you do understand these things, the things they say are easily disproved.

"You know witnesses can say anything. Especially when they've been threatened like Beckett, Troxel, and Clevenger were by the police. Or if they had been bribed with the deals like McCune, Troxel, and Beckett. But the science does not lie."

Strout said the science showed that Della was likely killed twenty-four hours before her body was found, meaning that she was killed on Thursday or Friday, but not on Tuesday or Wednesday, as many of the state's witnesses had claimed. "As for the state's witnesses, the gangsters ... they're all connected, and their stories are all out the window once the scene and the science about the body is understood. Because it's not a matter of being a little confused about the dates.

"At the end of the day there is not one shred of physical evidence, not a bit of forensic evidence, and no recorded confession as the state now concedes. The physical evidence excludes Wade. It is not his DNA. It is not his pubic hair. It is not his fingerprint in the victim's wet blood. Shouldn't the confession be wholly reliable before they ask you to convict a kid of first-degree murder? Joshua Wade had nothing to do with the death of Della Brown. He didn't kill her. He didn't rape her or do anything else to her. We must focus on the real issue. Josh was not involved in Ms. Brown's death. There is no lesser included offense for a person who is not involved. No breaks. We are not asking for a break. Because Josh did not do it."

Strout elicited gasps from the gallery during a dramatic presentation about the cuts found on Della's neck and leg and challenged the medical examiner's testimony that the cuts likely were caused by a dull knife. "You can take out this dull knife and you can saw on your arm all day long and it is not going to cut the skin," Strout said as she pressed a butter knife against her upper arms and moved it back and forth. "What made these marks is something that had a point. Like a nail, or a pointed branch." Strout took out a sharp branch and swiped it across her arm, drawing blood.[56] Strout argued that a small branch found on Della's body might have caused the injuries but was discarded by police at the crime scene.

"That's what made those marks. And that's what happened here."

Strout outlined a number of missteps made during the investigative process, including the failure to compare Wade's DNA, fingerprints, or shoe prints to any of the physical evidence that had been gathered until well after the case had gone to the grand jury. Some of the tests, including tests to compare Wade's DNA with the pubic hair found on Della's body, or tests to compare his fingerprint to the bloody print found at the scene, had still not been performed more than a year later, once the trial was underway.

"We did our own testing of the fingerprint in blood. And it said Mr. Wade cannot be matched to that print. And then we come to trial. Then the state decides to test the pubic hair from the vagina of Ms. Brown. It is not Joshua Wade's. The police finally compared shoe prints to Joshua Wade's, and they weren't his. So what you can see from this investigation

---

56 Strout told me she did not intend to actually scratch herself, saying, "I think in this heat of the moment, in closing arguments, I may have scratched it harder than I was practicing."

is that the state never really investigated this case until we were here at trial."

"Della Brown was a human being, and her memory deserves respect. And that includes unbiased, comprehensive investigation. And locking onto a suspect with a big mouth dishonors that memory."

For his part, Jim McComas focused on the alternate suspects in the case.

"Who really killed Della Brown? The defense strongly believes that someone should make a real effort to find out the answer to that question. The state took the easiest suspect and believed in the confessions brought in by a bunch of thugs, started to test some evidence and then stopped for two years until the trial started up. Now, I don't claim that the defense can definitively answer the question, 'Who killed Ms. Brown?' And the law does not require that we do that. But we have made progress. We came up with facts that forced the state to start testing evidence once the trial started, evidenced that it had never tested before."

"The prosecution can say this is sleight-of-hand or magic. They can call me any name they want to. I've heard them all. We're going to rest upon who has been following the rules in this courtroom, who is trying to do a good job of bringing the facts out."

McComas began by discussing the person who might have left the bloody fingerprint at the scene, who, he posited, was the same person who was the source of the semen found inside Della Brown.

"Instead of the 'unknown man' I think we should talk about him as 'the man whose name is not yet known.' Because I think he will be found someday. What do we know about this man? We know that he was in the scene. When I say in this scene I don't mean just at the scene. Like he stuck his head in ... for a better look. His print is in wet blood. His footprints are in wet blood, and he was in Ms. Brown. His semen was in her vagina, and his semen was in her anus. And his pubic hair was recovered. Why isn't this our murderer? How can anyone with common sense vote to convict Mr. Wade without evidence that identifies who this person is?

"So what does the state do to address this problem? They dishonor the memory of Ms. Brown. The stage has already characterized her and presented her to you as a drunk, as a liar, as an exaggerator. Why would the state be doing that to their own victim? To protect Rudy. They told you that they can explain the DNA and the pubic hair because, according to their argument, Ms. Brown sold her body for crack cocaine on Thursday. I think you know and I think the family knows that that is not true. That was an outrageous statement to make, unsupported by any kind of evidence. There is no indication that she ever sold her body for alcohol or crack or anything else. It's just a desperate attempt to get a conviction where the prints, the DNA, the footprints in the pubic hair, belong to someone other than the man on trial.

"Where is Rudy while Ms. Brown is being killed? The only evidence is his word that he is home alone. The police don't even ask this man where he was when they go to interview him. But when they do come to interview him a very interesting thing happens. Right at the beginning of the interview."

McComas played an audio recording of the police interview in which Rudy asks how Della died, and when the officer said, "Blunt trauma," Rudy immediately responded, "To the head?"

McComas stopped the tape.

"Lucky guess, for Rudy. The officers didn't even tell Rudy that she had been murdered. Just thought she was dead. How did she die? You would think that he would assume she was hit by a car or something. Blunt force trauma to the head. The very same head that Mr. D'Apice has been beating on all these years. That's called a clue in our business.

"Let's move onto the next individual, and that would be Mr. Poindexter. The serial rapist who always attacks from behind. There are at least five proven and known victims of his, and Della Brown was probably a victim, as well. He is motivated by great anger. He wants to punish, degrade, and humiliate women. And the crime scene bears that out. He usually rapes his victims anally. We know his anger level often results in retarded ejaculation. And what do we know, four out of the five victims there was no semen from Mr. Poindexter. So the fact that there was no semen from Mr. Poindexter in Ms. Brown in no way eliminates him. Although it's the smallest classification of rapists, the anger rapist is the most likely to kill."

If anyone was trying to mislead investigators, McComas argued, it was Timothy "Romeo" Beckett.

"One of the stranger things in this trial is that it's Romeo Beckett who says on September 2nd, to an officer who he seeks out to tell it to, that he saw an African American male who is six feet three, heavy build, short hair about thirty years old, walking on Dorbrandt in the direction of the shed with an Alaska Native woman, carrying a shirt. And this was before Ms. Brown's body was found on September 2nd. He gives this very specific description to the police, and he volunteers it. Here is the description of Gregory Poindexter: he is 250 pounds, short hair. He's seventy-five inches tall, which is six feet three, and he's within a month of being exactly thirty years old. Did Romeo Beckett see Della Brown walking with Gregory Poindexter? Is this just a flight of fancy that it comes up with someone who misdirected the police? Whatever it is, it is a hugely significant fact that has not been explored in this investigation. By anyone.

"Romeo Beckett is someone who could have very well

killed Ms. Brown. What is his motive? He doesn't need a motive. What's the motive for doing a home invasion? What's the motive for robbing the Spenard Hotel? This shed could be where the violence of the GTS gang began. Robbery could be a motive for Mr. Beckett. He also enjoys beating people up.

"None of these witnesses had immunity. They said something in court that incriminated themselves. All deals are off. They could've been prosecuted for Della Brown's murder. How much truth do you think you're going to get out of people who may have done the crime?"

TWENTY-ONE

The seven men and five women of the jury filed out of the courtroom to begin deliberations. Two alternates were excused from further duty and were free to go.

Anne Gore was the woman a fellow juror had described as young, attractive, and "yuppy-ish." Gore and another man, who was described as the nice young man who had a ponytail, always wore Dockers, and drove a red truck, were unaware of their positions as alternates during the entire three months, and felt shell-shocked after being thanked for their service and escorted out of the courthouse.

"It was pretty horrifying," Gore recalled. "Because it was like no, no, no, no, no. I just listened to three months of this testimony, and I have no way to process it. The other alternate, we walked out, and we're just standing on the sidewalk with our heads spinning, and I sort of said, 'So what do you think?' And he said, 'Not guilty.' And I was like, 'Are you fucking kidding me?! Guilty!' And he was like, 'What?! How can you say that?!' And I'm like, 'Did we just listen to the same trial? For the last three months?'"

Once in the jury room, one of the older and more respected members of the panel, Richard Hensel, polled his fellow jurors. Hensel, a retired civil servant, asked who thought Wade was guilty, and nine jurors raised their hands. Hensel, along with two women on the jury, felt from the onset that Wade was not guilty.

"The main reason I felt he was not guilty was by virtue

of the fact, and this is my personal opinion, that the police work was woefully inadequate," Hensel told me. "Just as an example, there was a pubic hair found on the victim. It did not have the same DNA as the alleged perpetrator. And I felt that that, by itself, was enough of an argument to say that he was not guilty."

The jury deliberated for a full week. The foreman had emerged just once, toward the end of deliberations, to ask a question of the judge: Could they convict Wade under the theory that he was an accomplice or somehow involved in the crime? The judge explained they could not. The jury instructions were clear; a murder conviction required that they find Wade was personally responsible for the victim's death.

****

On April 16, 2003, there was word that the panel had finally reached a verdict. Daisy Piggott had been tormented during the trial, imagining what her daughter had endured at the hands of her killer, and Daisy hoped the nightmare would soon come to an end. She nervously dressed, and when she and her husband arrived at the courthouse, they filed into the courtroom along with a group of reporters and photographers. The mumblings of conversation fell silent as the jurors filed into the jury box.

"I understand the jury has reached a verdict?" Judge Wolverton asked.

Mike Rodriguez, the jury foreman, stood up. "Yes, Your Honor. We the jury, in the matter of the State of Alaska versus Joshua Wade, find the defendant not guilty."

Quiet gasps could be heard in the courtroom, and then the faint sound of sobbing, which grew louder and louder.

There were a total of nine charges, and Rodriguez

uttered the words "not guilty," for all but one. Wade had been acquitted of murder and rape, but the jury had found him guilty of tampering with evidence.

It was soon clear that the sounds of despair were coming from Daisy Piggott.

"When the foreman kept saying, 'Not guilty ... not guilty ... not guilty ...' The last 'not guilty,' I think it was manslaughter ... I just broke down. My husband grabbed my arms, and said, 'Time to go, Daisy.' He ushered me out. It was awful."

One juror, who asked that I not use her name, recalled with striking clarity, watching the scene play out from the jury box:

I remember looking over the room and spotting Daisy Piggott, and I couldn't help but feel dread. I was anticipating seeing her face after she'd heard our decisions. The judge brought the room to order and everything became absolutely silent. I think Mr. McComas and Ms. Strout bowed their heads, possibly in prayer, and each put an arm around Wade. Mike stood up and began reading each count, I think there were twelve or thirteen, and after each charge, except the last, he paused and said, "Not guilty." After about the third charge and the third not guilty, there was this low-pitched wail coming from the gallery. It was faint at first, it gradually got louder, and it was absolutely heartbreaking. It sounded like an animal in pain. I realized then that it was Della's mother. I thought Mike would never finish saying "Not guilty." I remember thinking at the time that in addition to getting such horrible news, she was completely taken by surprise. I think the police and prosecuting attorneys had convinced her that, without a doubt, Wade would be found guilty. Maybe it's become exaggerated over the years, but to me I hear it like it was yesterday and I wonder if I'll ever get that sound out of my mind.

The nine jurors who felt from onset that Wade was guilty had apparently realized as deliberations continued over the course of the week that there was a difference between feeling Wade was guilty, and finding him guilty of first degree murder, based on what had been presented in court. Richard Hensel told me that after a week of deliberating all but one juror felt the verdict should be "not guilty," but ultimately, with some convincing, that juror decided to switch his vote to a "not guilty" verdict.

"The other jurors who felt he was guilty were convinced otherwise by the fact that there was 'a shadow of doubt' in the way the case was prosecuted," he said.

The defense team embraced in a long hug with their client, who seemed, according to one account, "temporarily overcome with emotion."[57]

Daisy Piggott would later refer to the day of Joshua Wade's acquittal as "the worst day of [her] life" and one that would signal the beginning of a long downward spiral. When asked how she felt about the jury in the case, Daisy told me she hoped the jurors would never have to endure what she had experienced. "They should feel guilty," she said. "It was devastating."

---

57 This quote is taken from an article in the *Anchorage Daily News*, dated April 17, 2003.

PART TWO: OUTRAGE AND APATHY

TWENTY-TWO

On September 4, 2003, five months after the jury had found Wade guilty of evidence tampering, Daisy Piggott was back in court for the sentencing hearing. Wade had agreed to the maximum penalty for that offense, which was six-and-a-half years in prison.

At the hearing, Della's family was permitted to speak, as part of what the court refers to as the "victim impact" statements.[58] Daisy knew she would never be able to address a crowd without breaking down in tears, but she had written a statement, which she asked to be read by an advocate from the Alaska Native Justice Center, Marty Willis. Daisy stood next to Marty as she read her words:

"The jury came to a verdict that I disagree with. So be it. I am learning to live with it. The crime that we are now addressing at this instant is tampering with evidence. What is described here it is not the run-of-the-mill tampering with evidence. This was the manipulation and degradation of the physical shell that housed my daughter, Della Marie. To come to terms with the fact that someone cared so little for her body after her spirit was gone has been a horror for me and I have no capacity to understand. It has caused me to question my values and the values of our society, that a body could be treated this way. There were questions at times about this being racially motivated. Yes, no? We don't know. But aside

---

58 In Alaska, as in many jurisdictions, the judge can take into account the feelings of the victim's family when considering an appropriate sentence for the crime.

from that, I tried to consider what prompts a human being to treat the body of another [in] such a fashion. I question what did I do that was wrong? Was I somehow responsible?

"I feel that I was failed by the judicial system from the start. From the quality of the investigation, to the multitude of delays and postponements, to the verdict, that here we are at sentencing for a crime that occurred over three years ago, almost exactly to the day. I felt I had to be [here] for the trial and to be here today, because I felt that somehow my presence would honor the memory of my daughter that was already so dishonored."

Daisy wrote of all she and her family had sacrificed to be there: relocating from New Mexico to Alaska, leaving behind two adult children and a slew of grandchildren in Albuquerque, pulling her two teenaged children out of school and forcing them to move and start over again in a new place and climate, where they experienced racism for the first time in their lives. She spoke of the anger and grief her children felt related to the death of their sister. Daisy admitted the verdict had so devastated her that she had turned to prescription drugs for relief.

"This has affected me in that now I go to sleep and wake up and go through the day with the companionship of pills. Some days I get through without the extra pills and medication but they are rare. For a while, especially during the months of January, February, and March, I got by with one therapy session a week. But after April I spent time in a residential crisis center, have changed medications many times in order to be functional, and I am now seeing a therapist at least twice a week. We all know that stuff runs downhill, and throughout this whole process I felt that I was at the bottom of that hill.

"I also looked unfairly for targets for my feelings. And unfortunately, I found them, as most of us do, in the people who are closest to us. My husband and my children were the unfortunate targets of my anger and my rage and my grief. Not even the dog was left out. We were a family before. Strong and close. Since this has occurred we have separated from each other and in our pain each to their own corner. We have lost our family life, and I'm sure my children at times have felt that they lost their mother. Instead of being able to navigate the turbulent years of their youth with the strength and trust that came from our bond as a family, I was emotionally absent from them too much. When I should've been going to high school activities, parent-teacher conferences and such, I was going to hearings and arrangements and returning home so full of pain and sorrow that I missed seeing so much of what they needed."

Daisy concluded her statement by thanking the people who had come to support her through the ordeal, and then ended with a simple plea to the judge.

"I would like to ask the court to sentence Mr. Wade to the maximum sentence possible. Again I thank the court for this opportunity to speak."

Daisy's youngest daughter, Keenak, then addressed the court. She recalled fond memories of her big sister and said that her death had torn apart the family.

"If I could have only one wish and I knew it was going to come true, I would wish for my sister to come back so it could be the same again and we can be a family again. We all miss her and loved her very much and she will never be forgotten."

Wade then addressed the court. He began his statement by thanking the judge.

"Number one, I want to thank you for being fair to me during the three years that I've been in your courtroom. Whether it's for me or the DA, you've been more than fair. I want to say from the beginning of my case I was not given a fair chance because of the media. They convicted me before I even stepped foot in a courtroom. Two, the DA making me out to be a racist when I have a best friend who was a Native, and that's given me nothing but problems in jail.[59] You make a big deal about my fights in jail, but you invoked every single one of them. Three, even though that twelve people said I was not guilty, everyone thinks I am guilty because of everything that was put out in the media. I've been rejected from every program possible as an option instead of doing time, and I've been rejected because they think I am guilty. I've been rejected at institutions because of the Native population, so I took this agreement because I didn't want to put myself or my family through any more humiliation. Especially myself because they want to rape my past. And when I was a kid horrible things happened to me. I had no counseling for that, and I don't think there's anything wrong with that, but they want to make it seem like it's bad because I needed help because something bad happened to me. So I want the maximum sentence because I don't want to be humiliated anymore, I don't agree with it, but that's about the only reason that I'm doing it. The only thing at all with this case that I'm sorry for is that I did not call the police whenever I found that lady's body. The only person I'm sorry to is her mother, that's it. And the family. But other than that, I'm not sorry for all the hell you guys had to go through, for lying and trying to get a conviction on me. The family and you, for the inconvenience, are the only people that I apologize to for all of this. And I just want to say thank you to my jury for being fair. That's it."

Judge Wolverton said the case had taken an "overwhelming toll" on the community and especially on Della's family.

---

59 Wade is referring to Jesse Ackmann, whose mother, Ruby, was a Native Alaskan.

"I can't imagine your pain. I'm sorry," he said, making eye contact with Daisy Piggott.

He then sentenced Wade to five years behind bars, with two years already served. Wolverton explained the sentence would run consecutive to another eighteen-month sentence for a gun-possession conviction in June of 2000.[60]

As Wade was escorted out of the courtroom in handcuffs, a woman in the gallery who was a crime victim and a frequent spectator in the courtroom, shouted at Wade in disgust.

"You're a fucking pussy!"

---

60 The judge sentenced Wade to the maximum penalty; five years is the standard two-thirds of a six-and-a-half year sentence.

TWENTY-THREE

There were few people more outraged by the jury's verdict in the Della Brown case than Native activist Desa Jacobsson. The sixty-seven-year-old—whose first name is pronounced *Deesa*—is a wonderfully eccentric woman, a descendent of the Gwich'in and Yup'ik tribes, who can dispense motherly advice and utter a string of four-letter epithets in the same breath. Often the sole protester at government events in Anchorage, she keeps her salt-and-pepper hair in a fashionable bob and is never without one of her signature pink scarves around her neck. Before following her political aspirations—which included a run for governor as the Green Party candidate in 1998—Jacobsson headed a citizen crime-prevention brigade she dubbed the "Rat Patrol." The group was made up of five women, who in white T-shirts patrolled the main thoroughfare in downtown Anchorage late at night, trying to protect Native women from predators. One night, Jacobsson said, she watched as a group of more than a dozen men lined up outside a bar frequented by Native women, ostensibly ready to pounce when the bar closed its doors.

"One of them had a case of beer, and I thought, what are they waiting for? At first I thought for a cab or something, but no, they were waiting for vulnerable Native women to come out … so they could do what they wanted with them. Nobody said a thing."

Shortly after Wade's acquittal, Jacobsson announced she was beginning a hunger strike to protest the verdict. She vowed to live on only coffee and water until the police chief resigned and until federal prosecutors indicted Wade for violating Della Brown's civil rights.[61]

"It wasn't a strike, it was a fast," Jacobsson clarified. "The word 'strike' has violent connotations."

Jacobsson's feud with Anchorage Police Chief Walt Monegan stemmed from what she deemed a "sloppy police investigation" and from comments Monegan made on a radio program suggesting that Native women should not put themselves in the vulnerable position of being drunk and alone at night. Jacobsson considered this victim blaming.

"I don't care what kind of life you lead," Jacobsson quipped. "Nobody deserves to be slaughtered."

Monegan insisted that Jacobsson had misconstrued his comments, telling the *Anchorage Daily News*, "I think it's part of my duty. If there's a threat out there, I should be warning people about it. … No one deserves to be a victim."

Most important, Jacobsson saw that Della Brown's murder was already fading from the public's consciousness and she didn't want Della to be just one more Native woman the public would forget. Two weeks into her twenty-eight-day fast, weak yet determined, Jacobsson led a ten-mile memorial walk in memory of Della Brown and the other five women who had been slain. Thirty-five women, mostly Native Alaskan, followed Jacobsson quietly in a solemn procession from the foothills east of Anchorage to downtown and then on to Spenard, where Della Brown's body had been found. There, the women held candles and some of them wept under a darkening sky.

"We were all screaming inside, 'Someone do something! Say something!' And no one did," Jacobsson recalled. "Even

---

61 Jacobsson reasoned that federal civil rights charges were a possibility since there had been testimony during the trial that Wade had disdain for Alaska Natives.

the Native leaders said we were being purely reactionary. And we said, 'No, we can do something, we can hold a candlelight vigil, and let everybody know that this is not okay.' You see, it's the silence that's dangerous."

****

In December of 2004, after serving time for his conviction for tampering with evidence, Joshua Wade walked free. At the DA's office, Assistant Attorney General John Novak was apprehensive. He was sure Wade had gotten away with murder once and worried he would strike again.

"When he got out, we all got together and said, 'Hey look, we need to watch this guy.' You know, probation and cops, and we were very concerned."

Authorities had reason to worry.

PART THREE: MINDY

TWENTY-FOUR

August 7, 2007, 5:30 p.m.

Detective Pam Perrenoud had just picked up her four-year-old twin girls from preschool and was driving home after a grueling day at work when her cell phone rang. She had worked hard to balance the demands of work and family, but as a homicide detective for the Anchorage Police Department, she knew the work often required long and odd hours. Still, as her car barreled down the Glenn Highway nearing her home in suburban Eagle River, she hoped it wasn't her boss calling to summon her back to work.

"Hello?"

"Pam, we have a missing person case that's suspicious. And this one sounds interesting." It was her boss, Sergeant Pablo Paiz. Detective Perrenoud knew how strapped the department was for resources, and she realized if it wasn't her, someone else would have to work the overtime.

"Alright," she said with a sigh. "I'm just going to drop the girls off with John and I'll be right in."

Perrenoud, (whose last name is pronounced *Perr-new*) is unpretentious, with a round, kind face, and she possesses the rare quality of seeming instantly relatable to most strangers. She has a keen investigative mind and can exude a sense of calm in the most stressful of circumstances. Being the mother of twins helped her refine this latter skill, and it had served her well on the job; it put others at ease, and often, made the most hardened criminal or witness more willing to talk.

152

She had come to Alaska from her hometown of Seattle in the late 1980s and spent two-and-a-half years in the Army getting money for college before attending the University of Alaska Fairbanks. The Anchorage Police Department hired her in 1990, and, at first, she worked undercover drug cases, often posing as someone trying to buy drugs or supervising informants as the case officer. She loved the work and considered it a kind of mental challenge—unraveling the mysteries of a case, exploiting the perpetrator's weaknesses, and ultimately beating a criminal at his own game.

In 1999, while working a drug case, Perrenoud met John Eckstein, an FBI agent based in Anchorage, and the couple soon fell in love, married, and started a family. It wasn't long before Perrenoud had moved on to homicide investigations. She had served as the lead investigator in at least twenty such cases, and she found the work both exhilarating and stressful. Homicide cases contained the elements of many different crimes and she felt that uncovering a motive— whether it was based on money, drugs, domestic violence, or whether it was completely random—was a challenging and rewarding endeavor. The downside was it also was the kind of work that demanded an intense amount of energy and attention, and there was little room for error.

After dropping the twins off at home with her husband, Perrenoud immediately returned to police headquarters. There, she met Sergeant Paiz, who explained the department had received a call from a woman in Fairbanks named Kathy Hodges who was concerned about her co-worker and good friend, Mindy Schloss. Mindy was a 52-year-old psychiatric advanced nurse practitioner who worked at Tanana Chiefs Conference,[62] and she split her time between Fairbanks and Anchorage. Mindy was expected at work in Fairbanks on

62 Tanana Chiefs Conference is a non-profit organization that serves the Native Alaskan population in forty-two villages of Interior Alaska.

Monday morning, but it was already Tuesday night and she hadn't shown up nor had she called to explain her absence. Mindy was scheduled to meet with psychiatric patients, and there was just no way she wouldn't have shown up without an explanation, Kathy had explained.

It was not Kathy Hodges' first call to police. She had called them late on Monday, asking if officers could go to Mindy's house in southwest Anchorage to check on her. An officer had obliged, and even walked around the house on the quiet, tree-lined cul-de-sac on Cutty Sark Street, but the officer said the doors were locked and that he couldn't enter the home without a warrant or unless he felt someone's safety was immediately at risk. Even so, the officer looked into the house through the windows and didn't see any signs of a struggle, anyone passed out on the floor, or anything that appeared suspicious.

"Mindy had high blood pressure. And I was afraid that maybe she had had a stroke or something," Kathy recalled, frustrated that police had not broken the door down to see if Mindy was all right, especially given that she lived alone. By Tuesday, with still no word from Mindy, Kathy's concern had deepened. She called police again, and said she wanted to file a missing person's report. An officer explained she would have to wait forty-eight hours and, meanwhile, advised her to call area hospitals, to see if Mindy had been admitted as a patient, given her health problems. Kathy did, but no hospital reported having a patient named Mindy Schloss.

"At that point, I knew something was really wrong," Kathy recalled. "So I told my boss, 'I'm taking time off and I'm going to go to Anchorage and I'm going to look for her.'"

It was a six-hour drive to Anchorage from Fairbanks, so Kathy booked a flight, convinced that Mindy had gone berry picking and had possibly fallen and hurt herself. Mindy was known, at this time of year, to perform her annual tradition of picking blueberries and making jam, which she enjoyed sharing with her friends and coworkers.

"Mindy loved to go blueberry picking," Kathy said. "And I thought that stupid girl has gone out blueberry picking by herself in the hills around Anchorage and fallen and broken her leg and she's out there in need of help."

Mindy Schloss was a petite woman with a fair complexion, big eyes, and dark, wavy hair. She was open-minded and generous, loved to travel, and she relished new experiences. Her openness to new things had resulted from the influence of her mother, who was a self-taught New Age "spiritualist."[63] The Schloss family had moved from Brooklyn to upstate New York in the late 1950s after Mindy's father contracted tuberculosis. Apparently shunned by others in their tight-knit, orthodox Jewish community due to the stigma of the disease, they had relocated to Syracuse, New York, so Mindy's father could receive treatment and the family could have a new start. Mindy was slow to judge others and open to perspectives that differed from her own; qualities that had proved invaluable in her work with psychiatric patients. She did not subscribe to any specific spiritual practice or follow any organized religion, but she was fond of crystals and tarot cards. She also took heed in the practice of *feng shui*; she had even paid a feng shui consultant to make sure the furniture in her home was placed in harmony with the surrounding environment.[64]

Despite the seriousness of her profession, Mindy was playful and fun loving. Kathy recalled they had once gone to a local park in Fairbanks and in a beautiful garden Kathy had taken photos of Mindy wearing what Kathy described

---

63 This term was used by Kathy Hodges to describe Mindy's mother.
64 Feng shui is one of the Five Arts of Chinese Metaphysics considered to govern spatial arrangement and orientation in relation to the flow of energy.

as "a pretty dress that might be worn by a wizard woman during the Middle Ages" while holding a crystal ball. Mindy thought the photo might make a fun Christmas card, and Kathy remembered with humor the ruckus Mindy had caused with the TSA at an airport security checkpoint when she attempted to bring the large glass orb onto one of her bimonthly airplane rides from Anchorage to Fairbanks.

****

After Kathy's second call to police, Sergeant Paiz decided to drive by Mindy's house. He found a way in through the door that entered the house from the garage, opening the locked door with a credit card, sliding it down the edge of the door, near the lock. Once inside, he didn't see anything he considered suspicious inside the home or any sign of struggle, but given Kathy's level of concern for her friend, Paiz decided to call in the homicide unit.

When Detective Perrenoud arrived at Mindy's house, she met Mindy's best friend, Gerri Yett. Like Kathy Hodges, Gerri was a nurse who had worked with Mindy, and like Kathy, Gerri was becoming frantic about her friend's disappearance. Gerri was a dependable and sincere woman, and although Gerri and Mindy were close in age, Mindy often jokingly referred to Gerri as "Mom," because she was such a thoughtful and loyal caretaker.

"After Mindy's mother died, I inherited the role of being Mindy's guardian angel," Gerri recalled.

Their friendship was deep and had developed over the course of fifteen years, as Gerri and Mindy traveled together all over the state of Alaska as nurses for Alaska's Section of Epidemiology. Their work investigating outbreaks of infectious diseases such as tuberculosis and hepatitis took them to the most remote Native villages of Alaska. They often would stay in one place for weeks at a time; many of the villages had no running water or power, and Gerri and Mindy slept on the floors of schools or clinics. During these trips, and partly due to the harshness of the conditions, they had grown incredibly close. Gerri's two teenaged children considered Mindy an adopted aunt, and they often would stay with Mindy when their mother was out of town.

"She was a part of my family, and I was a part of hers," Gerri said.

Detective Perrenoud listened to Gerri recall details about Mindy's routine. It was summer in Alaska, and so although it was nighttime, the sun still blazed in the sky as they stood outside Mindy's house at 6852 Cutty Sark Street. At this time of year, the days were at their longest; the sun wouldn't set until 11:30 p.m. Gerri explained that Mindy typically alternated her weeks between Fairbanks and Anchorage and Gerri had the habit of coming over to Mindy's house every morning and every evening when Mindy was out of town to feed Mindy's fifteen-year-old cat, Willy, and to give him his medication.

Gerri explained that Mindy typically took a flight from Anchorage to Fairbanks on Sunday. Gerri and Mindy had planned to attend a mutual friend's fiftieth birthday party the past Friday evening, but at the last minute, Gerri said she had called Mindy and told her she couldn't make it.

"I'll call you tomorrow," Gerri had promised.

The next day, Gerri called Mindy and the call went to voicemail.

"I just figured, people get busy," Gerri recalled. "Then Sunday, when I called again, she didn't answer and that was unusual for Mindy. She would usually respond to her calls, but I didn't know what time she was leaving for Fairbanks. So I thought she could be in transit."

Gerri told Detective Perrenoud that on Monday she

went over to feed Mindy's cat and noticed the doorknob of the front door appeared to be loose. Knowing that Mindy was not the handy type, Gerri retrieved a screwdriver and tightened it. As she walked through the house, Gerri said she noticed the kitchen was not as Mindy would have left it; there were papers on the table and an empty wine bottle on the counter. It was also part of Mindy's routine, when she left for Fairbanks, to leave a check on the counter for Gerri's daughter, Desi, who did some housecleaning for her. Mindy was also known to leave chocolate kisses and a nice note for Desi, along with the check, Gerri said. This time, there was no note, no chocolate kisses, and no check.

Detective Perrenoud wondered if Mindy had been unhappy with her life or distraught for any reason, knowing that depressed people can sometime disappear of their own accord. Gerri said Mindy had never been happier, and in fact, had just signed a lease for office space, hoping to settle more permanently in Anchorage by establishing her own psychiatric nursing practice. As far as Mindy's future was concerned, only promise lay ahead.

****

Gerri and Detective Perrenoud entered the house. Gerri began to point out the things she thought were amiss: the unsorted mail and unpaid bills; some glasses that were out on the counter and not put away; and the empty wine bottle on the counter she had already mentioned. Mindy would have never left the house in this state, Gerri explained.

Detective Perrenoud looked for signs of a break-in. Gerri remembered she had tightened the loose doorknob, and immediately felt a pang of guilt, fearing she had done something wrong. Detective Perrenoud assured her that she hadn't, but that the information was helpful if indeed someone had pried open the front door. Detective Perrenoud saw a number of Native carvings and artifacts on the mantel that Mindy had accumulated during her extensive travels across Alaska. Knowing such items were worth thousands of dollars, Detective Perrenoud thought it was strange that a would-be robber wouldn't have taken them. As a psychiatric advanced nurse practitioner, Mindy was able to dispense psychotropic medication and it was also strange, Detective Perrenoud thought, that a prescription pad lay on the table. If someone had burglarized the house, wouldn't they have also taken the prescription pad?

In the bedroom, Mindy's bed was made with military precision, with the corners of the sheets tightly folded in a meticulous fashion. This was bizarre, Gerri said, because Mindy was a restless sleeper, and she never made her bed that way.

"Somebody else has done things in here," Gerri told Detective Perrenoud. "I'm sure of it."

In addition, knowing that Desi was coming over to clean and to do laundry, Mindy would have left the bed unmade anyway, Gerri explained. Gerri also remarked that the suitcase Mindy usually took with her to Fairbanks was gone.

It was also notable that Mindy's car was not in the garage. This was odd, Gerri explained, because Mindy's house was only a five-minute drive from the airport. She would have taken a cab to catch her flight, rather than paying for airport parking for a full week.

As Detective Perrenoud and Gerri looked for other things in the house that might have provided clues, they came across a rumpled up apron in the garbage. Gerri immediately recognized it; she had made the apron for Mindy as a gift for her birthday. Adorned with bright moons and stars, Gerri told Detective Perrenoud that she had made the apron for Mindy the year Mindy's cheesecake had won a second-place ribbon at the fair. Gerri told Detective Perrenoud that Mindy valued her friendships, and there was just no way she would have ever thrown something with such sentimental value in the garbage.

Mindy did not have close family ties, Gerri explained. Both of her parents were dead, and she had a brother who lived in upstate New York with his wife and children, but they did not visit often and were not particularly close.

Detective Perrenoud asked if Mindy had a significant other. Gerri explained that Mindy was single, but she remained close to her former boyfriend, Bob Conway. In fact, the couple had moved to Alaska together in 1980 after meeting and falling in love in Seattle, she said. Long after they cut romantic ties, Gerri said, Bob would often run errands for Mindy when she came home to recuperate from the numerous surgeries she had to remove cysts from her kidneys, which resulted from a disorder called polycystic kidney disease. Her condition was chronic, and Bob was always there for Mindy, a loving and devoted friend.

At this point, Gerri was feeling restless, so she said she was going to make some calls to Mindy's other friends, to see if they had heard anything from her. Detective Perrenoud could see the pain and worry in Gerri's face. Being a detective meant remaining somewhat hardened to the circumstances and people she encountered; still, Detective Perrenoud empathized. She promised Gerri if she had any significant update to share, Gerri would be the first to know. Gerri left, and Detective Perrenoud stayed behind, combing through the house for any additional clues.

Methodically, Detective Perrenoud went through every room in the house. In a back room, which appeared to be used as an office and for storage space, Detective Perrenoud found an old wallet on a desk. There was no sign in the house, anywhere else, of a purse or pocketbook, so the wallet piqued Detective Perrenoud's interest. It was not a billfold, but of the larger variety many women carried, dark purple with a clasp on top. Inside, Detective Perrenoud found a small scrap of paper pushed all the way down in one of the pockets. The small paper had a four-digit number written on it: 4-1-4-7. Detective Perrenoud jotted the number down in her notebook. In Mindy's papers, Detective Perrenoud also found a bank statement and noted the account numbers. *We'll check her accounts*, Detective Perrenoud thought, knowing that tracking a missing person's ATM withdrawals was usually a good place to start.

TWENTY-FIVE

August 8, 2007

The next day at police headquarters, Detective Perrenoud contacted Mindy's bank to see if there was any unusual activity. She discovered a $500 ATM withdrawal on Friday, August 5 at 5:01 a.m. The amount of the withdrawal and the time of day it had occurred both seemed strange to Detective Perrenoud; Mindy's friends had said that she typically used her debit card to make purchases and didn't usually carry around a lot of cash. Detective Perrenoud called the Anchorage office of the FBI, knowing that they were better equipped than the police department to track down more detailed financial records. Special Agent Mike Thoreson, who mostly investigated white collar crimes, took the information Detective Perrenoud provided and began an examination of all of Mindy's bank accounts, debit cards, and credit cards.

In the meantime, Detective Perrenoud already had heard from Mindy's former boyfriend, Bob Conway; she had talked to him the previous night after finally returning home. It was after 11:00 p.m., and dispatch called to say the missing woman's former boyfriend had called, requesting to talk to her. Although it was late, Detective Perrenoud called him back.

"There's nothing more we can do tonight," she assured him. "We'll pick this up in the morning." At that point, Detective Perrenoud didn't know if Bob Conway had anything to do with Mindy's disappearance, so she remained guarded. Any suspicions she may have had initially, however, quickly evaporated when she checked out Bob's alibi. He worked for a company called Quality Asphalt Paving and managed road construction projects in some of the most remote areas of Alaska. At the time of Mindy's disappearance, he was managing a project hundreds of miles away. He had just returned to Anchorage, to help search for Mindy, and Detective Perrenoud could sense his concern for Mindy was deep and genuine.

Bob was a rugged outdoorsman, a quiet type, with a distinctive white mustache and a rosy complexion; he hadn't heard from Mindy but was distressed by the thought some terrible fate had befallen her. His coworkers had road construction and repair projects all over the state, and so Bob alerted them to be on the lookout for Mindy or her car, a red 2000 Acura Integra. One group of contractors even shut down their project along the Seward Highway early to search the area for any sign of her.

Detective Perrenoud also discovered that Mindy had planned to remodel her kitchen and was in the process of taking bids from contractors. Detective Perrenoud was able to identify three contractors with whom Mindy had recently met. The most recent worked at Home Depot and had seen her the same weekend she had disappeared. Mindy's bank records showed she had made recent purchases at a local Costco, so Detective Perrenoud obtained surveillance footage from the store that showed a woman, who appeared to be Mindy. The contractor from Home Depot described what Mindy was wearing and the surveillance video appeared to show Mindy doing errands earlier that same day, wearing the clothes he had described. The contractor had come over to Mindy's house to provide an estimate of the remodeling work on the very night she had vanished.

Detective Perrenoud determined the Home Depot contractor was the last known person who had seen or talked to her.

A close friend of Mindy's, Susan Oliver, said she had recommended another contractor to Mindy. Susan said she later regretted making the recommendation because Mindy and the contractor had disputed over his pricing. The argument had become so heated, Susan said, the man had even called Mindy a "bitch" and left a somewhat threatening note on her door, demanding that she not discuss his prices with others. Detective Perrenoud discovered that man had a criminal record.

The last contractor, however, was the one who had really raised a red flag with Detective Perrenoud. He had an unforgettable name: Red Tiger-Chase. He was short in stature and covered in tattoos, the most prominent of which depicted a life-sized Glock handgun across the left side of his shaved head. A member of a Latino gang, he had a long list of infractions including assault. Apparently unaware of Tiger-Chase's criminal past, Mindy had awarded him the contract to do the remodeling of her kitchen.

All three contractors appeared nervous when they were interrogated by police. Despite their uneasiness, after the interviews, each man agreed to provide a sample of his saliva for DNA analysis.

****

Detective Perrenoud decided to return to Mindy's neighborhood and knock on a few doors. Most of the neighbors had not seen or heard from Mindy in days, but one man who lived across the street said he saw Mindy's car pull into her driveway at about 9:15 a.m. on Saturday, August 4. He was so sure of the time, he explained, because his father had recently passed away, and he was sorting through some files, making sure the records were all in order. He was loading some of the papers into the bed of his pickup truck, on his way to a ten o'clock appointment with an accountant, when he saw Mindy's red Acura come down the street. He said he watched the car come up the driveway, and although he couldn't say for sure whether Mindy was behind the wheel, he said he saw a "slender arm" reach up and press the garage door opener inside the car, and then watched the car pull into the garage.

No one else in the neighborhood had seen Mindy that weekend or had noticed anything out of the ordinary. There was, however, a common theme emerging from the neighbors: the young people who lived in the house next door, just to the south of Mindy's, were troublemakers. They lived there unsupervised, and they drank and smoked and had loud parties that sometimes lasted all night long. In fact, one such party had disrupted the neighborhood that past Friday night.

Detective Perrenoud knocked on the door of the house that was the source of the complaints, but there was no answer. She resolved to keep trying to reach the occupants, even if she or another officer had to visit the home several times a day.

As she was wrapping up her interviews with Mindy's neighbors, Detective Perrenoud's phone rang. It was Agent Thoreson.

"We've got video footage from the ATM," he said. "And you're going to want to see this."

TWENTY-SIX

Detective Perrenoud's instincts were right; the bank records had led to their first big clue in the case. The video, taken from an ATM at the Sand Lake branch of Wells Fargo bank, just three blocks from Mindy's house, showed someone making a $500 withdrawal from Mindy's account. Detective Perrenoud's eyes widened as she watched a figure walk into the frame from the left; the person in the footage was a man, with a blue and white bandana tied around his face and a dark baseball cap with four wide, white pinstripes down the bill of the hat. The cap was pulled down low on his forehead, and he was wearing a quilted, dark jacket. Agent Thoreson explained that, for a moment, the suspect in the footage would approach the ATM, and just briefly, would pull down the bandana, revealing the bottom half of his face.

"Right there," Agent Thoreson said, freezing the frame. "Guess he couldn't see over his bandana." Detective Perrenoud squinted to see more clearly the grainy image of the man's face. Just the tip of his nose was visible; the top half of his face was off-frame. It was obvious the man was Caucasian, but she knew identifying anyone from a grainy photo of their mouth and chin was going to be a challenge. Plus the shot of the man's face only lasted two or three frames. The man had quickly pulled the bandana back up over his face, taken the cash, and walked out of the bank. As he turned around, she and Agent Thoreson could see he was wearing a black and white backpack. Bank records showed that the suspect had checked the balance, and was aware that Mindy had about $20,000 in her account.

Agent Thoreson discovered other activity related to Mindy's account, as well. At 4:16 a.m. the following morning, August 6, the same masked figure had entered an ATM kiosk at Credit Union 1 on Eide Street, about four miles northeast of Mindy's house. Aware of the daily maximum cash withdrawal from an ATM, again the man withdrew $500. This time, though, cameras positioned above the ATM kiosk and on the ATM itself had shown something unexpected. After the man retrieved the cash, he had left the small enclosed kiosk and returned several times. The footage showed him pacing back and forth, in an agitated state. A bank official had told Agent Thoreson it was likely the man had forgotten to retrieve the debit card after taking the cash, and that after a few seconds, as a security measure, the ATM machine had swallowed the card. Knowing that $20,000 remained in the account, the man was likely frustrated and kept returning to the ATM in an apparent attempt to retrieve the card.

Given the early morning hour, it was not likely anyone had witnessed this scene, but Agent Thoreson checked with the bank and was surprised to learn someone else had used the same ATM just fifteen minutes after the suspect, at 4:30 a.m. Agent Thoreson got his name and was able to track him down. The man explained that he was having trouble sleeping and had stopped by the ATM on his way to get some early morning breakfast. As he entered the ATM kiosk, he said another man was exiting and told him that the ATM wasn't working. The witness said he entered the kiosk, successfully withdrew some cash, and, as he left, the man was still hanging around outside.

"Hey, it worked for me," the witness had said to the man, before getting into his car and driving off. Agent Thoreson said the witness reported the man was not wearing a bandana or a hat when he saw him, but that he was Caucasian, about five feet ten, had on white tennis shoes, "Levi's style jeans," and a dark jacket. He was also riding a bicycle, the witness said.

Detective Perrenoud knew the man in the footage had something to do with Mindy's disappearance; she also knew she would have to show the ATM footage to Mindy's friends, to see if any of them recognized him. It was a conversation she knew was necessary, but she also was dreading it. She called them all, one by one, and asked if they could come down to the police station.

****

It was Wednesday and no one had heard from Mindy in five days. Local TV stations in Anchorage reported her disappearance simply as a missing person's case, devoting thirty seconds or so to the story during their evening newscasts. Police had not indicated foul play as a factor, so reporters had not been assigned to dig any deeper than that. On KTUU's 5:00 p.m. newscast the anchor read the following script, as Mindy's photo flashed on the TV screen:

New at five ... Anchorage police are looking for a nurse who has not been seen since Sunday. Fifty-two-year-old Mindy Schloss is a nurse who frequently travels to Fairbanks to see patients. She was scheduled to fly to Fairbanks on Sunday but didn't get on the plane. Schloss hasn't made any of her appointments since then, and police say her car and cell phone are missing, too. She is described as extremely reliable and unlikely to take off without letting people know.

Bob Conway had returned to Anchorage from his road construction project, and Kathy Hodges had arrived from Fairbanks. Along with Gerri and Susan Oliver, they had all been searching tirelessly for Mindy. They spent hours combing Cook Inlet bluffs and beaches, looking for her in Arctic Valley, where she loved to pick blueberries, and they wandered miles of railroad tracks and hiking trails. Thinking the worst, Bob even began digging through Dumpsters, and looking in ditches. They were all, by the end of the day Wednesday, physically and emotionally exhausted.

When Kathy Hodges got the call a detective wanted to meet with Mindy's friends at the police station, she had a sinking feeling. She was frustrated because she felt police reacted slowly to her phone calls concerning Mindy's whereabouts earlier in the week and just now seemed to be showing a sense of urgency.

"For people who paid no attention to me for two days, I knew it had to be something bad," Kathy recalled.

When Gerri, Bob, Susan, and Kathy arrived at police headquarters that evening, Detective Perrenoud escorted them into the police chief's conference room and asked them all to have a seat.

"I have something to show you," Detective Perrenoud said. She pulled out a photo, a still image from the video footage from the first ATM withdrawal, showing the suspect with the bottom half of his face exposed. "Do any of you recognize this man?"

No one did. Detective Perrenoud explained the man had used Mindy's debit card to withdraw $1,000 from her account. A shiver traveled down Bob's spine, and he immediately felt sick to his stomach. His eyes filled with tears. Gerri and Susan broke down and began to weep. Kathy, too, was overcome with emotion, but she hadn't given up hope.

"I thought maybe she had been kidnapped by this guy and that maybe she was still alive."

TWENTY-SEVEN

On August 9, 2007, almost a week after Mindy vanished, Anchorage police released a photo of her red 2000 Acura Integra to the media, along with a photo of Mindy wearing a black dress and a diamond pendant necklace and with a beaming smile on her face. The flyers, which were posted all over town, had the word MISSING as a heading, in large letters and outlined in red. The story of the missing nurse had made the front the page of the *Anchorage Daily News*, and all the local TV stations had taken notice, too, sending reporters to Cutty Sark Street to interview neighbors and to do live shots on the progress of the investigation.

The public was responding to the story with both intrigue and concern. Gerri Yett cultivated this public sentiment on behalf of her best friend, granting interviews with the local media. She didn't share her deepest feelings, but the anguish in her face was evident as she appeared on camera, urging anyone with information to come forward. She reminded viewers that this could have been their sister, their daughter, or their mother who had mysteriously vanished. As Gerri described how Mindy had dedicated her life to helping others and the baffling circumstances of her disappearance, it was impossible not to share her heartache.

Bob Conway had made sure his colleagues at the paving company had all seen the photo of Mindy's car, knowing that they covered the state and were frequently driving local roads in and around Anchorage. On the very day police

170

released the photo of the car to the public, the image of the red Acura was foremost in the mind of one of Bob Conway's good friends and colleagues, Jeff Roskelley. Bob had called him personally three days before to say that Mindy was missing and to please keep an eye out for her car. Roskelley was driving down Old International Airport Road and as he passed the parking lot of the Sky Chef's building, the company that provided passengers' meals for the airlines, he caught a glimpse of a red car. Roskelley figured he should go back and check, so he turned his truck around and pulled into the parking lot. As approached the car on foot, he called Bob on his cell phone. Bob answered, and when Roskelley read to him the license plate, Bob told him to immediately back away from the car.

"Hang up and call 911," Bob told him. Roskelley began to tremble, realizing he had just found Mindy's car.

****

The Sky Chef parking lot was cordoned off with crime scene tape until the police department's forensic team could arrive and search the car for evidence. In the meantime, Detective Perrenoud talked to a manager inside the Sky Chef building and discovered that there was surveillance video of the parking lot. The manager scanned through hours of footage before finding a grainy image of the red Acura driving into the lot at 12:45 p.m. on Saturday, August 4. Mindy's car was captured at the very top of the footage, passing from left to right; it pulled into a spot at the top right-hand corner of the screen. After about a minute, the door opened and a man exited the car. The image was much too grainy to decipher the man's face, but he appeared to be Caucasian and was wearing a dark, short-sleeved shirt and jeans. Once out of the car, he lingered for about thirty seconds and appeared to be doing something to the door, possibly wiping the driver's side door and handle of fingerprints. He then appeared to put on a backpack, walk across the parking lot the same way the car had entered, and disappear off the screen.

It was a strange place to park Mindy's car, Detective Perrenoud thought, if someone was trying to make it look like Mindy was catching a flight. It was where Sky Chef employees parked their cars, and there was no direct access to the terminal. Perhaps the man knew the airport had surveillance cameras in all of the passenger parking lots, Detective Perrenoud reasoned, and had chosen this lot, not realizing it, too, was under video surveillance.

Police swiftly obtained a search warrant for Mindy's car, and crime scene investigators found Mindy's purse in the backseat with her car keys and wallet inside. The items in the wallet all appeared to be intact, with the notable exception of her ATM card, which was missing. In the trunk of the car, they found Mindy's suitcase with some rumpled up clothes inside, along with Mindy's laptop computer. Also in the trunk, there was a medium-sized garden shovel, which investigators later determined had been taken from Mindy's garage. Three cigarette butts were in the ashtray, which was strange, according to Mindy's friends, since she had quit smoking in 2005.

In the backseat, crime scene technicians found more troubling evidence. A substance that appeared to be blood was discovered on a floor mat behind the front passenger's seat. There was also a dusty print of a woman's shoe on the armrest, just behind the passenger-side door. The shoeprint was sideways and facing forward, as if someone had been lying across the backseat, on her side, facing the driver.

None of this information was released to the media, but the next night, the CBS affiliate, KTVA, reported that Mindy Schloss could be in "grave danger," while the NBC station ran an interview with the police department's spokesman Paul Honeman, who suggested it was possible that Mindy had been kidnapped and was being held against her will.

TWENTY-EIGHT

August 14, 2007

It was about noon, and Kathy Easley was getting ready for her evening shift as a clerk at Sadler's furniture store when there was a knock at her front door. She had dressed, but she hadn't yet dried her hair and was already running late. In addition to being a single mom and working at the furniture store, Kathy attended nursing school and had just returned home from an early morning clinical. She had just enough time to change her clothes and wash her hair before heading off to work.

When she answered the door, she was surprised to see a young man she only knew as "Josh" standing on her front porch. Josh had moved into the place next door about a month prior, and although she knew the family who lived in that house well, she rarely talked to the new tenant and she didn't even know his last name. He was twenty-eight, but she thought he looked much younger and she had to admit he wasn't bad looking—a tan and well-groomed "California boy"—but he always puffed his chest out when he talked and she found him to be arrogant and even creepy. Once, when she was next door visiting, he had made a comment about a tattoo she had on her lower back, and it made her skin crawl. *Wow he really likes himself,* she had thought. *I better steer clear of this guy.*

"Can I help you?" Kathy asked with a curious look on her face.

"I wondered if the police had talked to you yet," he said.

Kathy thought the question was strange, but she was in a real hurry and her hair was still dripping wet.

"No, why?" she asked.

Kathy was aware that the woman who lived two houses down had been missing for more than a week. Detectives had been talking to neighbors, but Kathy had just returned from a family reunion in Idaho, so she hadn't yet talked to them.

"Don't tell the police that I live next door," he said.

It sounded more like a command than a request.

"Why wouldn't I tell them that?" Kathy asked.

"I've been in some trouble, and there's a warrant out for my arrest," Josh said.

"Look, I'll talk to you later," she said dismissively, cutting the conversation short. "I'm late for work."

Kathy shut the door and returned to drying her hair.

Not more than two minutes later, there was another knock at the door. *What the hell does he want now?* Kathy thought, annoyed, thinking it was Josh again. She opened the door and was greeted by two police officers.

"Hi, I'm Detective Pam Perrenoud, and this is Detective Tim Landeis. Do you have a minute to talk?"

"I'm in a hurry," Kathy said. "But okay. This is about the missing woman?"

Kathy came out onto the front porch. She explained that she had been away for five days, at the reunion, and that her eleven-year-old daughter and seven-year-old son had stayed behind there to spend some time with her folks. Kathy said that she didn't know Mindy Schloss and had only seen her in the neighborhood.

From her vantage point on the porch, Kathy glanced up, beyond the officers, across the lawn to the house next door. Her chest tightened. She could see Josh peering out of the kitchen window. *This is crazy*, she thought. *He's watching me. Are you fucking kidding me?*

He was too far away to hear what she was telling the police, so Kathy began to shake her head and make hand gestures indicating a negative response. *No, I don't know anything. I don't know shit,* she was trying to say nonverbally.

"Do you know who lives at 6902?" Detective Perrenoud asked, referring to the house where Josh stayed. "We've heard complaints about that house from other neighbors, and no one has answered the door for days."

In truth, Kathy had known the owner of the house at 6902, Shawni Phillips, for almost a decade. Kathy's children had grown up with Shawni's eighteen-year-old son, Shane, and Kathy had recently taken in Shawni's brother, Jeremy Lyon, who was recovering from knee surgery. In return, Jeremy had agreed to babysit Kathy's children while Kathy worked and went to school part-time. The Phillips family had experienced its share of turmoil; and after two failed marriages, Shawni had gone to Whittier, sixty miles south of Anchorage, to live with her new boyfriend. Shane had stayed behind and lived in the house with a friend, nineteen-year-old Eric Holmstrand. Eric's girlfriend, seventeen-year-old Jenna Wamsgams, was a frequent visitor. At first, Jeremy lived in the house as well, but Kathy had offered to take him in for part of the summer, until his health improved.

The teenagers were friendly with Kathy because of her connection to the family, and on occasion, they even helped her unload groceries from her car. But they had no supervision, had the run of the house, and often partied until all hours of the night. In fact, on the very night Mindy Schloss had gone missing, Kathy recalled holding a study session at her house with some of her fellow nursing students, and she had to go next door to tell Shane and his friends to quiet down. They were blasting their music and were out in the driveway being drunk and obnoxious.

"Hey you guys, cool it!" Kathy had admonished. "It's too loud!"

With Jeremy temporarily living next door with Kathy, there was an empty bedroom at 6902 Cutty Sark Street. Shane's father, Shawn Phillips, who had been in and out of prison, said he had a friend from jail who needed a place to stay, so the decision was made to rent out the spare bedroom. Josh had only been staying there for a few weeks.

Of course, Kathy wasn't about to go into any of this as she talked to the officers on her front porch, especially not with Josh glaring at her.

Kathy told police that the owner of the house had moved to Whittier, and that her teenaged son Shane lived there with his friend Eric. As for why they weren't answering the door, Kathy said she thought the boys had perhaps gone fishing or hunting.

"Does anyone else live in the house?" Detective Perrenoud asked.

"Well, Eric's girlfriend is there a lot, but she usually spends the night at her parents," Kathy replied.

"And that's it? No one else?" Detective Perrenoud asked.

"No."

Detective Perrenoud thanked Kathy for her time and handed her a business card.

"If you think of anything else, please give me a call," Detective Perrenoud said.

Kathy closed the door and let out a big sigh. Now she was really late for work. She quickly gathered her things and was about to leave, when there was yet another knock at the door. Exasperated, she opened the door, and there Josh stood, with a scowl on his face.

"What did you tell them?" he asked, accusingly.

"They were asking about the missing woman. I told them

I didn't know anything," Kathy replied, trying not to seem rattled.

Josh said he knew the male officer who had come to the door, Detective Landeis, and that the officer would certainly recognize him. He repeated that there was a warrant for his arrest.

"What'd you do?" Kathy asked.

There was a pause.

"I robbed a drug dealer's house."

"I didn't realize drug dealers reported things to the police," Kathy responded doubtfully, without thinking.

This seemed to anger Josh, and so Kathy quickly excused herself, explaining she was really late for work.

"Really, I have to go," she insisted.

Josh glared at her, then walked away.

****

Kathy hurried off to work at the furniture store, where she recounted her troubling encounter with her neighbor to her coworkers.

"Something about this really doesn't add up," one of them said. "I think you need to call the police."

Kathy had Detective Perrenoud's card, so she called and left a voice message, saying that she was "weirded out" by something that had happened, and that she wanted to talk further. She said, "Please, call me back, just don't come to my house."

****

When Kathy returned home from work late that night, she was alone in her house. Her two children were still in Idaho visiting her parents, and Jeremy, whom Kathy had taken in while he recovered from knee surgery, was down the road at a friend's. She was tired from a long day of school and work, but she thought she'd take advantage of the rare few hours of uninterrupted solitude to catch up on some nursing school homework.

It was almost midnight when she heard the unmistakable creaking sound of the wood panels of the front porch. Thinking Jeremy had just arrived home, she waited for what typically followed: the click of the dead bolt, turn of the door knob, and the door swinging open, then closed. She waited, but there was just silence.

Kathy had been studying in a back room of the house, on her computer, so the room she was in was illuminated but the rest of the house was completely dark. She slowly got up from her chair, and tiptoed through the house, making her way through a bathroom that connected to her daughter's bedroom. Once in the bedroom, through a window, Kathy could see the shadowy silhouette of a man standing on her front porch. The porch light was off, and as her eyes slowly adjusted to the dark, a face she recognized slowly came into focus.

What the fuck is he doing here? she thought. She watched as the man she knew as Josh stood, facing her front door. He was completely still, and because the house was dark, Kathy was fairly sure he couldn't see her. For several excruciating minutes, he just stared at the door. She thought, *He must know I'm home, my car is in the driveway. Why is he just standing there?*

After what Kathy can only describe as a "very long time" of watching Josh linger on her porch, she was overtaken by a sense of dread. She watched from the window as Josh leaned up against one of the posts on her porch and puffed on a cigarette. He glanced around as if he was casing the place, then leaned slightly forward and rang the doorbell. The sound echoed down the hallway, and Kathy inhaled. Then she watched as he stepped off the front porch, not waiting for someone to answer the door, disappearing into the darkness.

Had he come to intimidate her? Or worse? Kathy could hardly catch her breath. She immediately phoned Jeremy, and said, "I need you to come home, NOW."

PICTURES

Above: Childhood photos of Della Brown. *(Photos: Daisy Piggott)* **Bottom Left:** Della's mother, Daisy Piggott, outside her home in Anchorage in 2015. *(Author Photo)* **Bottom Right:** Della Brown's DMV photo, taken near the time of her murder. *(Photo: Anchorage Police Dept.)*

Above: Mindy Schloss. **Top Right:** Mindy's house on Cutty Sark Street. **Right:** Mindy's Red Acura, found abandoned in a parking lot near the Anchorage airport. **Below:** The back seat of Mindy's car. Detectives found a footprint on the armrest which matched Mindy's shoes. *(F.B.I. Photos)*

Above: Surveillance footage of Joshua Wade cashing a check at a Northrim Bank branch. The footage was used to help identify him as the person in the image, **(bottom left)** at an ATM withdrawing $500 from Mindy Schloss's bank account. **Bottom Right:** This photo of a Glock .45 pistol with a red laser sight was found on Wade's cell phone, and although the gun was never found, it is believed to be the weapon used to kill Mindy Schloss. *(F.B.I. Photos)*

Above: A bullet casing matching a .45 Glock pistol was found in a wooded area in Wasilla, less than 20 feet from where Mindy Schloss's body was discovered. **Below:** A gold Seiko watch found in Wade's house was identified through photographs as belonging to Mindy Schloss. *(F.B.I. Photos)*

ANCHORAGE POLICE DEPARTMENT
786-8500

WANTED
$2,500 Reward

Joshua Alan Wade
Date of Birth: 3-18-1980
White Male Adult
6'1"; 225 pounds

Anchorage Police are looking for Joshua Alan Wade who has outstanding warrants for his arrest relating to bank fraud, fraud with access device, and aggravated identity theft. He is also wanted for questioning in the disappearance of missing nurse Mindy Schloss.

Wade is a 27 year-old white male adult, 6'1" tall and 225 pounds with blue eyes and sandy-blonde hair. He has a scar on his right hand and a tattoo of a snake on his left hand between his index finger and thumb.

The FBI is offering a $2,500 reward for information as to the whereabouts of Joshua Alan Wade. In addition, Crime Stoppers will pay up to $1,000 for information on the whereabouts of Joshua Alan Wade. To remain anonymous, call Crime Stoppers at 561-STOP or submit a tip using our secure on-line website at www.anchoragecrimestoppers.com.

W A N T E D

The search for Wade was considered one of the largest manhunts in Alaska history. *(F.B.I. Photo)* **Above:** Authorities plastered these fliers all over town and even handed them out at the Alaska State Fair.

These photos were taken of Joshua Wade on September 2, 2007, at the time of his arrest. Wade took hostages inside an Anchorage apartment complex before surrendering to police. *(F.B.I. Photos)*

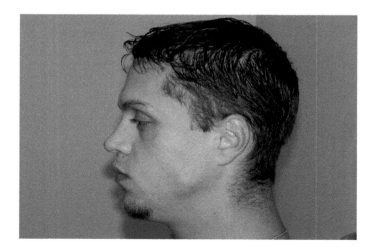

Above: Law enforcement raided Wade's house and found every room to be in disarray with the exception of Wade's bedroom, which was meticulously clean and orderly. **Bottom Left:** Artwork penned by Wade while in jail. **Bottom Right:** A short story written by Wade while in jail, with apparent parallels to the murder of Mindy Schloss. *(F.B.I. Photos)*

Top Left: Detective Pam Perrenoud, the lead police detective in the homicide investigation of Mindy Schloss. *(A.P.D. Photo)* **Top Right:** Special Agent Jolene Goeden, the lead F.B.I. detective in the Mindy Schloss case. *(F.B.I. Photo)* **Below:** Native Activist Desa Jacobsson, going over her notes from the Della Brown murder trial. Jacobsson went on a 28-day hunger strike to bring attention to the murders of six women in 1999-2000. *(Author Photo)*

A childhood photo of Joshua Wade with his sister, Mandy Huson, taken circa 1983. "It was unfair how we were raised," Mandy told me. *(Photo: Mandy Huson)*

Above: Michelle Foster Butler was stabbed to death while walking home from an Anchorage grocery store on September 26, 1999. Her murder is still unsolved. *(Photos: Claude Butler and A.P.D.)* **Bottom Left:** Annie Mann was found murdered on August 8, 1999, behind a building on Post Road in Anchorage, and the case remains unsolved. *(A.P.D. Photo)* **Bottom Right:** Also still unsolved, is the mysterious death of Vera Hapoff, whose body was discovered in Ship Creek in June of 1999. An autopsy revealed the cause of death to be drowning, however, she suffered injuries that indicated an assault prior to her death. *(A.P.D. Photo)*

TWENTY-NINE

The next day Detective Perrenoud returned Kathy's phone call and asked if they could meet. Kathy reiterated her desire not to meet at her house for fear that Josh might see her talking to the police, so Detective Perrenoud suggested that they meet at Sadler's, the furniture store where Kathy worked, and Kathy agreed.

Kathy had been shaken by her encounter with her neighbor the previous night and was relieved when Jeremy arrived home.

"I really don't like that guy," she explained to Jeremy, glad she was no longer alone in the house. "What a creep."

Jeremy was not in prime physical condition because of his recent surgery, but he didn't like Josh and Kathy knew, if need be, Jeremy would stand up to him. In fact, she had seen the two men clash before. Josh had a habit of declaring to the younger occupants of the home next door, "This is my house," and Jeremy had, under no uncertain terms, reminded Josh that he was just renting a room and the house belonged to Jeremy's sister.

"Who the hell are you?" Jeremy would demand.

"I don't think he was used to having people talk back to him," Kathy recalled.

When Detective Perrenoud arrived at the furniture store, Kathy told her, "His name is Josh. I don't know his last name, but he's wanted on a warrant for something." Kathy explained she knew Josh was friends with Shane's father,

Shawn Phillips, and guessed that they had probably met in jail. She said Josh had recently been released from jail and was on parole and that he was apparently living in the house to "watch the boys" and to make sure they didn't act up. Kathy described Josh, saying he was twenty-eight, with short, blondish hair that was spiked on the top, a muscular build, very tan skin, and that he worked for a construction company. She also related what had happened the previous night with Josh standing on her front porch. Kathy said the whole situation made her feel uneasy.

"Can't you check if there's a warrant out for someone named Josh who's also twenty-eight?" she asked. Detective Perrenoud promised she would check and, in the meantime, would put the house where Josh lived under surveillance.

That evening, officers staking out the house at 6902 Cutty Sark Street saw a man who appeared to fit the height and weight of the individual in the ATM footage and the footage from the Sky Chef parking lot. They tailed his car and followed him to a local gym, the Alaska Club, on Northern Lights Boulevard. Officers took surveillance photos as he entered the gym and later, as he left, they stopped him, and discovered his name was Joshua Greene. The eighteen-year-old was wanted on a warrant for underage drinking, and so officers placed him under arrest.

Thinking this was the man to whom Kathy had referred, Detective Perrenoud immediately called Kathy and asked her to stop by the police station after work to look at some photos.

"That's not the right Josh," Kathy said with certainty, looking at both the surveillance photos and a booking photo. She said the Josh who lived next door looked older and had longer hair which was more spiked on top. It turned out Joshua Greene was a friend of Shane Phillips who did not live at the house, and had just come by for a visit. To add to the confusion, Shane's stepfather, Josh Hershleb, had been around to check on his stepson in recent days but was also not the Josh to whom Kathy had alluded.

Detective Perrenoud then showed Kathy a number of booking photos of other men, none of whom she recognized.

"No, I don't know any of those people," Kathy said, shaking her head. "Sorry."

At this point, officers had finally reached the teenaged occupants of the house, Shane and Eric, and neither boy had mentioned a third male lived with them.

"Why wouldn't they tell us this?" Detective Perrenoud asked Kathy. "They said no one else lived there."

"I don't know why," she replied. "[Josh] told me he was in trouble. Maybe that has something to do with it."

In fact, that evening at about 9:30, Shane Phillips and his roommate Eric Holmstrand would finally relent, admitting to Detective Landeis and two other officers that a third male, a friend of Shane's father, had recently moved into a bedroom of the house. His name was Josh, but Shane and Eric claimed to not know his last name. They also admitted that they were aware he had previously been in trouble with the law. Shane told the detectives Josh had made it clear he didn't want the police to know where he was living. He had not been home since about four o'clock that afternoon, they said.

There was a reason Shane and Eric were not completely forthcoming with the police: their new roommate had established an intimidating, even threatening presence in the house. Shane would later confess to Kathy Easley that he felt tormented by Josh, relating an instance in the living room one night when he noticed a beam of red light on his chest. Shane glanced up and saw Josh standing out on the deck, pointing a gun at him, with a big smile on his face. Shane did not initially recount this story to police, however, simply stating that Josh kept to himself and spent a lot of time alone in his bedroom, working on his art and listening to rap music.

Detectives tracked down Eric's girlfriend, Jenna Wamsgams, where she worked. They knew she frequented 6902 Cutty Sark Street, and they asked her what she knew about the third male who lived in the house. She said his name was Josh and confirmed that he didn't want the police to know that he lived there.

"Do you know his last name?" one of the detectives asked. She hesitated.

"Yeah, it's Wade," she replied. "Joshua Wade."

THIRTY

As a member of the FBI's Evidence Response Team Unit, Special Agent Jolene Goeden had been working behind the scenes on how best to collect evidence in the case. Agent Goeden was sharp and unflappable, with long, blonde hair; she possessed a relaxed demeanor and an attractiveness that must have seemed disarming to the criminals with whom she came face-to-face. Her undergraduate degrees in psychology and sociology, along with a masters in forensic psychology, equipped her for such difficult interactions, and, in her first five years with the FBI, she worked mostly on cases involving sex and human trafficking.

The bureau's ERTU specialized in not only collecting forensic evidence but also in processing crime scenes. The police department's crime scene investigators had already examined Mindy's house, finding no obvious signs of a struggle, or blood, nor any evidence of a cleanup. Analysts had collected thousands of hairs from the living room carpet, in hopes of finding some trace of DNA belonging to Mindy's assailant. The FBI's lab painstakingly processed many more hairs than usual, in fact, because Mindy had a cat, and detectives knew the majority of the hairs would turn out not to be human.

Agent Thoreson, who had examined Mindy's bank transactions, now turned his attention to the laptop computer that had been discovered in Mindy's suitcase, in the trunk of her car. The web history displayed a number of websites related to nursing, and it suggested that Mindy was online until about 1:30 a.m. on Saturday. No one had seen or heard from her after that time. Gerri had mentioned that Mindy had done some online dating, so Agent Thoreson looked but found no dating sites in her browser history.

One of the other agents who served on the ERTU with Agent Goeden, Chad Joy, had just returned from training with human-scent dogs in Los Angeles, and he suggested that the dogs could be helpful in the search for the missing nurse. Agent Goeden was interested to see what the dogs could do, so she told Detective Perrenoud she thought it was worth a try.

The notion of collecting scents in jars and deploying dogs to track those scents, a week or more after Mindy Schloss had disappeared, seemed absolutely ridiculous to Detective Perrenoud. She didn't hide her doubts, but she wasn't about to refuse help from the FBI.

"If you guys are going to help me, I'll do whatever you want to do," she had told Agent Goeden.

Agent Goeden thought the discovery of Mindy's car provided the perfect opportunity to collect scents of Mindy's alleged abductor, and there was no time to waste. The red Acura had already been processed by police for trace evidence such as fingerprints and DNA and had been towed to an evidence garage near the Anchorage Police Department's headquarters. There, Agents Goeden and Joy used a contraption called the "STU-100" to collect scents from inside the car. The STU-100, or Scent Transfer Unit, was a small 12-volt electronic device about the size of a DustBuster. The tip of the device was placed within an inch of any item of evidence, and the vacuum sucked air into a Teflon-coated attachment containing a sterile surgical pad. After about thirty seconds, the pad would contain the scent or scents present on that particular item of evidence.

Knowing that Mindy was not the person last seen driving her car, Agent Joy used the STU-100 on the driver's seat, drawing the scent into three sterile gauze pads. Wearing surgical gloves, Agent Joy placed the gauze pads in jars, which were then tightly sealed. Changing gloves and cleaning the STU-100 each time, Agent Joy also collected scents from the steering wheel, parking brake, and the gear stick. Agent Goeden assisted, sealing and labeling the jars. They also collected scents from items found inside Mindy's car: three cigarette butts found in the ashtray, a shovel found in the trunk, and the floor mat from the driver's seat.

Later, Agent Goeden contacted Special Agent Rex Stockham, who headed the human scent evidence team. She related some basic facts about the case, and he agreed the dogs could be useful in the search for Mindy Schloss and perhaps for her alleged abductor.

On August 17, the team headed by Special Agent Stockham arrived in Anchorage with five specially trained dogs and four dog handlers from Southern California. That afternoon, Agent Goeden was holding a briefing at the FBI building downtown to discuss how the investigation would proceed.

Detective Perrenoud was in attendance, and just as the briefing was getting underway, her cell phone rang. She could see it was her colleague, Detective Kristi Ratcliff, so Detective Perrenoud stepped out into the hallway to take the call.

"Pam, you're not going to believe who Jenna[65] just identified as the guy who lives next door," Detective Ratcliff said with a sense of urgency.

"Who?" Detective Perrenoud asked.

"Josh Wade."

---

65 Jenna Wamsgams was Eric Holmstrand's girlfriend and was a frequent visitor at the house where Joshua Wade lived.

"Oh my God."

This is so bad, I need to get back to APD, Detective Perrenoud thought, but the briefing was just starting and she knew she had to get Agent Goeden's attention. Detective Perrenoud sat impatiently, knowing that her phone was about to ring any minute. There was a chain of command, and certainly her superiors would be trying to reach her. As soon as she had the chance, she pulled Agent Goeden aside.

Most of the residents of Anchorage would have recognized the name Joshua Wade because of the Della Brown case and the amount of media coverage it had received. Agent Goeden, however, did not share this familiarity because she didn't live in Anchorage at the time of the Della Brown case.

"We've figured out who lives next door," Detective Perrenoud said. She explained who Joshua Wade was, that he had been acquitted in the killing of another woman, and that it was widely believed he had gotten away with murder.

"This is really bad," Detective Perrenoud said, shaking her head, still trying to process the news. After checking in with their superiors, Detective Perrenoud and Agent Goeden quickly excused themselves from the briefing, retrieved the most recent booking photo of Joshua Wade, and drove to Kathy Easley's house.

****

Kathy Easley could tell her neighborhood was under surveillance. It seemed, all of a sudden, there were utility workers working on the phone lines across the street, passing cars, (which was odd on a dead end street) and people she didn't recognize taking leisurely walks past her house. When Detective Perrenoud called and said she wanted to meet, initially Kathy thought they could meet around the corner at the "Tastee Freez" frozen yogurt shop, but then realized there was little danger of meeting at the house, given so many officers were secretly watching.

"Sure, come on over," she said.

Minutes later, Detective Perrenoud and Agent Goeden arrived at Kathy Easley's front door.

"This is Agent Jolene Goeden from the FBI," Detective Perrenoud explained. Hearing "FBI" took Kathy aback. *Wow, this must be really serious,* she thought. Kathy invited them in.

"I'd like to show you a couple more photos," Detective Perrenoud said. She pulled the first photo from a folder, and without hesitation, Kathy said, "Yep, that's him."

Agent Goeden and Detective Perrenoud exchanged a concerned look, realizing Kathy had just confirmed what they suspected, that the Joshua Wade who had stood trial for Della Brown's murder was, indeed, Mindy Schloss's neighbor.

"Should I be worried? Am I in danger?" Kathy asked.

"Let's put it this way," Detective Perrenoud said. "If you've got another place to stay tonight, I would."

THIRTY-ONE

Two weeks had passed since Mindy's disappearance, and news that an elite team of search dogs and their handlers had been flown in from the Lower 48 to assist in the search intensified the local media coverage. Operating on a tip, the Anchorage Police Department and the FBI searched Kincaid Park, a sprawling wooded area with thirty-five miles of trails near Mindy's house. The story led KTUU's late-night newscast on August 17:

> Good evening. A K-9 team from the FBI is tonight joining the search for missing Anchorage nurse Mindy Schloss. And at this hour, Anchorage police and FBI agents are focusing on Kincaid Park. Tonight APD searches a wooded hill at the entrance of the park near Mindy Schloss's home, where a jogger detected a foul odor in the forest.

Tips were pouring in, but none had led to anything substantial. Divers had even plunged into DeLong Lake, a body of water just 350 yards north of Mindy's house, and had found nothing.

Detectives discovered that since living on Cutty Sark Street, Wade had been working on a construction site mixing mortar for bricklayers for a company called Diamond Masonry. In fact, Wade had been sent home for having an attitude problem on August 3, the same night Mindy disappeared. No one at the construction site had seen him since.

While the missing nurse was a frequent topic of discussion around town, one person who was not closely following the developments was Christina Greaser. Christina was a naive twenty-year-old with doe-like eyes, olive skin, and long brown hair who had dated Joshua Wade when she was seventeen and he was twenty. After they broke up, they remained friends.

"I was working at a pretzel stand at the mall, and he was always coming in," Christina recalled, explaining how she met Wade. "I was seventeen, and he was just a good looking, attractive guy. He told me he was in a halfway house for possession of a firearm. I guess I wasn't mature enough to say, 'Let me look at this guy and check out his background.' He had a really clean appearance. He was really well kept; he took very good care of himself. He was very smart, very intelligent, and a really good artist."

Christina admitted her own ignorance to Wade's criminal past when she talked about their ongoing friendship, telling me, "I knew he was acquitted for the murder of Della Brown, but I didn't judge him for that. I was raised in a Christian school so my thoughts and the way things were for me growing up ... I never felt in danger around him and I was young so I didn't understand the terminology of 'acquitted of murder.'"

As the search for Mindy Schloss intensified, Christina had been giving Wade rides in her car, not realizing he was wanted by the police and the FBI. She had, out of the blue, received a call from Wade asking her if she could swing by the Century 16 cinema and pick him up. Christina agreed. She knew Wade didn't have a car, and his requests for rides became more frequent in the coming days. Despite her naiveté, Christina found some of his behavior strange. For example, he seemed overly concerned that her Ford Explorer had a tail light that was burned out; he insisted that they have it fixed because he didn't want to be pulled over by the cops. He also refused to use a public bathroom; he would ask her to pull over in a park and he would urinate in the woods. And a few times had asked Christina if he could sleep in her SUV.

I met Christina during my first visit to Anchorage. She had refused previous interviews with television and documentary crews, but I had set up a meeting at a Starbucks with her mother, Tina Greaser, and was surprised when Christina also showed up. I was most struck by Christina's genuine gullibility with regard to Joshua Wade and her willingness to admit that she never felt threatened by him, even after discovering he had killed multiple times.

"I know this sounds weird because he probably has other victims out there," Christina told me. "But this is what I still honestly believe, the way I was to him ... he saw that I would accept him for who he was ... so he trusted in me. I know that's weird to say."

"You weren't afraid of him," I said.

"No, I wasn't."

"You didn't think he was going to hurt you?"

"No, not at all."

Christina's feeling that Josh Wade wouldn't hurt her was what had sustained their friendship, and had also made her tolerant of his paranoia, which reached its peak when they attempted to stop by his house on Cutty Sark Street one afternoon and saw four police cruisers outside.

"Keep driving," Wade urged Christina.

"Okay," she agreed, noticing at least one vehicle that appeared to be an unmarked police car.

When Christina questioned his panicked reaction, Josh initially didn't answer, but he eventually explained that a neighbor woman had gone missing and he thought, because of his criminal record, police would consider him a suspect.

****

Ann Anderson, an attorney and member of the FBI's Human Scent Evidence Team, had just arrived in Anchorage from Southern California with her two bloodhounds: Casey, a trailing dog, and Jack, a cadaver dog. As one of the dog handlers deployed by the agency in response to the disappearance of Mindy Schloss, Anderson had already used her dogs to search Kincaid Park for any sign of the missing nurse, but they had not presented any indications that Mindy Schloss was nearby. By mid-afternoon, a team leader told Anderson to go to Cutty Sark Street, to stay in her car and await further instruction. Another cadaver dog was being used to run a trail, and for the moment, she and her two dogs were not needed. Anderson sat in the passenger seat of an unmarked car, parked outside Wade's house, for hours.

"At some point, I was sitting there, and I noticed that from my left a car approached very slowly," Anderson recalled. "I thought, that's odd, because this car was going so slow."

Anderson turned to look, and the slow-moving SUV was just a few feet from hers; a man in the passenger seat glared at her with an intensity that seemed to suggest he was sizing her up. She noticed a young woman was behind the wheel of the SUV. Anderson couldn't shake how odd she felt about the brief encounter. It wasn't until much later, while reading a news article on the internet, that she would recognize the man in the other car as Joshua Wade.

Despite the presence of the police, Wade was insistent that he needed to pick up some of his belongings, so Christina and Wade drove past the house a couple of times that night but didn't stop because the police cars remained parked out front. Later, on their third attempt, it appeared the coast was clear. Using his cell phone, Wade called one of his roommates and asked him to gather some of his things in a backpack and bring it out to the car. Christina couldn't hear what was being said on the other end of the line, but it was clear whomever Wade was talking to didn't want to come outside, probably because, Christina thought, one of the items Wade had requested was his pistol.

Hearing that a gun was involved, Christina refused when Wade asked her to run inside to get his things. Frustrated, Wade jumped out of the car, went into the house, and within a few minutes returned with a black and white backpack.

"Let's go," he urged. "Hurry!"

As Christina pulled out of the driveway, Wade pulled from his bag a Glock .45 pistol with a red laser sight and held it in his hands. He wrapped the gun in a bandana and tucked it into the waistband of his pants.

It was getting late, and, given police had swarmed his neighborhood, Wade explained he couldn't go back to his house and asked if he could spend the night in Christina's SUV. She said he could, told him goodnight, and left him parked outside her apartment building.

****

Christina woke up the next morning and found Wade still sleeping in her SUV. He wanted to avoid going home, so he went along as she ran some errands. During the course of the day, Wade asked Christina to drive by Cutty Sark Street to see if there was any kind of police activity. First, though, he wanted to stash his gun, in case they were stopped by the cops. Wade directed Christina to a street not far from the neighborhood. When they reached an intersection with a stop sign, Wade got out and stashed the gun in some nearby bushes.

They drove around Anchorage for a few hours, and at one point along a busy thoroughfare, they were startled by the sight of officers rushing into the road, holding up their hands to stop traffic. Christina's SUV and the other vehicles on the road slowed and came to a halt. Then, wide-eyed, Christina and Wade watched as a parade of police officers and FBI agents came rushing across the street, trailing behind a bloodhound on a fifteen-foot leash. The dog appeared to be hot on the trail of a scent. What neither Wade nor Christina realized was the K-9 was heading straight for Mindy Schloss's neighborhood, and the scent it was trailing belonged to Joshua Wade.

THIRTY-TWO

At the FBI briefing with the Human Scent Evidence Team, Agent Goeden had been careful not to divulge that a prime suspect had just, minutes before, been identified. Under instructions from the team leader, Special Agent Rex Stockham, she shared only the basic information: the missing woman had last been seen on August 3; someone had used her debit card at two separate ATMs; and that the same individual was suspected of stealing her car and abandoning it near the Anchorage airport. A bloodhound's sense of smell is more than one thousand times stronger than that of a human, but the dogs had been known, on rare occasions, to falsely alert to a location due to unconscious signals from their handlers. If the handler was unaware of a location or a particular suspect, the danger of such false positives was removed from the equation.

Although the use of bloodhounds in criminal investigations had faced scrutiny in the courts, the FBI's dog handlers stood by their methods and had even published their own studies, suggesting a person's own unique scent could exist in a place days, even weeks, after they had been there.

"The body puts off a lot of volatile organic compounds," Agent Stockham explained. "It also sheds millions and millions of skin cells and, as we walk along, all of that's coming off our body, so there is, if you will, a trail of our smell wherever we go."

Mindy had been missing for almost two weeks, and

Agent Goeden knew time was not on their side. She and Stockham decided to start with the ATM location at the Wells Fargo Bank on Jewel Lake Road, just a half-mile from Mindy's house. Agent Goeden had with her a number of jars containing scent pads she and Agent Joy had collected from Mindy's car with the STU-100, each labeled, indicating from where the scent had been taken: DRIVER'S SEAT, STEERING WHEEL, PARKING BRAKE, CIGARETTE BUTTS.

As head of the Human Scent Evidence Team, Agent Stockham decided to begin with the scent that was least likely to contain a scent from the victim. He realized Mindy's car would contain both Mindy's scent and the suspect's, but he had been told that Mindy did not smoke, and the cigarette butts found in the ashtray of the car were almost certainly not hers. It was important to Agent Stockham that the dog handlers were unaware to whom any particular scent might be connected; so without any preliminary explanation, he took the jar labelled CIGARETTE BUTTS and handed it to dog handler Dennis Slavin. Slavin's dog, a ten-year-old bloodhound named Tinkerbell, a large dog with a black and brown coat and long floppy ears, had her harness on, which was a signal to the dog that it was time to work. Standing outside of the door to the enclosed lobby of the bank where the ATM was located, Slavin unscrewed the jar and, using plastic forceps, retrieved the scent pad and presented it to Tinkerbell. The dog lifted her snout to the pad and sniffed; Slavin immediately returned the scent pad to the jar, which he resealed. Tinkerbell sniffed around a bit, but did not react. Slavin knew what this meant; Tinkerbell was presenting a "negative response," indicating she did not pick up a similar smell outside of the ATM.

As was his practice, Slavin took Tinkerbell out of her harness and gave her a five- to ten-minute break, and then he put her back in the harness, indicating it was again time to work. This time, Agent Stockham handed Slavin the jar labelled DRIVER'S SEAT. Slavin repeated the process, using the plastic forceps to remove the pad from the jar, letting Tinkerbell register the scent. This time, Tinkerbell had an immediate reaction, sniffing intently near the door leading inside to the ATM. She then "took trail" as dog handlers describe it, taking off, north on Jewel Lake Road. Slavin ran behind Tinkerbell, firmly holding her long leash; the pair was followed by Agent Goeden and several other members of the team. Anchorage police were ready to stop traffic and officers did so as the parade of FBI agents and members of the HSET made a left onto Raspberry Road with Tinkerbell leading the way. The dog then took a sharp left onto Cutty Sark Street, and slowed as she approached the house numbered 6852.

Agent Goeden couldn't believe her eyes. She had hoped the bloodhounds would be helpful, but she had no idea that right out of the gate one of them would lead the team straight to Mindy's house. She immediately called Detective Perrenoud to share the news.

"Pam, you're not going to believe where this dog is leading us," she reported in an excited voice.

"What are you talking about?" Pam replied incredulously.

Slavin followed closely as Tinkerbell approached Mindy's house. The dog climbed the stairs to the home's outside deck which led to the front door and paused briefly, sniffing the door knob. Slavin thought Tinkerbell might end the trail there, but he then noticed a change in the dog's behavior. It was almost as if she was picking up a stronger odor from somewhere nearby. The dog descended the stairs of the deck and made her way back down Mindy's driveway, as the entourage of FBI agents followed. The dog appeared to want to enter the yard next door but there was a long, tall fence blocking the way, so Tinkerbell went almost to the end of Mindy's driveway, made a sharp right, and led the agents through some brush and tall grass and into the front yard of the house next door. Tinkerbell made a beeline for the carport and circled a few times the area where a car might usually be parked, then paused to sniff the door and doorknob that led from the carport into the house. Tinkerbell lingered near the door, sniffing the base of the door and the one wooden step just in front of it, showing no real interest in any other location, indicating to her handler that this was the end of the trail.

To make sure the results were not some sort of fantastic anomaly, Agent Stockham had another bloodhound named Lucy run the same trail from the Wells Fargo ATM, this time using a scent pad taken from the gear shifter in Mindy's car. Just as Tinkerbell had done before her, Lucy would lead authorities along the very same trail: from the ATM, to the carport, and finally, to the side door of the house where Joshua Wade lived.

THIRTY-THREE

Since identifying Joshua Wade as their prime suspect, Detective Perrenoud and Agent Goeden had been working nonstop. Wade's house was under surveillance, but they knew they had to act fast to search the house, before he or someone else inside had the chance to remove or destroy any evidence. That meant first, however, that Detective Perrenoud would have to get a search warrant. Running on no sleep, at 2:21 a.m. on August 17, 2007, she testified before a magistrate, seeking permission to search 6902 Cutty Sark Street. Joining her to testify was Tinkerbell's handler, Dennis Slavin.

After explaining the background of the case, Detective Perrenoud asked for authorization to seize the following items from the home: a dark baseball cap resembling the one worn by the suspect in the ATM footage, a dark jacket, a dark-and-white patterned bandana, and possibly a pair of sunglasses. She explained that in the footage, you could see the very edge of what appeared to be rims of sunglasses. (In trying to determine why the suspect had pulled down the bandana to reveal the lower half of his face, investigators had speculated that his glasses had fogged up, preventing him from clearly seeing the ATM screen.) Detective Perrenoud also requested permission to seize cigarettes and cigarette butts, given that three butts had been found in the ashtray of Mindy's car and close friends had informed the police that Mindy quit smoking two years prior. Detective Perrenoud requested permission to take receipts or documents relating to any activity on August 3 or 4, the time during which it was believed Mindy had been abducted and/or killed. Detective Perrenoud also requested permission to seize photos of those residing in the home, so their images could be compared with the ATM footage and the footage from the Sky Chef parking lot.

Slavin explained a bit about the process of trailing a human scent and recounted that Tinkerbell had signaled Wade's residence as a place of interest earlier that evening. He also explained that in order to exclude other occupants of the home, he needed each of them to provide a sample of their individual scent. The process was simple and noninvasive; it was accomplished by simply rubbing a clean scent pad between a person's hands.

After hearing the testimony, Magistrate Brian Johnson said, "Based on the testimony of Officers Slavin and Perrenoud, I do find that there's reasonable grounds to believe that at 6902 Cutty Sark Street, there will be evidence of the crime of homicide, and I will authorize the search of that residence, for those items listed. I'll further authorize that search any time of the day or night, given the fact that this is a homicide and I expect it to be made immediately."

****

It was about five o'clock in the morning when the Anchorage Police Department and the FBI roused the young occupants of 6902 Cutty Sark Street out of bed to serve the search warrant. Wade was not home, but Shane and Eric were caught completely off guard, especially at that hour, and stood, somewhat dumbfounded, out on the lawn as Agent Goeden accompanied SWAT officers carefully combing through every room of the house.

Her first and most obvious observation was that the house

was a total mess. It was what one might expect from a pair of teenagers living on their own. There were unwashed dishes piled up in the sink, dirty clothes on the floor, and it appeared that no one had vacuumed or dusted in months. That held true for all but one room in the house: the bedroom that belonged to Joshua Wade, which was, in a word, pristine. The bed was made meticulously, the carpet had been recently vacuumed, and even the pornographic DVDs were lined up neatly on a shelf. Two books lay neatly next to the mattress and box spring: the sixth book in the *Harry Potter* series, *The Half Blood Prince,* and Jeffery Deaver's *The Cold Moon,* a novel about a serial killer. Two plug-in air fresheners on opposite walls kept the room smelling nice, and each article of clothing was hung in the closet with the utmost care, equidistant to the next. Lined up on the floor of the closet there was a pair of clean, white Adidas tennis shoes.

Investigators also found a number of drawings presumably penned by Wade. Detective Goeden could not help but notice the impressive yet misogynistic nature of the artwork: depictions of naked women posing seductively, all with large breasts, and many with demon horns protruding from their heads. One such "demon woman" was on her back sucking on two of her two fingers. Another resembled the mythological character Medusa, with strings of hair like serpents; yet another drawing showed a woman bent over on all fours, with massive angel wings spread out behind her. In every case, the woman's eyes were left blank, white as the page, vacuous.

Detectives also found a binder of newspaper clippings Wade had kept from his first trial—detailing the murder of Della Brown and his subsequent acquittal—but none having to do with the mysterious disappearance of Mindy Schloss. Gazing out of Wade's bedroom window from the northwest side of the house, Agent Goeden noticed the window provided a direct view of Mindy's house and reasoned it was an ideal place from which to secretly watch her and scope out her routine.

It was not in Wade's bedroom, however, but in the common areas of the home, where investigators found the most damning pieces of evidence. Draped over a couch in the living room, officers found a black and gray jacket that appeared to match the one worn by the suspect in the ATM footage. The garment was distinct in that both the front and back were black and the arms, from the shoulder to the cuffs, were gray. The collar also was gray, with two black stripes, and the material was quilted with small squares. In the inside pocket, detectives found a receipt for a $500 ATM withdrawal.

Another incriminating item was discovered almost by chance, as a SWAT officer searched a coat closet downstairs near the living room. When the officer climbed a ladder to enter a crawl space in the closet, his utility belt scraped against the molding on the inside of the closet door, causing an object to fall to the floor. The officer glanced down, and saw a woman's gold watch. Detective Perrenoud, who had gone home to get a couple hours of sleep, arrived later that morning, after the search of the house was already well underway. She called Gerri Yett and asked her if Mindy wore a watch, and if so, could she describe it?

"We are both old-school nurses, so of course we always wear watches," Gerri replied. She also confirmed that Mindy's wristwatch was gold.

"Mindy is petite," Gerri reminded Detective Perrenoud. "So the watch would have to fit someone her size."

Detective Perrenoud could tell by the circumference of the band the watch must belong to someone with a small wrist. She asked Gerri if she had any photos of Mindy wearing the watch and also phoned Kathy Hodges with the same request. They e-mailed Detective Perrenoud several photos, which showed Mindy wearing a watch that appeared identical to the one investigators had discovered.

Once all of the rooms of the house were thoroughly searched, Agent Goeden consulted Agent Stockham, and they decided to bring in a cadaver dog named Maggie. Unlike human scent dogs that detect the scents of individual people, cadaver dogs were trained to alert to scents of human decomposition or blood. As Maggie was not used to working on a leash or lead, her handler, Lisa Higgins, gave the dog free range. The K-9 went through almost the entire house, including the basement, scanning each room, passing over piles of dirty laundry and clutter, without alerting to any particular scent. When she reached the bedroom belonging to Joshua Wade, however, Maggie showed interest in the closet, conveying a "positive response." Because it wasn't clear to which item in the closet Maggie was responding, Agent Stockham instructed dog handler Lisa Higgins to remove Maggie from the room. The most uncluttered room in the house, besides Wade's, was the basement, so agents put down butcher paper on the floor and one by one, the items of clothing hanging in Wade's closet were brought downstairs and laid on the paper. Methodically, Maggie scanned each item, to alert to any signs of human decomposition or blood. The dog proceeded to linger over three items, alerting positively to a black baseball cap, a plaid shirt, and a black jacket (not the same jacket that was discovered on the couch).

Even though Mindy's body had not been found, Agent Goeden reasoned that Wade must have been wearing these items when he had killed her. Members of the HSET were able to retrieve scents from the cap, plaid shirt, and black jacket, and using human scent dogs, they determined Wade's clothing contained the scent of Mindy Schloss.

Detectives also would later discover the occupants of

6902 Cutty Sark Street never used the front door of the house, and always came in and out of the door where Tinkerbell and Lucy had signaled. Later, Tinkerbell was put through an exercise during which she connected Wade's scent to the parking lot near the airport where Mindy's car had been found; the bloodhound also excluded scents provided by the three other people who occupied the house: Shane Phillips, Eric Holmstrand and Eric's girlfriend, Jenna Wamsgams.

THIRTY-FOUR

Christina Greaser's mother, Tina, had an "open door" policy with her children's friends; young people would come and go and, when she could, Tina would listen to their problems and offer advice. She was aware that her daughter had been giving rides to Wade and also was aware of his criminal past. This was a source of worry for Tina, but Christina was twenty years old and Tina knew her daughter was headstrong and would do as she liked. Still, Tina would warn, "Be careful, keep your phone with you, and remember to call me."

Tina had three other children in the house and it was Saturday, so unlike a school day, the house was full of activity. She didn't like the fact Christina was hanging out with Josh Wade, but at least when they stopped by her house that afternoon, Tina took some comfort in knowing they were both in her living room, under her watchful eye. After a while, Christina told her mother she had a few more errands to run, and knowing Wade didn't want to go home, she asked her mother if she minded if Wade hung out at the house for a bit. Tina reluctantly agreed. Tina's three-year-old daughter, Sophia, was playing in the living room, and the toddler soon started bringing toys to Wade, who was seated on the couch. He sat patiently, playing with the little girl. The television was on in the background, and both Tina and Wade grew quiet when KTUU's five o'clock news came on:

Anchor: Good evening. There is still no sign of

missing Anchorage nurse Mindy Schloss. Police and the FBI continued the search early this morning, concentrating on Kincaid Park. And now, a house next door to Schloss's. Channel 2's Angela Blanchard joins us outside the home of Mindy Schloss's neighbor, with more.

Reporter: Police have been searching this house since early this morning. It's the house of Mindy Schloss's neighbors. Searchers are splitting their time between Kincaid Park and this neighborhood near the airport, where Mindy Schloss lived. She was last seen in her home two weeks from yesterday. Two teenagers in a car outside Mindy Schloss's house say they are neighbors and that police knocked on their door somewhere around five o'clock this morning and began searching the house on Cutty Sark off Raspberry Road. This afternoon, police asked the teens to come into the house ... other than that, police are questioning Schloss's neighbors. They are also using articles of clothing from Schloss's home to see if their search dogs in Kincaid Park can pick up a scent.

Anchor: Angela, you talked to those teenage neighbors. Did they know Mindy Schloss well?

Reporter: No, the teenagers are eighteen and nineteen. ... They said they knew Schloss enough to say hello, but otherwise didn't know her well. And they said they weren't aware she was missing for at least a week.

When surveillance footage from the Sky Chef parking lot came on the screen showing Mindy's red Acura, Wade made a comment that didn't sit right with Tina. (She told me she still struggles to remember exactly what the comment was.) "He said something about how the car was parked. And that really got me because I had been working at the airlines for thirteen years, and I knew that there were cameras in that parking lot. I thought, how would anyone know [what he was telling me] unless they were there and had seen the car or had parked the car?"

During the course of the conversation, Wade admitted to Tina that Mindy was his next door neighbor.

"I remember telling Josh, 'You need to get a hold of your lawyer. Because it looks crazy,'" Tina recalled. "'You live right next door to her, and with everything that's happened with Della Brown, you need to speak to your lawyer. Because if you didn't do this, you have nothing to be afraid of. And I think he said, 'I'll do that first thing on Monday.'"

Some time passed, and Christina still had not returned, so Wade left. Later that night, Christina returned to her mother's house alone.

"Do you realize he lives next door to that missing nurse?" Tina asked her daughter, in a concerned, almost accusing tone. "I told him he needs to call his lawyer, because you know police are going to want to talk to him."

"I know," Christina replied. "I told him, 'What does it matter if you live next door and you didn't do anything?'"

Tina then asked her daughter if she had noticed anything suspicious about Wade's behavior.

"Yeah, he has been acting all paranoid," Christina admitted. "He told me I needed to change my broken tail light, and we pulled over and he changed it for me." Christina also told her mother that when Wade had to go to the bathroom, he would ask her to drive to Kincaid Park, where he would urinate in the woods, to avoid being seen in public.

Tina raised an eyebrow. Sometime during the course of

their conversation about Wade, KTUU's ten o'clock news came on:

Anchor: APD is asking for your help finding a man officers are calling a "person of interest." Channel 2's Rebecca Palsha has more.

Reporter: Megan and Mike, fifty-two-year-old Mindy Schloss was last seen at her home in South Anchorage just over two weeks ago. Since then, police and the FBI have combed the woods and searched a lake. And friends say they think the worst has now happened. This photo is a possible lead. Investigators have been combing through photos taken at ATMs in the Sand Lake/Jewel Lake area and have come across who they consider is a person of interest ... a young man ... non-black ... and younger. [The photo shows] a partial face shot and clothing that appears to be unique.

Anchor: Rebecca, why do police believe the man has a link to Schloss?

Reporter: Police aren't saying what the connection is. They do say they are still looking for Schloss but are no closer to finding her.

"Oh my God, that's Josh," Christina said, her mouth gaping in disbelief. The ATM photo only showed the man's face from the nose down, but she recognized Wade instantly. She also recognized his black stitched jacket with gray sleeves from Foot Locker.

"Are you sure?" Tina asked her daughter, in a panicked voice. Christina nodded. She was 100 percent certain. *Could Josh have done something unspeakable to his next door neighbor?* Christina's mind was racing. Suddenly, a thought occurred to her that sent a wave of panic through her body. *His backpack.*

"Mom, I think Josh left some stuff in my trunk," Christina admitted, almost in a whisper. Tina could hardly believe what she was hearing. *Was this real?* Frantic, they both ran outside. Christina swiftly opened the trunk, and she and her mother stood side-by-side for a moment, staring at Josh Wade's backpack. Together, they lifted the bag out of the trunk and nervously unzipped it. They slowly pulled out the contents there in the trunk: an almost empty bottle of vodka, a wallet with Wade's correctional ID inside, headphones, a cassette player, a toothbrush, a bandana, some receipts in a Ziploc bag, and a cell phone. Christina breathed a sigh of relief, realizing Wade's .45 caliber Glock was not in the bag. However, when she flipped open the cell phone and examined the digital photos, she was startled to find a two close-up photos of the gun. The first showed a side view of the weapon, and it was being held upright by a man (whom she could only assume was Wade) with an unusual grip; his thumb was on the outside ring of the trigger and his four fingers gripped the back of the pistol. In the photo, the red laser sight of the gun was illuminated. In the second photo, a man (again, whom she assumed was Wade) was gripping the gun properly, aiming it out of what she assumed was his bedroom window. Again, the red laser sight was illuminated. The pistol looked exactly like the gun Christina had seen Wade wrap in a bandana and slip into his pants and then later hide in the bushes. She then thought of the missing woman. *That could be my mom. That could be me*, she thought. Christina knew she had no choice. She had to go to the police.

THIRTY-FIVE

Detective Perrenoud had submitted several items to the state's crime lab for testing. Knowing the case was a high priority, the lab processed the items with uncharacteristic swiftness, and Detective Perrenoud received the results on August 20, just eleven days later. A swab of DNA from the steering wheel of Mindy's car had come back with a mixed sample, which matched both Mindy's and Wade's DNA. A swab taken from a substance on the floor mat behind the passenger seat was found to have contained Mindy's DNA. The cigarette butts in the ashtray had come back with a male DNA profile, not Wade's, and also not one on file in the federal database known as CODIS, or Combined DNA Index System.

As for the evidence produced by the bloodhounds, Detective Perrenoud remained dubious. She had worked with police K-9s but she had never before encountered bloodhounds, and the accomplishments attributed to the human scent and cadaver dogs seemed inconceivable to her. She would have to see it for herself. On the same day they had served the search warrant at Wade's house, Detective Perrenoud drove to the second tracking location, the ATM at the Credit Union 1, where Agent Goeden and the Human Scent Evidence Team were preparing to deploy a human scent dog named Lucy. This time the ATM was much farther from Mindy's house, about five miles to the northeast, and the idea that a bloodhound could pick up a scent that was two weeks old and spread over such a long distance seemed outlandish to Detective Perrenoud.

Standing outside the door of the bank, and just outside the lobby where the ATM was located, Lucy's handler, William Kift, offered the dog a scent pad taken from the pair of Adidas tennis shoes investigators had found in Wade's closet. Immediately, Lucy had a positive response and "took trail," trotting across the bank's parking lot and toward the street, her long ears swinging back and forth as she moved. The dog made a right turn on West 36th Avenue, with Kift holding her lead and with members of the HSET trailing behind, along with Detective Perrenoud. Lucy traveled along West 36th Avenue for about five blocks before abruptly turning her head and thus signaling to Kift that she was changing directions. She then turned left onto Spenard Road.

Lucy was known to track a scent with an almost obsessive manner and at a swift pace. At 105 pounds, Lucy pulled on her lead with such force it was not uncommon for Kift to replace his leather gloves every three weeks. Anchorage police had the difficult job of stopping traffic along the way, not knowing exactly where the dog might turn. Up ahead, Spenard Road crossed Minnesota Drive, a four-lane parkway. Police officers ran ahead and rushed into the busy intersection just moments before Lucy led a line of law enforcement officers across four lanes of traffic. Then, signaling with another turn of her head, Lucy led the group off the road and onto a path to the left, which ran parallel to a set of railroad tracks.

Detective Perrenoud had been following skeptically, but her doubts began to melt away as she remembered that a witness at the credit union had seen Wade on a bicycle. Someone riding a bike would certainly take such a shortcut to get to Mindy's neighborhood and there's no way these dog handlers from California could have known to take this route, she thought.

Lucy popped her head to the side again, indicating to Kift she was about to make another turn, and then proceeded on a path that led to a parking lot of a strip mall. She continued down a residential street and then cut through the grounds of a recreation center, passing by a baseball field. It was an usual sight, and Kift couldn't help but notice some kids on skateboards who stood mesmerized by the spectacle as Lucy passed, followed by a group of both uniformed and plain-clothed officers.

As they passed a picnic area and playground, Kift became concerned because he could see ahead a gate between a construction area and a school, and beyond it, a busy highway. Lucy was moving at a quick pace, and so Kift yelled to the officers whose job it was to slow traffic to get ready. They ran ahead and, just in time, slowed cars to a halt as Lucy made her way across the highway. Kift could tell they were near the airport, and Lucy led them onto a small bike path that took them to Raspberry Road. She then made a left onto Cutty Sark Street, slowing her pace and sniffing more intensely. Kift knew Lucy well and realized this meant she was nearing the end of the trail. Lucy then turned up the driveway of 6902 and ended the trail five miles from the ATM, at the carport near the side door of Joshua Wade's house.

There were other police officers in the group following Lucy who initially shared Detective Perrenoud's incredulity; some of them even worked with police dogs and were skeptical about what the bloodhounds were purported to do. Yet, there in the driveway of the house where Joshua Wade lived, Detective Perrenoud and the other skeptics stood, staring at one another, too stunned to speak.

THIRTY-SIX

Despite her initial resolve, Christina Greaser told me that she later struggled with the decision to turn in her friend. In fact, the night she discovered Wade's backpack in her car, Christina decided she would "sleep on it" and take the backpack to police first thing in the morning. The next day, she drove to the Anchorage Police Department and identified Josh Wade as the man in the photo she'd seen on the news. She also turned over the backpack and its contents to Detective Ratcliff, who immediately contacted Detective Perrenoud. Christina also turned over Wade's cell phone, which she had been keeping in her purse.

Before talking to Christina, Detective Perrenoud carefully examined the backpack and its contents. To her, the item of most interest was the cell phone, which contained photos of what appeared to be a .45 caliber Glock pistol. The background of the photo showed liquor bottles on a window sill and part of a closet; Detective Perrenoud thought perhaps the photo had been taken inside Wade's bedroom. As she scrolled through the contents on the phone, she came across a dialed call in the log that had just four digits, which was strange, since it was clearly not a phone number. 4-1-4-7. Where had she seen those numbers before? She flipped through her notes. During the search of Mindy's house, she had written down the same four-digit code; it matched the numbers on the scrap of paper she had found inside Mindy's wallet, and the digits matched Mindy's ATM pin number.

214

Police questioned Christina at length and even took a swab sample of saliva from her as DNA evidence. Knowing that she had not cut off contact with Wade and that he would want to retrieve his backpack, Detective Perrenoud asked Christina if she would be willing to let them record her phone conversations with him. She hesitantly agreed. Detective Perrenoud knew that Christina would be in imminent danger as soon as Wade figured out that she had gone to the police. As a precaution, and for Christina's safety, Detective Perrenoud rented a hotel room and took Christina there, to keep her under guard. Christina was certain she had done the right thing, but the experience was starting to overwhelm her and she had doubts about how far she wanted to go to help the police. Detective Perrenoud recognized Christina's ambivalence.

"In the hotel room, she got a phone call which we later found out was Wade," Detective Perrenoud recalled. "She told us at the time, while she was on the phone, that it was her sister. But she spoke to Wade, and we didn't get it recorded."

Detective Perrenoud felt that Christina didn't clearly see what was at stake, nor did she fully understand the amount of danger she was in.

"You need to pick sides," Detective Perrenoud told her firmly. "I mean, right now you're in a very dangerous situation. You have a lot of information that Wade doesn't want you to give to us … but you're not being completely honest with us, either. You're in the worst of possible situations right now."

Christina claimed a few times that her phone rang and that no one was there when she answered, but denied that Wade ever called her while she was in the presence of police.

"They knew the only person Josh talked to and trusted was me," Christina recalled. "It was really awkward for me and uncomfortable."

Eventually, the pressure became too much for Christina to handle, and she decided she had done enough to help the police and was leaving the hotel. Detective Perrenoud urged her to stay.

"You're halfway there. You turned in his backpack; you turned in his phone that's got this evidence on it. You were there when he picked up the gun. Can't you see how much danger you're in right now?"

Christina had made up her mind. Before walking out of the hotel room, Detective Perrenoud looked at her square in the face and issued a stern warning.

"You don't get it," she chided. "You better watch out. Because if you stay with us, we can help you. But if you leave, you're on your own. And he's going to figure out what you did, and he's going to come for you."

In the meantime, Tina Greaser's concern for her daughter was growing. She knew Christina had decided to initially cooperate with police and then had withdrawn her offer to assist in the investigation. Thinking they should seek legal counsel, Tina phoned a family friend who was a tax attorney. Even though he had no experience in criminal matters, she thought he could offer some guidance. As Tina and Christina sat on the backyard deck of the attorney's home explaining the situation, Christina's phone rang. The conversation grew quiet, and she answered.

"It's Josh," she mouthed to her mother. Tina asked Christina to put the call on speaker phone.

"I want my backpack, Christina," Wade said.

"What's going on Josh? Why are police looking for you? Your photo is all over town," Christina said.

"I just need my backpack."

Christina continued to question him, as Tina and their attorney friend listened, and it was clear Wade was growing suspicious.

"What did you tell your mother? What does your mother know about me?" Wade asked.

A feeling of dread came over Tina. *He knows where I live*, she thought. As this was happening, the attorney and friend to whom they had come for advice had the presence of mind to quietly excuse himself and call 911. Within minutes, the police and FBI had arrived at the house.

When Tina expressed her fear to officers that Joshua Wade would harm her or her family, officers advised her not to immediately return home and to temporarily stay with family or friends. Two of Tina's children had just begun school, and she worried the teenagers would complain about having to wear the same clothes to their second day of class. She could figure that out, she reassured herself. More worrisome was Christina; Tina knew Wade would be furious once he discovered Christina had turned over his backpack to the authorities.

THIRTY-SEVEN

Christina Greaser was not the only person who recognized the bottom half of Joshua Wade's face in the image taken from the ATM surveillance footage. Lisa Andrews, who also went by the name Ruth, was a petite and shrewd woman, part Native Alaskan, who had died her long, dark hair platinum blonde. She met Wade in 2000 and initially knew him as her teenaged daughter's boyfriend. However, she had apparently fallen in love with the twenty-year-old delinquent herself, and they had soon commenced a passionate and tumultuous relationship. Wade shared Lisa's intense feelings, later describing her as the only person with whom he had experienced "real love" and "who gave [him] some of the most wonderful moments of [his] life."[66]

Lisa's connection to Wade was unconventional by any standard; not only had Wade first dated her teenaged daughter, Lisa was seventeen years older than Wade. Douglass Foster, who managed a restaurant called the Village Inn where Lisa waited tables and her husband, James, washed dishes, recalled visiting their home in Bear Valley, a rural, mountainous area on the southern tip of Anchorage. While there, Foster encountered Wade and recalled feeling a sense of foreboding in his gut.

"I couldn't get out of there fast enough," Foster said. "[Wade] made my skin crawl. I knew he was a criminal, and

---

66 Wade made the comments about Lisa Andrews to KTVA reporter Andrea Gusty during a jailhouse interview in February of 2010.

I just felt like calling the police and saying, 'There's evil up there.'"

According to Foster, not long after his visit, Lisa and James split up and eventually divorced.

"The most important thing for me was trying to maintain some kind of thread of attachment to James," Foster recalled. "I wanted to keep his mentality above ground because he was spiraling down."

Not surprisingly, the biggest challenge in the relationship between Wade and Lisa Andrews was Wade's uncontrollable temper. In April of 2005, Lisa filed a restraining order against him, stating:

On the evening of April 6, 2005, Josh held me against the bathroom closet door, using his fist, punching the door, leaving two holes. While I was in the bedroom with the door shut, he punched the door, leaving a hole. He forcibly took my cell phone from me and returned it with a broken antenna. On April 17, 2005, I asked him to leave my house as I am concerned for my safety, about him stealing items from my house, and destroying my property. He said he'd burn my house to the ground. He screamed at me on the phone calling me a "Native cunt bitch whore." He admits his temper is escalating. In [January] '05, he punched a hole in my bathroom wall.

Despite the violence, Lisa maintained that their relationship also had its good points. In her only interview about Wade, (I tried persistently but without success to reach her) Lisa Andrews told Megan Holland and Peter Porco of the *Anchorage Daily News*, that Wade had a "softer side," that they shared a "normal relationship, whatever normal is, until [they] had [their] outbursts." Lisa added that she and Wade enjoyed cleaning house together, doing laundry, and watching movies, and that Wade was an "exceptional cook."

Detective Perrenoud, who had multiple interactions with Lisa, was impressed by how intelligent she seemed, saying, "I didn't understand why someone like that would be with Wade. She was smart … both 'business smart' and 'street smart.' It shocked me that she was with him."

By the time the manhunt for Wade was underway, however, Lisa and Wade had ended their relationship. In another court filing, submitted earlier that year, Lisa stated she wanted to dissolve the restraining order:

> Our relationship is over. Josh and his personal items are out of my house. We have nothing to fight about. He is not a threat to me. I want the above referenced order ended. My locks have been changed.

Lisa had called police after seeing the fuzzy surveillance image from the ATM on the news to say she recognized the man in the photo as Joshua Wade. It was after 1:00 a.m. on August 29, 2007, when Detectives Alex Barbosa and Jade Baker tracked down Lisa at the Denny's restaurant where she waited tables.

"How are you this evening?" Detective Barbosa asked Lisa.

"I'm doing fine, how are you?" Lisa replied.

"Good."

"Have you picked up Mr. Wade yet?" Lisa asked. "I guess not," she continued, answering her own question. "Otherwise you wouldn't be here."

"You guys want some coffee?" Lisa asked.

"Oh, no thank you."

Lisa had already been visited by at least one other police officer, but detectives wanted to see in person if Lisa recognized Wade in the ATM photo.

"We can do it right here," Detective Barbosa said. "But if you want some privacy, we can—"

"It's okay, there's nobody here," Lisa interrupted, explaining that the restaurant was technically closed at the time, because the exhaust hoods in the kitchen were being cleaned.

She added, "Now's a good time to be looking for him, 'cause he's not going to come out during the day."

"Have a seat," Detective Barbosa said, motioning to a nearby table.

"Alright."

"I want to show you a photograph, to see if anything looks familiar to you." Detective Barbosa pulled out the grainy ATM photo.

"That's Josh," Lisa said matter-of-factly.

"How can you tell?"

"Well, that's the jacket he bought at the Foot Locker, and you guys are calling it a 'puffy' jacket. It's really not that thick."

"Okay."

"And uhm, that's definitely his mouth and his nose. And uhm, he's got blue and black bandanas like that."

"Alright."

"And the backpack makes sense because he would be on a bike. If you wanted me to, I have pictures of him from 2000 when he was really thin," Lisa offered.

"So you've known him for a long time, I take it?"

"Um hum."

"When was the last time you saw him?"

"June 5. My sister flew in from Idaho and I packed his shit and I told him to get out on June 5."

"And the name you know him by is?"

"Josh," Lisa replied.

"Josh," Detective Barbosa affirmed.

"Josh Wade. AKA asshole, liar, fake," Lisa said, then pausing. "So you guys can't trace the ... or you can't ... I don't know. It seems like you guys ... it must be hard to catch him, I guess."

"I don't know," Detective Barbosa replied.

"Anchorage is so small. It seems really hard to believe that one person can hide like this."

"Well, you know," Detective Barbosa said. "Some people are better at it than others," adding, "Now if you see him, you call 911."

"Alright," Lisa replied. "Well, good luck."

THIRTY-EIGHT

Authorities did not immediately announce to the public that Joshua Wade was wanted in connection with the murder of Mindy Schloss.

"When I obtained the arrest warrant on Josh, we initially tried to keep it quiet," Agent Thoreson recalled. "Even though he was already in hiding, we wanted to try to prevent him from going any deeper."

A few days passed, however, and Wade continued to elude authorities. Thoreson said that at that point they had no choice but to go public.

On August 30, 2007, a front page headline in the *Anchorage Daily News* announced: **EX-CON LINKED TO MISSING NURSE.** Just below the headline appeared a mugshot of Joshua Wade, along with a smaller photo of Mindy Schloss. The caption under Mindy's photo read: *Mindy Schloss was last seen Aug. 3 and is presumed dead by law officials.*

The public announcement that the police and FBI were looking for Joshua Wade in connection with the mysterious disappearance of Mindy Schloss triggered what many law enforcement officials still consider to be one of the largest manhunts in Alaska history. Billboards along two of Anchorage's busiest thoroughfares went up displaying WANTED signs with Wade's huge, looming mugshot. Officers had been reassigned from their usual beats and instead tracked down all of Wade's known associates, knocking on so many doors with such frequency, they hoped to spook Wade's friends, giving him nowhere to take refuge.

In the days that followed, Anchorage police received hundreds of tips of apparent sightings of Wade at grocery stores and on street corners. Agent Thoreson recalled that law enforcement had responded to many of these tips and calls, arriving at various locations, later to discover they had missed Wade by an hour or less. One such instance occurred during the early morning hours of September 2, 2007, when officers tracked Wade to the apartment of a woman who lived on Government Hill, a neighborhood in northwest Anchorage. When Agent Thoreson, accompanied by other officers, knocked on her door at about 1:00 a.m., she claimed that Wade had left her apartment just thirty minutes prior to their arrival. She admitted that she and Wade had watched the news together and that he seemed to be fascinated by the coverage. She granted permission for agents to come in, and inside the apartment they found a collection of newspaper clippings about the Mindy Schloss case and the manhunt for Wade, which Wade himself had apparently compiled.

Just two nights before, Wade's father, Greg "Bubba" Wade, appeared on KTUU's evening newscast. Distraught and looking directly into the camera, he pleaded, "I love you, Josh. I just want you to turn yourself in. I want you to do the right thing. By staying out and hiding from this, it doesn't make things any better."

KTUU reporter Jason Moore also interviewed Daisy Piggott, who said she felt it was "just a matter of time" before Wade struck again. "He needs to be found before anyone else gets hurt," Daisy said in her typical soft-spoken tone. Referring to Mindy's family, she added, "Hopefully this time, the judicial system won't fail them like it failed me."

The seven years since Wade's murder acquittal had been difficult for Daisy. Overcome by depression and anxiety, she had been prescribed antidepressants and other medications that rendered her a shell of her former self. Try as she could, she could not escape the overwhelming guilt of abandoning Della as a girl.

"You know, it's something I will never get over. Ever. And you know, people who say 'time heals all wounds.'" she told me, before pausing and breaking down in tears. After regaining her composure, Daisy told me when she learned Wade was wanted in connection with Mindy's death, she became concerned that she could be in danger.

"I made a call to the [police] department and told them who I was, and would you please check my surroundings, because I knew he did not like me, and I didn't want to become his target," she recalled.

Wade was still at large, and Daisy became convinced that he would come and find her. One day, as she sat in her living room, Daisy heard a popping noise, and then realized it was gunfire. A window shattered and a bullet whizzed by her head, missing her by just a few inches; one bullet traveled through her living room and into the kitchen, hitting the door of the freezer. Daisy dropped to the floor, crawled to the phone, and dialed 911. Her husband had gone down the road to the store, and there was no one there to protect her.

"He found me!" she told the dispatcher. "And I'm here alone!"

"Did you see anybody?" the dispatcher asked.

"No!" Daisy exclaimed. "I didn't see anybody, and I'm not going to go outside and look!"

Daisy would later discover that her neighbor, a young man in his twenties, had fired the shots in a drunken stupor, not meaning to hit Daisy's trailer. The realization came as a relief to Daisy, but she was already in a fragile state and the experience just escalated her feelings of anxiety.

****

Christina Greaser continued to struggle with guilt over having ratted on her friend. The truth was, she had not been completely forthcoming with police. Detective Perrenoud had been adamant that Christina needed to tell her if or when Wade called. He had, in fact, called her several times, each time from a different number, from what Christina assumed were different pay phones scattered across town. She wrestled with her decision but decided not to pass along this information to Detective Perrenoud.

On the same morning Agent Thoreson had tracked Wade to the apartment on Government Hill and more than two weeks after she had gone to the police with Josh's backpack, Christina awoke to discover about eight missed phone calls from numbers she didn't recognize. She assumed Wade was becoming frantic. He must have felt like the world was closing in on him, she thought, given his face was plastered on billboards all over town. A local printing company had even donated its services, printing thousands of WANTED fliers with Wade's mugshot that were passed out at the state fair. The reward for information leading to Wade's arrest was growing; the FBI had announced a $2,500 reward, and Mindy's friends had offered $5,000. In addition, there was a $1,000 Crime Stoppers reward, bringing the total reward fund to $8,500. Amid all the publicity, Christina hoped he would keep his distance from her, given he was, at the time, the most wanted fugitive in the state.

As she left her apartment that morning, however, she felt a sudden sense of alarm in the pit of her stomach. *Oh my God,* she thought. There, on the outside stairs of her apartment building, sat Josh Wade, with a scowl on his face. Not knowing what to say, Christina's face flushed. "Hi," she said weakly.

"I need my backpack, and I need you to give me a ride," Wade said, getting right to the point. "I need to go get something."

"Where do you need to go?" Christina asked.

"Wasilla," Wade replied.

Christina, who had been struggling with her decision to turn Josh in, at that moment, seemed to experience a moment of clarity; the gravity of the situation seemed to weigh on her, as it hadn't before.

"You stay here," Christina replied, somewhat nervously. "I just need to go back inside and get my keys."

Christina slid back into her apartment and pulled out her phone. Her hands were shaking. She had the number of the SWAT commander and called him directly.

"Joshua Wade is at my apartment," she said in a whisper, relating the address.

When she came back out of the apartment, Wade could tell something was wrong.

"What's wrong with you?" Wade asked.

"Nothing," Christina replied. "You just stay right over there."

"Who did you call?" he asked. Christina could tell he was becoming suspicious.

"I can't give you a ride, Josh." Christina said. "But just stay right there."

A sudden realization came over Wade's face.

"You're a rat," he said, and he turned from the parking lot and took off running in the direction of a nearby wooded area.

Christina knew she couldn't let him get away. She got into her car and watched him make his way across an empty lot across the street from her apartment building. He stopped a few times to glance back at her. Again, she dialed the number of the SWAT commander on her cell phone.

"He's headed across the empty parking lot and toward the woods behind the Alaska Club on Tudor Road," Christina reported.

Although police claim they responded within minutes of Christina's call, Christina said it felt like an eternity before the police and the FBI arrived. She didn't want Wade to escape so she backed her car out of its parking space and drove as far as she could along a dirt road, following him, until he disappeared behind a line of trees.

She called back the SWAT commander and said, "I lost him, but I think he's heading toward that apartment complex beyond the woods."

THIRTY-NINE

It was 8:00 a.m., chilly and drizzling outside, when twenty-eight-year-old Edward Michael Phillips finished a graveyard shift at McDonald's and started walking home to the apartment he shared with his younger sister, Elizabeth. The walk took about twenty-five minutes, and he was exhausted when he reached their first-floor unit at the Greenbriar Apartment complex. He smelled like grease but he was too tired to take a shower, so he took off his uniform and slipped into bed. About ten minutes later, he was just settling into sleep when he was startled by a knock on his window. The window of Edward's bedroom was situated just next to the front door of the unit, which opened directly onto a small set of stairs and a narrow lawn. The curtain was not drawn, and as he looked out of the window he could see several police officers standing outside.

"Open the front door," one of them said, his voice urgent but somewhat muffled by the barrier of glass. Edward's exhaustion seemed to compound his confusion, but he obeyed, and as he walked out of his bedroom and toward the front door, he encountered a man he didn't recognize, inside the apartment.

"I can't let you do that," the man said, motioning to the front door. For a second, Edward thought he could be dreaming. After all, these were the kinds of off-the-wall things that happened in dreams. He saw his sister Elizabeth sitting on the couch in the living room.

"What's going on?" Edward asked her.

"I don't know," she said, shrugging innocently.

"Who the hell are you?" Edward demanded of the man, not recognizing him as Joshua Wade, the fugitive whose image had been plastered all over town.

"Don't open that door!" Wade yelled, standing just to the right of the door, in the kitchen.

"No one's going to order me around in my own apartment," Edward replied defiantly. He swung open the door and saw three SWAT officers pointing assault rifles at him.

"GET OUT! GET OUT!" they yelled.

Out of the corner of his eye, to his immediate right and just a few feet away, Wade was pacing back and forth in the kitchen, clearly agitated.

"Get out of the apartment. NOW!" one of the officers repeated. Before Edward had the chance to respond, an officer grabbed Edward's right arm and pulled him out of the doorway and onto the grass. Within seconds, they had him in handcuffs. The apartment door slammed shut behind him.

****

Officers cordoned off the block with yellow crime scene tape. Edward was shocked to see dozens of police vehicles lining the road and filling the parking lot of his apartment complex; FBI agents and federal marshals had also responded to the scene. An officer escorted Edward across the street, still in handcuffs.

"What's going on?" Edward asked. The officer didn't answer. Edward was wearing only a T-shirt, his pajama bottoms, and socks. It was a chilly fifty degrees and still drizzling outside. He started to shiver.

"Can I get a blanket or something?" he asked the officer.

"Sorry, we don't do that," the officer replied.

After a half hour or so, the officer removed Edward's handcuffs and he could hear police referring to what was happening as a "hostage situation."

"My sister's in there, what's going on?" Edward kept asking. No one would answer. Neighbors had begun to gather, and a couple of them had passed by where Edward was sitting.

"That's Josh Wade in there," one of them said. "They've been looking for him all over Alaska, for drug stuff and possible murder."

This sent Edward into a fit of worry. "My sister's in there," he kept repeating to anyone who would listen. "And no one will tell me what's going on!"

****

It turned out that Edward's younger sister, Elizabeth, and Wade were not complete strangers. They had met a few weeks prior, according to Elizabeth, outside the apartment building where Wade had some customers to whom he sold drugs. They had exchanged pleasantries, and although they did not know each other well, he knew where she lived. When Wade came to the door, he asked to use the phone, but when Elizabeth hesitated, telling him she would go get the phone and bring it to him, he violently forced his way in. Witnesses on the street had observed Wade barging in and had called 911. Ten minutes later, an unsuspecting Edward arrived home from work and, exhausted from his overnight shift, he had walked directly to his bedroom, not realizing there was a stranger in the apartment. Given that Christina had indicated to police the direction Wade was headed, authorities quickly ascertained the intruder was likely Josh Wade.

SWAT officers had surrounded the apartment building

with their guns drawn, and Wade was frantic. He decided to call attorney Cindy Strout, who had represented him during the Della Brown case.

"I advised him to turn himself in," Strout recalled. "I also remember advising him to be sure to show his hands, you know, because I didn't want him to get shot."

Wade, however, wasn't eager to take her advice. He found a half-full bottle of white wine in the refrigerator, downed it, and then started in on a bottle of whiskey. He called Christina Greaser, who was outside, near the line of police cars, and he berated her for turning him in.

"He was telling me, 'You're a snitch, you're a rat,'" Christina recalled. "And I was like, 'Really? That's the way you're going to look at it?'"

Wade drank and listened to music for more than an hour, continuing a standoff with SWAT officers, who were taking every precaution, believing that he likely was armed with the Glock pistol which he had photographed with his cell phone and perhaps the same one he had used to kill Mindy Schloss. A negotiator talked to Wade by calling the landline in the apartment, but Wade remained defiant. Cindy Strout had a second phone conversation with him and urged him to surrender.

"I actually went to the scene, so he could see that I was there," Strout recalled. "I was at least a block away though, you know, because the police had the area blocked off."

Finally, about an hour later, Wade let Elizabeth go. Edward saw his sister emerge from their apartment and felt an overwhelming sense of relief. She was in shock, too numb to speak.

"She wasn't really talking to anybody," Edward recalled. "I could tell she was frightened."

Thirty minutes later, Wade came out of the apartment, wearing a white tank top and blue jeans with his hands up, ending his ninety-minute standoff with law enforcement. With bloodshot eyes, he glared angrily at Christina, who was standing near a group of police officers with her mother. Officers approached Wade slowly with their guns drawn, put him in handcuffs, and escorted him to a patrol car.

Overwhelmed with emotion, Christina embraced her mother. They then both hugged a police officer, standing nearby.

"It's all over," the officer reassured them.

Christina was glad the ordeal was over, but she still cared for Wade and knew he was furious with her. After the patrol car pulled away with Wade in the backseat, Christina remained at the scene, wiping tears from her mascara-stained face. As officers passed by, they congratulated her for helping to bring the intense manhunt to an end. Thanks to her, Alaska's most wanted fugitive was in custody.

FORTY

Joshua Wade was an experienced criminal; he knew how the game was played. So Detective Perrenoud and Agent Thoreson knew he was unlikely to talk. Still, after his arrest, officers took him directly to the FBI building in Anchorage and sat him in an interrogation room.

Agent Thoreson was a tall man with an angular face, short brown hair, and a strong work ethic; he investigated mostly white collar crimes such as bank fraud and money laundering. He was a firm believer that you shouldn't let a perp stew for too long; it gave the criminal too much time to consider his actions. He also knew you couldn't go into an interrogation with a thought-out strategy; such plans usually went out the window with the first question. Since Wade had been in and out of the system most of his adolescent and adult life, it was likely he would request an attorney before they even had a chance to ask him anything.

It was the first time Detective Perrenoud and Agent Thoreson had come face-to-face with Wade, who was sitting behind a metal table, kicked back in his chair. They pulled up chairs to the table and sat down.

"Hey Josh, I'm with the FBI," Agent Thoreson said.

"And I'm Pam Perrenoud with APD."

Wade didn't acknowledge their presence. Although he hadn't uttered a word, his body language conveyed a cocky attitude; he seemed to be saying, *Do what you've got to do and just take me to jail.* Agent Thoreson knew right away that sweet talking Wade wasn't going to work.

"You going to talk with us at all … or are you just going to sit there?" Thoreson asked. There was no answer. "You going to do the silent treatment? Do you want to talk with us?"

"About what?" Wade finally asked, facing to one side.

"About what you've been arrested for," Thoreson responded.

"I have no idea what I've been arrested for, man," Wade said.

"You've been arrested for two counts of bank fraud, aggravated identity theft … and access-device fraud," Thoreson informed him.

Wade perked up and turned his head, finally making eye contact. Thoreson knew most people weren't familiar with the term *access device fraud.*

"What the fuck is that?" Wade said.

"It just means that you used an ATM card of somebody that's not yourself … and that person did not give you permission to do so," Thoreson explained.

"You're assuming that," Wade quipped. As Wade spoke these words, Agent Thoreson had an idea. He thought, the only way to get something out of Wade, was to surprise him by saying something outlandish.

"No, we don't assume. We do a little bit more than assume," Agent Thoreson said. "We actually talked to Mindy, you know."

"Hmmm? What did you just say?" Wade asked, sitting up.

"I said we talked to Mindy," Agent Thoreson repeated.

A devious smirk came over Wade's face. If there was any doubt before that moment that Wade had killed Mindy Schloss, for either Agent Thoreson or Detective Perrenoud, it evaporated with one facial expression. Detective Perrenoud could see in Wade's eyes what he must have been thinking: *You couldn't have talked to her, because I killed her.*

"Are you guys trying to play games with me, man?" Wade asked.

"Why would we be playing games?" Thoreson returned.

"Can I have a cigarette, please?" Wade said dismissively, sitting back in his chair.

"No, you can't," Thoreson replied.

"Okay, well, I want my attorney, dude."

The interview was over.

****

It turned out that Wade was not armed when he was taken into custody. Investigators had searched Edward and Elizabeth's apartment for the .45 caliber Glock pistol as well as Wade's bedroom at the house on Cutty Sark Street. They had even retraced Wade's steps, with Christina's assistance, to the spot where Wade had apparently hidden the gun in the bushes near a street sign but had found nothing. The photos from Wade's cell phone, however, were revealing. In the photo of Wade aiming the gun out of window, there was a circular white and blue sticker on the bottom right-hand corner of the pane of glass. A photo taken of the exterior of Wade's bedroom showed the same decal, in the same spot on the window. In the background of the other photo of the gun, there was a cardboard cylinder leaning sideways inside a closet. Photos taken of Wade's bedroom when police served the search warrant of the house showed a similar cardboard cylinder in Wade's bedroom closet.

Wade was behind bars, but at this point, prosecutors didn't have much to work with, as far as a homicide case was concerned; there was no murder weapon and no body. Assistant U.S. Attorney Steven Skrocki knew what was at stake.

"I think the collective understanding between all of us is, we couldn't let this happen again. And [Wade] couldn't be let out, free on society again," Skrocki told me.

Because Wade had used Mindy's ATM card in the apparent commission of the crime of bank fraud, the federal government had jurisdiction. This was bad news for Wade. Although state prosecutors had their own separate criminal case to pursue, Alaska did not have the death penalty; the federal government, however, could pursue a capital case against him, once Mindy's body was found.[67] The government initially held off on murder charges, instead filing charges of bank fraud against Wade, related to the theft and use of Mindy's debit card.

On September 4, 2007, Wade was arraigned in federal court. Given that he had no assets to speak of, the judge assigned a public defender to the case. A preliminary hearing was set for the following Monday, September 10. The bank fraud charges alone carried with them a maximum penalty of thirty years in prison and a $1 million fine. The prosecution argued that Wade was a flight risk, calling the circumstances underlying the case "ominous," given that Mindy Schloss was still missing. But at the preliminary hearing, the judge said he also would hear arguments from the defense on whether Wade should be granted bail.

Christina Greaser attended the arraignment, and later that same afternoon, she went to the jail during visiting hours to see Wade, whom she still considered a friend. Wade was in protective custody, so she talked to him on the phone while watching him on a TV screen.

"He didn't refuse the visit, but he was mad. He called me

---

67 Murder, accompanied by what are considered aggravating factors, such as carjacking or bank fraud, make a defendant eligible for the death penalty in federal court.

a snitch or a rat," Christina recalled, adding that Wade was angry that he had been placed in solitary confinement.

Christina told me she was dismayed by how the local media had portrayed her, as a sympathetic friend to a killer, when she was the one who had turned Wade in. "I did it for him," she said of her decision to go to the police. "I thought it was in his best interest."

Christina told me that many years later she e-mailed Wade's father and confided in him that she never felt afraid of or threatened by his son.

"Well you should have been afraid," Bubba wrote back. "You're lucky he didn't take your life, too."

****

The following Monday, at the preliminary hearing, prosecutors outlined their case against Wade. Citing an "ongoing murder investigation," the government focused on the bank fraud charges. Agent Thoreson was called as a witness, and he testified about the ATM transactions and the surveillance footage that showed a man fitting Wade's description withdrawing a total of $1,000 from Mindy's account. Thoreson also testified that a jacket, believed to be Wade's, had been recovered from Wade's home and that inside the jacket investigators had found a receipt for one of the ATM withdrawals.

Under direct examination by Assistant U.S. Attorney Crandon Randell, Thoreson told the court that Wade had gone to his own bank on August 6 to cash a check from his employer. Surveillance footage from the Northrim Bank on West Dimond Boulevard showed a man appearing to be Wade making such a transaction with a bank teller. In court, a still image from the surveillance footage flashed on a screen, as Agent Thoreson narrated.

"You see that Mr. Wade is wearing a blue baseball cap that has white pinstripes on it, which resembles the hat as seen in the two ATM transactions that were performed on Ms. Schloss's bank account," Thoreson testified. "When he came in, he was approximately $104 in the hole, meaning he had a deficit of $104."

"Okay, so what did he do?" Randell asked.

"He cashed a check from ... I believe it was an employer of his ... paid the $104 with cash he had, then cashed that check, and then closed his bank account, and then walked out of the branch."

"Shut it down?" Randell asked.

"He closed his bank account."

Wade exploded. "I didn't close my account, man! That's a fucking lie! I'm sitting here listening to this lie, and you got a smirk on your face—"

"All right," the judge chided.

"You think something's funny, man?" Wade shouted at Thoreson.

"Mr. Wade," the judge said.

"If this lady's missing, why do you have a smile on your face, dude?"

"Mr. Wade," the judge insisted. "Take a moment to talk with your lawyer. It's not your time to talk right now. Take a moment."

Wade wasn't listening. "There ain't nothing funny about this, man! This is my life, dude. I'm trying to sit here and listen, man."

"And that's your job right now," the judge instructed. "To *listen*. And then later if you want to say something and talk to your lawyer, we'll permit you the opportunity."

"I would appreciate it," Wade said, sneering, "if these people could act like professionals and quit smirking at me. There's nothing funny about this. This is some serious shit, and this is my life on the line."

Agent Thoreson told me he didn't recall smirking on the witness stand and that he had the feeling Wade's outburst might have been premeditated.

"It was interesting that he accused *me* of smirking, given what he did in our interview with him. At any rate, the judge told him to calm down, and he did." Thoreson went on to explain that perhaps Wade didn't understand that withdrawing all your money from a bank account was equivalent to closing it down.

The judge ordered Wade held without bail, pending a trial on the bank fraud charges. Even though Mindy was presumed dead, Wade remained free of murder charges, with police continuing to refer to him as a "person of interest" in her death.

****

More than a week had passed since Wade's arrest. The air was turning brisk, and soon the ground would begin to harden under a ruthless cold and would be buried by a torrent of snow, which would not relent until April. Alaska's winters are unforgiving.

"We knew that we were running out of time," Detective Perrenoud recalled. "Because it was about to snow. And we knew if we didn't find Mindy soon, we may never find her."

FORTY-ONE

September 13, 2007

Detective Perrenoud was at her desk, rolling her eyes, and holding the phone receiver a few inches from her head, as she listened to the latest theory a member of the public had phoned in about where police might find Mindy's body.

"*Schloss* means castle in German," the male caller advised. "That's got to mean something." The department had received hundreds of calls to its hotline with useless tips such as this, and as the lead detective on the case, Detective Perrenoud felt a responsibility to follow up on most of the calls herself, in case someone had something truly helpful to offer. It meant spending valuable time listening to psychics and people she could only describe as *quacks*, who claimed among other things, that they had seen Mindy and Wade together in Texas and in other states in the Lower 48. The man on the line was rambling on when Detective Kristi Ratcliff waved to get Detective Perrenoud's attention.

"Pam, you need to get off the phone," she said quietly, but mouthing the words clearly. "It's important."

Detective Perrenoud was glad to end the call. "What is it?"

"A trooper just called," Detective Ratcliff replied. "A body's been found in Wasilla." Detective Ratcliff explained the body was decomposed, but based on the description she had heard from the trooper, it could be Mindy. "I think we should go," she advised.

241

Detective Perrenoud agreed, and they made the hour-long drive north to Wasilla. As they drove into the area where the body had been found, they could see it was an undeveloped neighborhood. There was a cul-de-sac on a dead-end street called West Murray Drive that had been paved years before, but there were no homes anywhere in sight. Discarded beer cans and trash suggested that the cul-de-sac had been a place for teenagers to drink and party in secret. Thirty yards beyond the edge of the cul-de-sac in a heavily wooded area and along a game trail, a utility worker had happened upon the body and called 911. Alaska State Troopers, who had jurisdiction over the region, had responded to the scene.

"We thought at first it was a juvenile," one of the troopers told Detectives Perrenoud and Ratcliff. "But you said your victim was petite. It could be a woman."

The trooper led Detective Perrenoud along the trail to where the victim had been found. The body was face up, near a small grove of birch trees. One leg was bent backwards, and the other was straight; both arms lay at the victim's side. Detective Perrenoud could see remnants of burnt garbage on the body, what appeared to be a bathrobe, and she noticed a distinctive necklace around the victim's neck. A bullet casing had been found less than twenty feet from the body that matched a .45 caliber gun. The victim also had on one shoe. The other shoe, belonging to a pair of black leather clogs, was found nearby.

The body was too decomposed to identify. Knowing that they would need dental records to make an official determination, Detective Perrenoud called Mindy's friend Kathy Hodges and asked about the necklace. Kathy knew the necklace Detective Perrenoud was describing and even had a photo of Mindy wearing it. She e-mailed the photo but was too afraid to prod Detective Perrenoud for more information.

"I thought maybe they just found a necklace," Kathy

told me. "I never really asked, because I didn't want to compromise the investigation and Pam couldn't probably tell me anyway."

Based on the photo, Detective Perrenoud concluded, they had, indeed, found Mindy's body.

****

Detective Perrenoud knew it wouldn't be long before the media got wind of the discovery and would start speculating that the body was that of the missing nurse. She dreaded the thought of Mindy's friends finding out the news from TV, so she and Detective Ratcliff drove from the crime scene in the direction of Bob Conway's house in Eagle River. Just about five minutes before they arrived, Detective Perrenoud called Bob.

"Can we stop by?" She asked. "We need to talk."

When they arrived Detective Perrenoud said, "A woman's body was found tonight in Wasilla. We don't know for sure, but it's probably Mindy."

Bob broke down in tears.

"I'm so sorry," Detective Perrenoud said. After a while, she said, "We need to tell Gerri. How do you want to do it?"

"I want to come with you," he said.

****

It was about 11:00 p.m., and Gerri was getting ready for bed when the doorbell rang. She answered the door and saw Detective Perrenoud and Bob; she immediately knew why they were there. Gerri began weeping, and she and Bob embraced. Gerri had been holding up a good front, granting interviews with the media and staying strong, hoping her efforts would help find Mindy. Now, there was no reason to be strong. She wept for the loss of her dearest friend.

Gerri thought the discovery of Mindy's body would provide some comfort or closure, bringing the torture of not knowing to an end. This was not exactly true. Gerri began to have nightmares about what Mindy had suffered during her last hours, what she must have been feeling during that hour-long car ride to Wasilla, tied up and gagged in the backseat of her her own car. Gerri's medical experience granted her the unwelcome knowledge of what a body would look like after six weeks of decomposition, out in the elements; she couldn't get the horrifying image out of her mind.

"You read about this stuff in the newspaper; it doesn't happen to you," Gerri recalled. "You see it on TV, and it's like, 'Did this really happen in my life?' It stays with you the rest of your life."

Detective Perrenoud called Kathy Hodges.

"Kathy, I have some bad news. We found a body in Wasilla, and we're pretty sure it's Mindy."

Kathy was devastated.

"I always thought about how Mindy worked so hard to help mentally ill people," Kathy told me. "And then obviously the person who took her was mentally ill. Whether he was the psychopath or whatever. You know, he killed the very person who helped people like him."

The case had also affected Detective Perrenoud. Usually, as a cop, she kept an emotional distance from her cases, but this one was different. Mindy's friends were so compassionate and helpful and Detective Perrenoud felt a connection to them, and in a strange way, she felt like she knew Mindy.

"Mindy could've been my friend or my sister," she said. "She was just a regular person going about her life and her business, and she just happened to have the bad luck of living next door to a killer."

FORTY-TWO

The next day, Detective Perrenoud and Agent Thoreson went to Mindy's dentist, who confirmed the x-rays of the deceased taken by a forensic specialist matched those he had on file for Mindy Schloss. They did not immediately release this finding to the media, but reporters, who had come to the crime scene in Wasilla, already were speculating and making the connection to the missing nurse. As difficult as it had been, Detective Perrenoud was glad she had broken the news to Mindy's friends the previous night.

Agent Goeden had responded to the crime scene where technicians were busy processing evidence. The team had determined Mindy's body had been burned with use of an accelerant, perhaps lighter fluid, and reasoned the assailant had used garbage nearby to help ignite the flames. It had been raining, however, and given Mindy's body had been left in the woods for almost six weeks, it suffered mostly from decomposition.

There seemed to be no forensic evidence to place Wade at the crime scene in Wasilla. Given the previous success of the Human Scent Evidence Team, Agent Goeden thought the dogs could again be helpful. She called Agent Stockham, who decided to dispatch Dennis Slavin and Tinkerbell back to Anchorage. In preparation of their arrival, and before Mindy's body was taken from the scene, Agent Goeden and Agent Joy collected scents from her corpse, using numerous sterile pads to do so, from her head, torso, limbs, and also from her clothing.

Mindy's remains were taken to the morgue, where Dr. Franc Fallico, the same coroner who had examined Della Brown's body, performed an autopsy. A forensic anthropologist who specialized in examining decomposed remains assisted, as did a forensic nurse, who attempted to collect evidence of a sexual assault. Unfortunately, given the degree of decomposition, experts were unable to determine if Mindy had been sexually assaulted.

Considering Wade's history, both Agent Goeden and Detective Perrenoud had their suspicions about that, and there were, in fact, reasons to believe Wade had sexually violated Mindy. Among the thousands of hairs that had been recovered from the living room carpet of Mindy's house, were two pubic hairs, which, when tested for DNA, matched Wade. It was suggestive, not conclusive evidence of a sexual assault; but at the very least, it placed Wade inside Mindy's house. Also, a few days before Mindy's disappearance, the young occupants of 6902 Cutty Sark Street were out on the front porch with Wade, when Mindy's car pulled into her driveway. Wade, referring to Mindy as she entered her house, reportedly made the comment, "I'd like to spread those cheeks."[68]

Wade's roommates had related this story to police, and Kathy Easley, the neighbor, had heard a similar story from Shane Phillips.

"They were laughing [at Wade] because they were like, 'She's an old lady,' cause to the boys, she was a forty-something-year-old woman," Kathy said. "And they were like, 'You're disgusting.'"

In addition, police had heard from a witness, who, during the early morning hours of August 4, saw a small red car

---

68 This quote is taken from a court document in which the government outlines its allegations of sexual assault against Wade.

near the ATM at a branch of Wells Fargo Bank, matching the description of Mindy's Acura. The location was just a short distance from Mindy's house, and the witness reported hearing a woman scream "Rape! Call the police!"[69]

With speculation swirling among the local media, Anchorage police announced the body found in Wasilla was the missing nurse, Mindy Schloss. The front page banner headline in the *Anchorage Daily News* the next day read **SCHLOSS' BODY FOUND IN WASILLA: Nurse is Identified Through Dental Records**. Mindy's friends and supporters planned a public memorial service.

****

The day before Mindy's body was discovered, a federal grand jury had indicted Wade on charges of bank fraud and identity theft. He was still being called a "person of interest" in Schloss's death but thus far he had avoided facing a murder charge. The state of Alaska had taken a backseat to federal prosecutors and hadn't filed any charges at all, while Assistant U.S. Attorney Steven Skrocki and his colleagues were scrupulously building a capital case against Wade.

"The case that we had built, was built upon a number of small pieces of evidence, which turned into pixels ... which turned into a picture of homicide," Skrocki told me.

****

Dennis Slavin and his bloodhound Tinkerbell arrived in Anchorage two days after Mindy's body had been found, and Agent Goeden accompanied them to the crime scene. The wooded area near the cul-de-sac remained surrounded

---

69 It's hard to know what to make of this witness's statement given the withdrawal of $500 from Mindy's account was made on August 5, 2007. Perhaps Wade attempted to make the ATM withdrawal just after abducting Mindy but was scared off when he saw someone nearby.

by crime tape. Standing in the cul-de-sac with Slavin and Tinkerbell, Agent Goeden first performed a number of "dismissals," a process by which scents from other individuals are excluded by the K-9. Tinkerbell did not respond to any of these scents, including those of Wade's roommates Shane Phillips and Eric Holmstrand. Then Agent Goeden handed to Slavin a jar containing a scent pad taken from Wade himself. (An agent had collected the scent by rubbing a sterile pad directly on Wade's skin after his arrest and when Wade was in FBI custody.) Slavin presented the scent pad to Tinkerbell, and the dog immediately reacted, taking off from the cul-de-sac and into the woods. Tinkerbell went about thirty yards along a game trail then paused, circling near a grove of birch trees, precisely the spot where Mindy's body had been found. The dog then trailed the scent back to the cul-de-sac, across the pavement, and into the woods on the other side, for thirty yards or so, then turned around and returned to the cul-de-sac, where Mindy's car was presumably parked.

Again beginning at the cul-de-sac, Agent Goeden handed Slavin another jar, this one containing a scent pad taken from the apron Gerri had given to Mindy as a gift. Again, Tinkerbell trailed the scent into the woods and to the spot where Mindy's body had been found. This time, though, the dog stopped near the grove of birch trees and sat. Agent Goeden realized what this meant: Wade had walked out of the woods but Mindy had not. They had just retraced Mindy's last, terrified steps.

****

As prosecutors built their first degree murder case against Wade, they faced one of their most critical challenges when Lisa Andrews, who had positively identified Wade in the ATM surveillance footage, decided she would no longer cooperate.

She and Wade had an on-again, off-again relationship; the two had apparently rekindled their affection during frequent phone calls and Lisa's visits to the Anchorage jail. Knowing that Lisa could connect him to the murder of Mindy Schloss and concerned the government would seek the death penalty, Wade decided he and Lisa should marry so he could exercise spousal privilege, the legal right afforded to married couples to keep their communications private.

The feds had in their possession a "large number" of recorded phone calls between Lisa and Wade, during which Lisa had admitted she was afraid of testifying, concerned she would "get beat up by the lawyers and [wouldn't] have any integrity." She also told Wade, perhaps jokingly, that she was "looking into countries that don't allow extradition."[70]

The couple filed for and obtained a marriage license, and in January of 2008 at Wade's urging, Lisa arrived at the Anchorage jail with two witnesses and an officiant to perform the wedding ceremony. The witnesses, required by law, included Lisa's daughter (not the daughter Wade had dated), a friend, and the officiant, who was a cook from the Denny's where Lisa worked. Jail officials turned the wedding party away, however, because regulations stipulated an inmate could have no more than three visitors at a time. Later that evening, Wade called Lisa and the couple exchanged vows over a speakerphone and in the "presence" of their two witnesses.

The jailhouse marriage prompted a legal fight between prosecutors and Wade's defense team. Prosecutors claimed the marriage was performed illegally over the phone, and was thus invalid. Wade's attorneys contended the couple had followed the letter of the law and denied that Wade had instigated the marriage as a ploy to prevent Lisa from

---

70 These quotes are taken from a court document filed by federal prosecutors.

testifying against him.

At some point, Wade was taken to SeaTac Federal Detention Center near the Seattle airport, where federal inmates from Alaska typically awaited trial. Lisa Andrews, who was now going by Lisa Wade, decided to uproot her life and follow him there, making the more than 2,000-mile trek south.

Detective Perrenoud and Agent Thoreson knew how important Lisa was to their case. She had previously told police Wade was an "asshole" and a "liar," and given the couple's violent history, Perrenoud and Thoreson decided to take the three-hour flight to Seattle to see if they could convince her to change her mind and to cooperate with the investigation.

Lisa was surprised when two detectives from Alaska, whom she immediately recognized, walked into the Denny's restaurant where she had found a job waiting tables.

"That chapter of my life is over," Lisa insisted. "I don't want to be involved in this anymore."

Agent Thoreson tried to appeal to her sense as a mother.

"Think about your own kids," he said. "I know you may not want to cooperate. You just want to move on, I understand. But think about your children. Would you want someone else not to say anything if one of your kids was killed?"

Lisa kept shaking her head and glancing down; she wouldn't budge. It seemed Agent Thoreson and Detective Perrenoud's long voyage to Seattle had been a waste of time. They returned home, discouraged.

They had spoken to other women who had been drawn in by Wade's "bad boy" charm, and they knew he had a way of manipulating them into doing what he wanted. On one hand, Lisa was considerably older than the other women Wade had been with, but on the other hand, she had relocated her entire life for him. Maybe, they thought, she was simply under his spell, unable to break free.

Late the next day, however, Agent Thoreson received an unexpected call. It was Lisa on the line. She couldn't stop thinking about what he had said.

"I've changed my mind," she said. "I'll tell you everything."

FORTY-THREE

Lisa Andrews was much more important to the prosecution's case than Agent Thoreson and Detective Perrenoud could ever have imagined. The fact that she could identify Wade from the ATM surveillance footage was just the tip of the proverbial iceberg; Wade had also confessed to Mindy's murder and shared with Lisa the graphic and disturbing details of how he had done it. The confession from Wade had apparently happened during one of Lisa's visits to the prison; they met in a visiting room where conversations were not recorded. What follows is the narrative gleaned by law enforcement from Lisa's account of her conversation with Wade:

During the early morning hours of August 3, 2007, a party was underway at 6902 Cutty Sark Street, which lasted well past midnight. That afternoon, Wade had been sent home from his job at a construction site for having an attitude problem. He was broke and decided to burglarize the house next door. Wade broke into Mindy's house, claiming he was unaware that Mindy was home at the time and asleep in her bedroom. When he began to rummage through her belongings, Mindy awoke from the commotion, emerging from the back bedroom. He made her lie down on the bathroom floor and restrained her with an item of clothing.[71] Wade said Mindy recognized him, and that he was worried

---

71 Court documents do not make clear what the item of clothing was.

about being sent back to prison.

Wade then returned to his house next door where he retrieved gloves, black zip ties, a shop rag, a roll of blue painter's tape, and his .45 Glock pistol. He re-entered Mindy's house. He bound Mindy's hands and feet with the zip ties. He obtained her debit card and forced her to tell him the pin number before shoving the shop rag into her mouth and securing it with the blue painter's tape. Wade then forced Mindy out of the house and into the garage, where he placed her in the backseat of her red Acura. She was wearing only a bathrobe and her black leather clogs; her arms and feet remained bound with zip ties. He placed a blanket over her. Wade drove one hour north to Wasilla and parked the car in a cul-de-sac in an undeveloped wooded area off of Knik-Goose Bay Road.

Wade took Mindy from the backseat of the car, removed the zip ties from her legs, keeping her arms restrained and the gag in her mouth, and marched her a short distance into the woods. He told her he was going to let her go, that he needed her to kneel down so he could cut off her restraints. Once on her knees, he cut the zips ties, then aimed his .45 Glock pistol at the back of her head and pulled the trigger. She fell to the ground. He then attempted to burn her body, using lighter fluid as an accelerant.

Wade drove back to Mindy's house and parked her car in the garage. He made efforts to conceal his presence; he swept footprints off the front porch, he cleaned and vacuumed, made the bed, and before leaving, stole Mindy's gold Seiko watch. At 12:45 p.m. the following day, he drove Mindy's red Acura to a parking lot off of Old International Airport Road and left it there, with several of Mindy's belongings, including her purse, inside.

On August 5 and again on August 6, Wade used Mindy's ATM card at two separate locations to withdraw a total of

$1,000 from her bank account.

It was a sterile sequence of events that left to the imagination the horror Mindy had experienced.

"When she was in the back of the car, she must have known she was going to die," Detective Perrenoud said. "It's at least an hour-long ride, and she must have been so scared. And we knew [from the evidence] he walked her down that path to where he eventually shot her."

The dusty footprint found on an armrest in the backseat of Mindy's car matched the black leather clogs found at the crime scene and detectives would later determine that the victim had been marched to this spot in the woods (they reasoned the clogs would have both fallen off had the victim been carried) and shot execution style—once in the back of the head. The FBI's crime lab would determine, based on the trajectory of the bullet, that the victim was on her knees when she was killed.

There was something about the timeline, however, that didn't make sense to Detective Perrenoud. As she reviewed her notes, she remembered the neighbor who had reported seeing Mindy's car pull into the driveway on August 4 between 9:00 and 9:20 a.m., describing a "slender arm" reaching up to press the garage door opener. That was the day *after* Wade had killed Mindy. *It must have been Wade behind the wheel,* she thought.

As for why he had divulged all of these details to Lisa, Detective Perrenoud figured it came down to a simple idea: he just needed someone to talk to. He knew once he was charged with murder, a possible death sentence was hanging over his head, and he was probably worried.

"He needed to figure out: How am I going to get out of this? What am I overlooking? And he knew that Lisa was very smart. So maybe he was looking for her help."

****

About a month after Mindy's body was found, a federal grand jury indicted Wade again, this time on charges he, as a convicted felon, illegally possessed a gun—namely the .45 caliber Glock pistol—and on charges he had possessed marijuana while in jail.[72]

Anticipating the murder charges, Wade's public defender, Mary Geddes, made a motion for a change of venue, arguing her client could not get a fair trial in Anchorage because of the media attention and due to Wade's public notoriety. In her motion, Geddes cited hundreds of comments from the internet, made mostly on the comment section of the *Anchorage Daily News's* website, to demonstrate the vitriol her client elicited from the local citizenry. Here is a sampling:

"Dear Governor, I'd like to apply for the position of the Executioner … hell, I'll volunteer to shoot, hang, gas or poison this hateful man."

"He's a scumbag!"

"I hope he never sees the light of day ever again … scum of the earth."

"I hope this monster rots in hell!"

"Joshua Wade got away with Della's murder. Even the bigots know. Justice is about to be served …"

"Wade is ugly and a waste of human skin."

---

72 The government had not recovered the murder weapon, but based the weapons charges on the photograph of Wade holding the gun recovered from his cell phone, along with interviews with Christina Greaser and Wade's roommates who said that they had all observed him with the weapon.

"I will gladly pull a switch, inject or whatever it takes to rid the world of this scum."

"Hell on Earth, Wade. I pray you do not get an easy death by injection."

"Human sewage ... he should be flushed permanently."

"I used to oppose the death penalty. Then I started having nightmares about this guy after Ms. Schloss disappeared. The fact is, nothing we can do will ever make it less horrible for her family to know how she spent the last days of her life. String him up."

"If he had been put away the first time, this lady would still be alive. Shame on those who let him free!"

The federal judge overseeing the case, Ralph Beistline, agreed that finding a pool of jurors without strong feelings about Wade would be nearly impossible in Anchorage and decided to move the trial 350 miles north to Fairbanks. With still no murder charges filed, the defense argued that Judge Beistline should not set a trial date at all or set one at least a year down the road. The judge wanted to know how Wade himself felt about this.

"Mr. Wade, do you want me to set a trial date or do you care?" Beistline asked.

"I would like a trial date," Wade responded. "I'd like to know if these cocksuckers are trying to kill me. I don't want to be left in suspense here, man."

****

On April 17, 2008, more than seven months after

Mindy's body had been found, the U.S. Attorney's Office filed first-degree murder charges against Wade. The charges included special allegations of carjacking and use of a gun to commit murder, making Wade eligible for the death penalty. Prosecutors also made allegations that Wade had tortured Mindy, stating in the charging document that the offense was committed "in an especially heinous, cruel and depraved manner, in that it involved torture and serious physical abuse to Mindy Schloss."

After the hearing, Skrocki noticed Daisy Piggott in the gallery. He knew she was Della Brown's mother, so he approached her and introduced himself. Daisy had vowed to attend every one of Wade's hearings, even though her daughter's case had ended five years before. Skrocki was a tall, well-groomed man with a full head of hair parted neatly to one side; he wore stylish, half-rimmed spectacles, and well-tailored suits. He towered over Daisy, who stood not even five feet tall. He promised he would do his best to give her and her family some resolution.

"I trust you," she replied, her eyes filled with hope.

****

In a number of pre-trial hearings, members of the FBI's Human Evidence Scent Team defended their practices and procedures, and the specific results the bloodhounds had produced during the investigation. The defense, hoping to demonstrate the unreliability of such evidence, filed a motion citing a 2001 case in which the FBI's dogs led agents to government researcher Steven Hatfill, who was then suspected of causing an Anthrax attack that killed five people. Hatfill was exonerated and later won a $5.8 million settlement from the government. It just so happened that Tinkerbell and Lucy, the very dogs that had worked on Hatfill's case, had singled out Joshua Wade as Mindy Schloss's killer.

State prosecutors watched the case proceed in federal court, worried the feds were relying too much on the evidence produced by the dogs.

"The evidence in the Mindy Schloss case was triable. That was not a slam dunk by any stretch of my imagination," Alaska Assistant Attorney General John Novak told me. Novak was not the assigned prosecutor for the state, but when I suggested the lack of evidence in the Della Brown case made that case much harder to prosecute, he chuckled.

"No, [in the Schloss case] you have key evidence from the dogs," he said. "You had a track that was performed a month later, and the person was transported in a vehicle. You had the dog, Tinkerbell, basically that was able to say that Joshua Wade went from 'A to B'… and they were able to establish that by this dog that made the track a month later. Okay? Look at all the weather that happens. And Mindy Schloss rode in a car. So I was concerned about the state court even allowing admission of that evidence and what a jury would do with it. Let's put it this way: I've had jurors return guilty verdicts on less persuasive evidence and I've had 'not guilty' on much stronger cases. The longer I do this … any time you go to trial, it's a crap shoot."

Steven Skrocki did not share Novak's doubts; he was "absolutely" confident in the case his office had put together.

"Even without the dogs, it was still a strong case," Skrocki said. "We saw the dog evidence as the tipping point."

Unlike the Della Brown case, there was, this time, forensic evidence connecting Joshua Wade to the victim. His DNA had been discovered on the steering wheel of Mindy's car; two pubic hairs belonging to Joshua Wade had been discovered on the living room carpet of Mindy's home. There was also Wade's coat, found with an ATM receipt displaying a $500 withdrawal. There was the backpack turned over by Christina Greaser and Wade's cell phone with the photos of him holding the .45 Glock handgun that matched the bullet casing found near Mindy's body. ATM surveillance footage showed a man dressed with clothes resembling Wade's; and the gold Seiko watch found in Wade's home had been identified by Mindy's friends as belonging to her. A family member would later confirm the watch was a family heirloom.

****

In July of 2009, prosecutors filed documents with the court demonstrating that Wade was making threats of violence against potential witnesses in his case. In one letter written by Wade, and intercepted by jail officials, Wade related to a friend on the outside the address of a person whom Wade considered a "major suspect of being a lying rat in my case," though just who that was isn't clear in the documents. Jail officials also intercepted a book sent to Wade in jail, entitled *Hacksaw: The True Story of America's Greatest Escape Artist*. The book detailed one convict's repeated escapes from more than a dozen jails and prisons. Prosecutors did not disclose who had sent Wade the book.

Of greatest interest to prosecutors was a blue Mead notebook found in Wade's jail cell, in which he had written a short story. The entry was dated "Nine-nine-O-Seven," exactly one week after his arrest. The story, which had gone through a couple of drafts, was told from the perspective of someone running from a captor or captors. The chase scene ended with descriptions of tear gas and "deafening explosions" that rendered the narrator unconscious. The story abruptly ended with the narrator waking:

Before I can even begin to gain vision, I am being ripped from my bed and tossed to the ground ... arms stretched behind my back and legs pulled up behind me so oddly angled I thought they'd snap ... then the burning pain from the zip ties being put on way too tight ...

Eerily, some of the final details of the first-person account seemed to parallel reality; Mindy was apparently asleep when Wade broke into her house and he later restrained her with zip ties around her wrists and ankles. Prosecutors seized the notebook as potential evidence.

Wade would have to wait months to learn that prosecutors did, in fact, plan to pursue the death penalty against him. Dying by lethal injection was clearly something Wade wanted to avoid; so the fact it was on the table gave prosecutors the leverage they needed to cut a plea deal. If Wade would plead guilty to the murder of Mindy Schloss and admit, despite the "not guilty" verdict, he had killed Della Brown, the government would take the death penalty off the table. Wade would have to plead guilty in both state and federal court to Mindy's murder and also have to agree to spend the rest of his life in prison, without the possibility of parole.

FORTY-FOUR

On February 17, 2010, just one month shy of his thirtieth birthday, Wade pleaded guilty in both state and federal court to the murder of Mindy Schloss. Sentencing was scheduled in both courts on the same day, first, in state court, where Superior Court Judge Philip Volland asked Wade a number of questions to make sure he understood the terms of the plea agreement.

"Do you understand the nature of this state court charge, including the maximum penalty from murder in the first degree, which has a sentence of ninety-nine years and potentially restriction on parole eligibility? Do you understand that?"

"Yes sir."

"Do you need any more time to think about the plea you're about to enter?"

"Absolutely not."

"Count one and the information filed yesterday charges you with murder in the first degree in the death of Mindy Schloss. As to that charge, how do you plea this morning?"

"I plead guilty."

"And did you murder Della Brown, Mr. Wade?"

"I am admitting to the murder, and to the murder alone, of Della Brown, Your Honor."

Hearing this, Daisy Piggott broke down and began sobbing.

"In signing this agreement, Mr. Wade, you acknowledge

that this state will not make any representations or promises regarding the facilities at which you may serve your sentence. Do you understand?"

"Yes, Your Honor."

"You also recognize that the recommended sentence in this case is ninety-nine years with the restriction on your eligibility for discretionary parole. Do you understand that? And that means, Mr. Wade, that you would serve sixty-six years in prison as a minimum. Do you understand that?"

"Yes, Your Honor."

Assistant Attorney General John Novak then introduced a number of friends and family members who wished to address the court, beginning with Bob Conway.

"Your Honor, John Wayne once said, 'Life is tough, it's even tougher if you're stupid,'" Conway began. "The parasite that brought us all here together today has made life tough on an awful lot of people. Della Brown and Mindy Schloss were taken from this world under the most brutal and violent terms imaginable. That had to be incredibly tough on both of them. This whole ordeal has been tough on the families and friends of both of these women. The fear and mistrust that his acts have spread through this whole community have been tough. It was also very tough on me. I was lucky to meet Mindy in 1978 in Seattle. In 1980, we moved to Alaska to pursue our dreams. I went into the construction industry, and Mindy got her nursing degree at UAA.[73] Mindy worked most of her career in public health traveling almost the entire state. She went on to earn another three degrees: a master's in public health from Johns Hopkins, an advanced nurse practitioner degree in adult nursing and the psychiatric degree. She did a lot to help people less fortunate than herself and to have her dream cut short by stupid actions and for cash machine withdrawals, it's a tough way to go. I do not

---

73 The University of Alaska Anchorage.

have the words to describe what it's like when someone you love is all of a sudden missing without a trace. Or what it is like after my friend, Jeff Roskelley, found her car out at the air freight terminal. To go crawling through the Dumpsters in the area, looking for her body. I have to tell you, that was a tough six weeks. I was actually relieved when Detective Perrenoud came to my house at 11:00 p.m. that night to tell me they found her body. I thought things were going to get a little better until I realized that this was far from over."

Conway sighed and his voice began to tremble. "Because of the nature of the crimes carried out by this defendant, it took one and a half years to run all the forensic tests and to get Mindy's remains cremated and then scattered in the Mediterranean. That was way beyond tough. So Your Honor, I'm here looking for some justice. I'm hoping that this court can do everything possible under the laws to make this defendant's life as tough as possible. He's not tough enough to face a trial and the chance of getting the death penalty, and that would be too easy for him. I will sleep better knowing that once this idiot is in the general population in prison that he will understand what 'tougher' is. This defendant will get a trial by his peers who are in prison with him, and I hope to hell he feels the fear he has inflicted on others. He was the tough guy to commit two murders, but something tells me, there's going to be some guys who are a lot tougher. Thank you, Your Honor."

Gerri Yett then stood up and addressed the court. "Your Honor, it's difficult to put into words the impact that Mindy Schloss's death has had on my life. I personally have gone through many phases of grieving. I've lost a woman who was like a sister to me and my best friend. Whatever the outcome of this trial, I can never replace the loss of Mindy in my life. I cannot even really begin to express in words the emotions I am feeling. As I tried to write this statement, I was flooded with memories of the times we spent together. As I mentally reviewed many fond, warm memories, oh how the tears flowed.

"Mindy was a very special person who was always there for the people she loved. She loved me and my children unconditionally, and that feeling was mutually reciprocated by our family. The bond that Mindy shared, or the bond that I shared with Mindy, grew stronger through the years."

Gerri explained that Mindy had a chronic kidney disease, and that not long before her death she underwent a ten-hour surgery to remove thirty cysts from her kidneys.

"I spent a week with Mindy in Seattle as her private duty nurse. These surgeries were done for palliative care and never resolved Mindy's condition. She often worked with a high level of pain, but she never complained about her own health issues, continuing to work as a nurse practitioner and trying to help others."

Gerri said that Mindy had helped her through several personal crises. In 2001, when Gerri was struggling to complete her master's thesis in nursing while working full-time, Mindy cheered her on, providing constant encouragement. When Gerri was close to giving up, Mindy gave Gerri a candle with the inscription, "Make a Miracle."

"We lit the candle and laughed. Within a few weeks, I successfully finished my thesis and I graduated.

"So what have the last two years been like for me? Very few people can imagine. The first few days after Mindy's disappearance, I spent many, many hours reviewing information while being interviewed by the Anchorage Police Department and the FBI. As time progressed, my intuition told me that Mindy was dead. But I didn't want to believe it. And we couldn't confirm that without finding her body. Again, I lit the 'Make a Miracle' candle Mindy had given me, and I prayed daily for her return."

After Mindy's body was discovered, Gerri said, is when the true nightmare began.

"Because I loved Mindy so much, I couldn't walk away from my responsibility to do anything that would help to lead to the conviction of the person who did this. During this time, I have struggled to assure that my activities to assist with the investigation have not compromised my ability and integrity to maintain my devotion to my family, friends, and career. I have remained in weekly therapy for two and half years, still trying to deal with the ongoing nightmares and grieving process for Mindy.

"So far, I've talked about the past and the present. Now, I want to touch on how the loss of my dearest friend will affect the future." Gerri began to cry. "We will never have the opportunity to experience the dreams we shared. We talked about traveling together and writing our memoirs. I promised her I would always be there to take care of her in her old age, and she promised to do the same for me. She will never again travel with my family and share adventurous family moments or see my children grow up. Your Honor, my biggest impact so far is that when I have a hard day and life gets a little overwhelming, Mindy can no longer reach out and comfort me and say, 'It's all okay, Gerri, tomorrow will be better. You're not alone. I'll always be here for you.'"

Daisy Piggott was too emotionally fragile to address the court. Her son, Kenneth Piggott, stood up and read from a statement Daisy had written.

"I'm reading for my mother. These are her words," he began. "Your Honor, thank you for the opportunity to speak. When I learned of the death of Mindy Schloss, it was just another tragedy to me, until it was discovered that Mr. Wade was the suspect. It's a terrible loss because it has reopened wounds that were created ten years ago by him taking the life of my daughter, Della Marie Brown. It feels like salt is being poured into these wounds. I used to cry, and I still do sometimes. Unfortunately now anger is a common response from the stress and grief I've carried for so long. I've been in counseling and therapy since 2004, I've been diagnosed with post-traumatic stress disorder. It is time for the defendant to carry the guilt now."

In her statement, Daisy described her bouts with depression, admitting she sometimes couldn't muster the strength to leave the house.

"I sometimes can't even get out to go grocery shopping. My family has suffered all these years. I was placed on multiple medications that made me a different person. I didn't realize that I had changed, until one of my children pointed it out to me. Della left behind two children: Robert and Nora. Nora has two children of her own, and Nora has said it's sad they will never have the chance to meet or bond with Della. Before I close I would like to thank Robert Conway and Mindy's friends and family for thinking of me and embracing us through this time. We deeply appreciate it. Also thanks to the FBI and the investigators in the United States Attorney's Office for their efforts for bringing the case to this point. I think it's important that the defendant remains in jail till his last days so that no one else is harmed and no one else will ever have to go through we've endured."

Della's son, Robert, now in his late twenties, stood up and addressed the court.

"It's kind of hard to follow that. I didn't have anything prepared. I've thought about this for a long time. It's been ten years. You know, it's had quite the impact on me. The last couple of weeks, since I heard this trial was coming up, I tried to sit down and write and figure out what I was going to say because I didn't want to draw a blank. It's really done a number on me. It's nothing you could never get over. Something you learn to live with. I think the hardest thing is watching my family and seeing the impact this [has] had on them. I guess I can say I'm glad this is over. I'm tired. I'm just glad it's over."

Della's little sister, Keenak Feldt, was next to speak. She was just ten years old when Della was killed, and now, ten years later, she was a young woman.

"I am the baby sister of Della Marie Brown. I had met my sister when I was a little girl. I could never forget her beautiful face. Every time she smiled at me, or played with my hair, and the times we stayed awake to watch scary movies together."

Keenak described learning of Della's death and having to move from New Mexico to Alaska so her mother could attend the trial.

"Everybody in the family changed. I never thought Sissy would have been killed. It was really hard on me. That's when I got into the alcohol and drugs. After going to rehab I have learned to deal with my sister being gone. Joshua Wade was sentenced in 2003 for my Sissy. He was convicted of tampering with evidence. I could not believe it, but there was nothing I could do. He was back on the street by 2004. He got away with killing my sister. I was scared for my mom and I was also scared for myself, so I decided to move to Illinois. Shortly after I got to Illinois, my mom told me that Mindy Schloss was killed by Joshua Wade. Even though I didn't know Mindy, I cried so hard as if she was part of my family. I don't think anybody understands what Joshua Wade has done to us. Della's and Mindy's families, what we've had to go through. It is hard to say that we will never be able to see our loved ones again. Only in pictures. I don't even think that Joshua Wade understands or even cares what he has done. So I'm asking not only for me and my family, but also for Mindy's, that he spends the rest of his life in prison in Alaska. So my Sissy and Mindy can rest in peace."

Della Brown's older sister, Mary Montgomery, made a brief yet angry statement, speaking directly to Joshua Wade:

"What you took was very precious to me. A part of my life that could never be replaced. Joshua Wade, the wrath of God is upon you, you piece of shit for a human being!"

Della's brother, James Britten, addressed the court by phone from New Mexico.

"Since my sister no longer has a voice of her own I will be one of many who will speak on her behalf. Joshua Wade is a sexual predator and a murderer. He has taken a sister from me, a sister-in-law from my wife, and an aunt for my child. He has left a massive, empty hole in our hearts and lives. My family has had to deal with this nightmare and what Della was put through the night he took her life. The people of Alaska have had to deal with the thought of who might be the next victim. We were adjusting to life without Della when Joshua Wade committed another heinous murder. All of the grief and anger came flooding back. We feel like we will never have any sort of closure. He should never have been in a position to harm another person. Joshua Wade, he will never change. I ask you to do everything in your power to prevent him from harming another woman or their families again. It would be unconscionable and morally indefensible for anyone else to suffer as our family has suffered for the last many years."

Della Brown's sister, Gloria Durham, said she was angry at the jury for acquitting Wade of Della's murder.

"Maybe if they had served justice, Mindy Schloss would still be alive today. Now with the murder of Mindy, we are reliving nightmares and another family is going through a living hell. It is devastating to lose a family member in such a horrible manner. Yet to know Joshua Wade was not held accountable for the murder of my sister is more than anyone should have to live with. He had the opportunity to kill again. It's so sad, and a piece of my heart is gone. My whole family and I will never see Della again. She will never come back. We will never see her beautiful smile, hear her laugh, or speak with, or cry with, or have a holiday with Della again. Della will never see her grandchildren grow up, and they will never have a grandmother. Not only did he take my sister, he took my whole family.

"Our family moved to Alaska to try to make certain justice was achieved for Della. Yet Josh Wade got to live and kill again. He took her natural life on a whim that should've been God's will to decide when her life was done. Murder is so malicious, so cruel and so selfish. There is just no way to find balance. Your honor, I would ask you to impose the harshest sentence allowed by law with no chance of parole. Prison will be kinder to Joshua Wade than what my family and Mindy's family has to live with for the rest of our lives."

It was the defendant's turn to speak.

"If they will give me permission to talk, Your Honor," Wade said, gesturing toward the family members of his victims.

"I'm the person who gives permission," Judge Volland said.

"I'm not trying to be offensive, Your Honor. I'm not here to explain anything to you. I'm here to explain to them."

"You may do so," the judge said.

"In no way is what I'm going to read to you guys any form of excuse," Wade said, glancing down as his prepared statement. "I don't expect forgiveness from any of you. I don't deserve it. Today is not about me. It's about you and about my family. I don't want you to take it as any form of disrespect, but I don't address these women by name because I don't feel that I have the right to, and I think that would be a further insult to you if I spoke their names. So I won't. Again, anything I read and here is not a form of excuse. Maybe it will make you understand why I am who I am and what brought me to where those incidents took place." Wade's voice began to waver. "I don't think you believe me, but I am sincerely sorry for what I did. There's no excuse for it. I know I've made faces at you in court, and I apologize for that.

"I read in the newspaper [family members say] I'm only sorry that I got caught. Nobody commits a crime expecting or wanting to get caught. So I would initially say that I was sorry that I got caught. But then seeing how many people this has affected, my family included, my friends … I'm kind of glad I got caught. I know what my future is going to be now. And I hope to make the best of my life. I'm doing the rest of my life in prison. I'm asking all of you if you will listen to what I have to say. Can I please go on? The road to hell is paved with good intentions. That couldn't be a truer statement. I tripped and fell and decided not to get back up again. I was so busy feeding my codependency issues, but I lost sight of me. I totally dismissed the fact that God, for whatever reason, gave me a last chance at life. I let my family down and disappointed them again. Like a vast amount of others, I have had more people reach out and try to save me from me. I've had more opportunities to change the course of my life. But for reasons, even unknown to me, I chose the path of destruction and failure. I only hope for your forgiveness. But realistically I know that it's not likely. I deserve to suffer."

Wade referred to abuse he suffered as a young boy, sexually abused by a group of boys while he lived with his mother, before moving to Alaska.

"My mother did the best she knew how to. I wasn't raped at age five through seven because my mom was sleeping around or smoking crack or drinking. My abuse took place while I was trusted in someone else's care while my mother worked a man's job to support her kids. A single mother doing right. I chose not to deal with those issues, with those abuse issues, but instead to bury them and allow them to fester and build into a murderous rage. Which ultimately resulted in a lot of pain and suffering for others. No. I chose to be what I am. I'm not a product of a fucked up childhood or upbringing. I'm the product of one who decided not to overcome the past and succumbed to a fate that I created for myself."

Wade insisted he had never sexually abused anyone. Referring to his own abuse, he said, "Again, I could've risen above that but chose not to. But I can die knowing I never hurt anyone like I was hurt. Man, woman, or child.

"My doing life in prison will not give your loved one back, I'm sorry for that. But if it will be the cause of closure in this, then I've done the right thing. I'm guilty and I have killed people, but I don't leave the world. The free world is a ghost. In my life, I have also touched the hearts of many. Regardless of my actions, I am still a human being. A son, a brother, uncle, nephew, cousin, and a friend to many. And to those people, I also ask for forgiveness."

Wade concluded by saying, "Today is the first day of the rest of my life, and I go as a free man. I think you guys were way too kind to me with your statements. I deserve much worse. I'm sorry."

Judge Volland then delivered the sentence. "I sentence Mr. Wade to a term of ninety-nine years to serve. I specifically find, based on these two murders—that includes my recognition of his admission to Della Brown's homicide—that the normal principles of discretionary parole are insufficient to protect the public and rehabilitate the defendant and accordingly, under my power, I restrict the parole board's eligibility to grant discretionary parole at any time during Mr. Wade's incarceration. Accordingly, he must serve a fixed term of sixty-six years."

****

Later that afternoon, Wade faced sentencing in federal court. Many of the same family members made similar statements to the judge, urging him to impose the maximum penalty. Mindy's only living family member, her brother, William Schloss, sent a letter to the court, which was ready by Steve Skrocki:

"I will miss my sister greatly," the letter read. "Besides my wife and children, she was the only immediate family I have left. She was taken from me abruptly and nothing will ever be able to change that. We would see each other twice a year when she would visit my family and me in New York. She enjoyed being an aunt and doting over her niece and nephews, who also loved her very much. I regret not keeping in touch better between visits, and I will no longer have the opportunity to rectify that situation."

In his letter, William Schloss went on to explain that he was a Christian, and he invited Wade to "turn from [his] sin before it's too late." The letter ended with a direct appeal to Wade: "By God's grace, though I hate what you've done, I can love your soul enough to tell you of your need for Him. I pray that you listen to his voice."

Wade again, read his prepared statement to the court. When he finished, U.S. District Judge Ralph Beistline commended the families of Della Brown and Mindy Schloss for showing their strength and determination, and for "doing what Della and Mindy couldn't do for themselves."

"I suppose that even Joshua Wade deserves some credit for finally admitting his evil deeds. But what an evil thing he has done. What an evil person he became. I always tell people, you are what you do. And when I look, Mr. Wade, at what you've done over the course of the last decade, it speaks volumes, and it doesn't speak well of you. What kind of person could find pleasure in the random destruction of another human life? And what I see, what you've done is, become a heartless, selfish human being, and that's the truth. That doesn't mean you're not redeemable. That means you've become what you've done. We know that you are a coward by your attacks —"

"Don't push it, man," Wade interrupted, with a flash of anger in his eyes.

"I am going to push it," Judge Beistline said.

"Well, don't push it," Wade repeated. "First of all, I didn't come in here, apologizing to you, man."

"Okay," the judge said.

"I don't give a fuck about you," Wade said, now enraged. "I'm not here to say I'm sorry to you, man. I'm saying sorry to the people I've hurt and my family. I'm not saying sorry to you, so don't sit there and push it."

"So we know you're a coward by the fact you've killed defenseless women," the judge continued.

"What about the men?" Wade shot back.

Judge Beistline was taken aback. "I don't know. What … well, tell me about the men you've killed."

"Oh, don't sit there and act like I'm some predator on women, man," Wade said.

"I don't know about the men you've killed," Judge Beistline said. "I only know about the women. And I know they were defenseless. And I know that's the type of thing cowards do. We know that you're vulgar and depraved, and you've demonstrated that by your conduct during the last decade."

"Don't act like you fucking know me, man," Wade said.

"We know you are a liar and a thief and a bully and that you frequently have used drugs and alcohol. We know that you have no respect for authority."

"Your kids too," Wade interjected.

"We know that you have no respect for the law," the judge said. "We know that you're a danger and a threat to any civilized community."

"You too," Wade retorted.

"And we know that you are incapable of living among us. You can't be rehabilitated, and you can't be deterred.

"In contrast to you," the judge said, "let's talk about the victim in this case for a moment, Mindy Schloss. She was truly a good person. She was a bright spot on the earth. She was full of life. She was ambitious. She was engaged in new projects. She wanted to live, and she deserved to live. She loved people and was loved by people. She was a highly educated psychiatric nurse who spent her life in service. Some people in this life are takers and some are givers. Mindy Schloss was a giver. She would have likely helped you, Mr. Wade, had the opportunity presented itself. What right did you have to take her from her patients? What right did you have to take her from her family and her friends? What right? You're quick to claim due process rights for yourself. But you set yourself up as her judge, and as her jury, and as her executioner. You had no such right. And today, for the first time, I thought you were expressing remorse. That's not up for me to decide whether to believe you or not. I know you're an angry man. I know if you want, you can be well-spoken. I know if you want, you cannot be. You choose.

"I've tried other murder cases during my career," Judge Beistline said. "And I have dealt with some truly bad people; people who have had horrible and dysfunctional youths. But I have not encountered anyone as mean and as evil and as vile and as degenerate as you have become. So based on what I know, I would have had no difficulty imposing the death sentence, had the jury so found.

"But I also recognize the value of finality. And it is time to end this nightmare," the judge concluded. "And so here's the sentence. It is the judgment of the court that the defendant, Joshua Wade, is hereby committed to the custody of the Bureau of Prisons, to be imprisoned for a term of life without the possibility of release."

The judge offered one final thought. "This is just an observation. The anger that Mr. Wade has displayed here today is very revealing. It may have been the last thing that Mindy Schloss observed as well. So I think the community is safer by the fact that Mr. Wade will never see the light of day again."

PART FOUR: REGRETS

FORTY-FIVE

Mindy Schloss's murder brought with it renewed publicity of Della Brown's case and drew attention to the tragic mistake jurors had made letting Wade go.

"It was like I had killed her," a juror told a local newspaper. "I know that's an exaggeration. I know I didn't kill her. But I felt like I had a part in it, because we let him go."[74]

Even before Mindy Schloss's murder, the case had taken such a toll on many of the jurors in the Della Brown case, several of them decided to attend trauma counseling together after the trial was over. Anne Gore, one of the two alternates, organized the sessions.

"Because for me, not being able to process it through the deliberation process, you just have this shit in your head and it's crazy," Gore told me. "And I have a friend who does trauma counseling so I went to see her on my own, and she said that if you want to reach out to your other jurors and if there are any others who want to come in, I'm not going to charge you, just come in and we can group process this. And there were probably six or seven of us who went."

When she heard Wade had struck again, Gore said she was horrified but also felt relieved to have been an alternate.

"I know this sounds terrible, but I had such an instant feeling of relief that I was not part of the group that had to find him not guilty so that he was out again. I'm not trying to fault to my fellow jurors. Because I talked to the foreman

---

74 Quote in the *Anchorage Daily News*, February 17, 2010.

afterwards, and I said, 'Mike, I would have hung that jury.' And he just shook his head and he said, 'Anne, no you wouldn't have.' But never was I so relieved to not have been in the deliberation room."

As far as Wade's guilt was concerned, Gore said she had absolutely no sense of doubt, reasonable or otherwise.

"At the trial he, in my mind, seemed to convict himself as I just watched him over the course of three months. And really it was watching him while other people talked about him. When people would say things that made him seem afraid or nervous or less manly or something like that, it was an affront to him. You could see this look on his face that was just like—and I'm not going to throw out the cliché that it was a murderous look—but there was a look on his face and in his eyes that just spoke volumes to me. I had not one shred of doubt in my mind that he killed her. "

After Mindy Schloss's murder, the jurors in the Della Brown case faced public scrutiny and, still more than a decade later, many of them were unwilling to talk about the experience. However, in addition to Anne Gore, two other jurors spoke to me, and had opposing feelings about their decision to acquit Wade of Della Brown's murder.

Richard Hensel, now retired from civil service work at age eighty-five, told me that of course he regretted that Wade had murdered someone else, but he didn't at all regret the jury's decision.

"My regret was pretty much canceled out by the fact that the police work was sloppy and as a result of that, I voted my conscience," Hensel told me.

"Just to clarify," I asked, "Did you believe Wade was guilty, but the prosecution couldn't prove the case beyond a reasonable doubt?"

"Yes, that's correct," he replied. "To me, there was doubt."

Following our conversation, Hensel sent me an e-mail in which he was even more emphatic:

> Regarding the question who's to blame, obviously the police and prosecuting attorneys as well as the district attorney's decision to go forward even though there was conflicting evidence. Hell no, do I have any qualms about my decision of a 'not guilty' vote, the reason being that I followed the judge's instruction and had reason to doubt the prosecution.

A juror who helped manage her husband's business had quite a different reaction, saying she felt "duped" by Wade. She did not want me to use her name but spoke at length about the toll the case had taken on her personally:

> The trial lasted for a very long, drawn out few months and it took me even longer to get over it. Several jurors went for a session with a crisis counselor immediately following the trial. I was surprised at how many of us felt so traumatized by the whole ordeal. And then to find out a few years later that our decision allowed him to kill another woman was truly devastating.

The juror told me she wondered if the outcome might have been different if there had been at least one Alaska Native member of the jury and faulted the prosecution for not insisting on it during the jury selection process. She also faulted the attorneys who took over for Mary Anne Henry after she stepped down, saying they were "absolutely in over their heads" and that Wade's attorneys were "far more capable and simply did a better job." The juror added that at times in court, the behavior of the two prosecutors, Marcy McDannel and Keri Brady, was unprofessional.

"They'd put their heads together and giggle or whisper comments to each other, as if whatever was going on with a witness didn't warrant their attention," the juror recalled.

This is a complaint that was echoed to me by two jurors, several court spectators including Della's mother, and the defense attorney, Cindy Strout, who told me she agreed that McDannel and Brady's behavior was "completely unprofessional."

"I remember one instance where they were sort of talking at the bench and laughing at a moment that seemed pretty inappropriate," Anne Gore told me. "I don't remember what was potentially being discussed. But it really distracted many of the jurors, I know. To the degree that one of the other jurors, a woman, said, 'God, what are they laughing about? What is going on?'"

Della's half- brother, who listened in on most of the trial on a phone line from New Mexico, blamed McDannel and Brady for the trial's outcome, saying, "The attorneys lost the trial. He should've been put away after my sister's murder. Had they done what they were supposed to, no one else would have been hurt. That's the way I look at it."

Daisy Piggott referred to McDannel and Brady as "ding-a-lings" but contended the outcome wasn't entirely their fault. "I think the police investigation from the start was not a good investigation. I guess their thought was 'Oh well, it's just another Native woman who was drunk.'"

I wrote to Marcy McDannel and to Keri Brady to get their responses and to hear their thoughts about the case. After a few weeks, I received an e-mail message from Marcy McDannel that stopped me in my tracks:

I will talk to you about the case, but I'm starting a

murder trial and won't be available until mid-April. And by the way, Ms. Henry did not just have health problems but there were other issues that kept her from adequately investing the case, preparing for trial, and showing up for trial. These problems, my own lack of experience, along with the District Attorney's failure to provide adequate supervision, are what cost the state that case.

FORTY-SIX

When Mary Anne Henry stepped down from the Della Brown case after just one month, the DA's office told the Associated Press that she was doing so "due to persistent respiratory problems." Henry, who had made history in the late 1970s as the first woman to prosecute homicides in Alaska, suffered from asthma. In court, the jurors were given the explanation that "health problems" had made it impossible for her to continue. A line in an article in the *Anchorage Daily News* read:

> Neither Pat Gullufsen, chief of the state criminal division, nor Anchorage District Attorney Susan Parkes would say what is wrong with Henry, but she is known to have asthma and suffered a debilitating bout of pneumonia earlier this winter.

Henry died in 2011, so there was no way I could ask her about what ended her involvement in the case. She was just fifty-nine, and her obituary said she "suffered for years from asthma and died of liver failure due to chronic hepatitis, according to a close friend who was with her at the end."

When I finally reached Marcy McDannel, months after her initial message to me, she said she still felt guilty about what had happened with the Della Brown case so many years later. I could hear the pain in her voice. McDannel said that at the time she had only been prosecuting felony drug cases and it was her first time working on a homicide. She had come in to assist Ms. Henry just a few weeks before the trial began, hoping to learn from Henry's decades of experience prosecuting homicides, but right away, McDannel realized something was wrong.

"Mary Anne would call me after court, and she would be very emotional, sometimes slurring, and almost incoherent," McDannel recalled. McDannel acknowledged that she knew Mary Anne Henry had health problems and was probably also burned out at work, but McDannel also told me that Henry would occasionally show up to court smelling of alcohol.

"I remember prior to the actual trial starting, [Mary Anne] had taken off a bunch of time and was spending it all at home on the theory that she was preparing for the case. But it turns out, that's not what was happening, because the case was completely unprepared for trial."

McDannel said she was shocked to discover most of the evidence in the case had not even been tested by the time the trial was underway; they didn't even know if Wade's shoe prints, his DNA, or his fingerprints connected him to the crime scene. The defense, on the other hand, had spent two years preparing its case.

McDannel told me the responsibility of testing the evidence lies with the prosecutor assigned to the case, not the police. "The way it worked back then was the prosecutor was assigned to the case from its inception. You helped direct the investigation, you helped prepare the warrants, you interfaced with the crime lab and discussed what needed to be tested and how you wanted it tested. That was all Mary Anne's responsibility."

As McDannel struggled to get up to speed, she told me Ms. Henry's incoherent calls became more frequent and troublesome, and then one day, Henry failed to show up for court.

"We were in the middle of a witness, and it was a crucial day in court. She had called me the night before, and she was just incoherent. And I was like, 'Oh my God.' So the next day I show up to court. I think the court clerk said, 'Mary Anne called in sick so we are not having court today.' And I was like, 'Oh my God. I can't do this. This can't go on. It's ridiculous.' So I went back to the office, and I went into Susan Parkes's office and I said, 'This is a nightmare. You have to do something.'"

According to McDannel, Susan Parkes, who was the district attorney at the time, ultimately removed Henry from the case. Parkes would not tell me what had caused Henry's departure from the case, calling it a "confidential personnel matter" and that "both state and federal rules" prevented her from discussing it. There were, in the DA's office, attorneys with more than a dozen years' experience prosecuting homicide cases, but the decision was made to move McDannel into the "first chair" position and to name as her co-counsel, Keri Brady, who also had never tried a homicide case before. Parkes, who has since left the DA's office and has worked for Alyeska Pipeline Service Company since 2007, defended this decision in an e-mail to me, writing:

[Marcy McDannel] was the most knowledgeable and experienced attorney with the case that we had in the office. The question was who could be assigned to co-counsel it with her. We determined that Ms. Brady had the ability to drop everything else that she was working on (without doing harm to another victim's case) to devote all of her time to this case. We believed that she and Ms. McDannel would work well together and would make a strong team.

Keri Brady, who is still close friends with McDannel, told me she was on maternity leave at the time and that McDannel was venting to her about what was happening with Mary Anne Henry. Brady realized McDannel was struggling with the case, and so, in an effort to help her friend out, Brady made the decision to end her maternity leave early and return to work.

"Marcy was telling me what was going on, and I was getting more and more horrified about what was developing. I actually asked to be put on the case second chair because no one else was stepping up and I didn't want her over there all by herself doing it."

"So why didn't someone with more experience step up?" I asked Brady.

"Exactly," she replied. "Why *didn't* anyone step up? We were so stupid. We didn't realize that they had already decided that that case was a loser and it was on TV every night. You know what I mean? The 'Wade update' every night. And so, we didn't realize that [our superiors] had already decided that the case was going to be a highly publicized loser."

Susan Parkes conceded the case was going to be a tough one to win but disputed the notion that McDannel and Brady weren't up to the task:

With the benefit of hindsight, it is always easy to second-guess how a trial was conducted and decisions made in the heat of the battle. However, this was a very difficult case for the state to win under the best of circumstances. My recollection is that some of the state's most compelling evidence was suppressed by the court. Our "star" witnesses were all in the criminal milieu and impeachable to varying degrees. I believe that Ms. McDannel and Ms. Brady did a good job under difficult circumstances on behalf of the state.

Part of the reason McDannel and Brady looked back with such regret on the Della Brown case was that they both believed if one of the more experienced prosecutors in the office had been assigned to the case, perhaps the outcome would have been different.

"It's just so tragic, and it was so avoidable," McDannel told me. "All it took was, 'Let's put our best person on this case. Let's put our best prosecutors on this. Let's dedicate resources to this.'"

Although it was her first murder case, McDannel had six years' experience at the DA's office including one year in the drug unit. Brady had five years' experience, including one year as an intern. Parkes insisted that just because neither McDannel nor Brady had ever tried a homicide case before, it didn't mean they were unqualified:

The rules of evidence are the same in all cases. Frankly, if you surveyed prosecutors, I think that you would find that many would tell you that homicide cases as a rule are not necessarily the most difficult cases to prosecute.

There is no dispute, however, that the defense team was, in fact, much more experienced. During the jury's deliberations, an article in the *Anchorage Daily News* had been devoted to profiling Wade's defense counsel, with the headline: "Joshua Wade is very lucky in his lawyers, but will that be good enough?"

Mike Doogan, who authored the article, wrote, "[Jim McComas] has a reputation as a man who can turn dodgy defendants into free men," and went on to write that the prosecutors had been "outclassed" by the defense team.

"We got out-lawyered," Keri Brady told me. "And I'm not ashamed to admit that as a five-year-out lawyer that I got totally out-lawyered."

"Keri and I, you know, God, when I think back, that trial almost killed both of us," McDannel told me. "I mean, no sleep for months. Not only was the defense more experienced than us, they had this enormous head start on us. They were so prepared that they could just keep attacking us and keep filing motions, you know. We would come in every morning, and there would be some new preposterous motion on our desk waiting for us. And we were just trying to do stuff that should've been done before the jury was ever seated. We *really, really* tried. But in the end, we just couldn't pull it out."

I asked both McDannel and Brady about complaints I had heard from several court observers that at times in court they had acted unprofessionally. McDannel said she regretted the inappropriate banter, explaining it was a "survival mechanism." Brady was quick to admit she had made inappropriate comments to McDannel in court as a way of using humor to help them both diffuse the incredible amount of stress they were both feeling. She also chalked it up to their inexperience.

"We did not know that the mics were live all the time," she said, referring to the microphones on the counsel table. "We thought that if you were not on the record that the mics were not on. So we were idiots. Like I said, inexperienced attorneys. You just can't imagine what an incredibly stressful situation it was, and the only way I knew to sort of defuse things and make them bearable was to use humor. And that was always the sort of relationship we had. You know we would just laugh about what we didn't want to cry about."

I asked Brady what kinds of things she was whispering

to McDannel.

"If having to recollect exactly, it was just things like, 'Wow McComas really got us on that point. I hope next time he—an inappropriate reference to anal sex—us, we get to use the Vaseline, not the sand,'" Brady recalled. "But I don't think there was anything like that in front of the jury." Brady paused. "Did any jurors say anything like that to you?"

I told her two of the three jurors I had interviewed couldn't recall any specific comments but did remember inappropriate banter between her and McDannel during the trial.

"I didn't realize the jurors had heard anything like that," Brady said, lowering her voice.

FORTY-SEVEN

One thing that had struck me during the course of my reporting was that there was not one piece of evidence that tied Joshua Wade to the shed where Della Brown was killed. Clearly, he had gone in and out of the shed numerous times. Not only had he attacked and killed Della Brown, he had also moved her body, so it was surprising that there wasn't a fingerprint or, at the very least, a shoe print that could be traced back to him.

Wade himself also apparently found it surprising, telling KTVA in 2008, "[The police] found semen, a pubic hair, and a fingerprint, but it didn't match any of the 'rats' or their supposed suspect. The prosecutors didn't do their job. The cops didn't do their job. It's incompetence on their part. That's on them."

Brady told me the lack of any physical evidence tying Wade to the crime scene could be explained, at least in part, by the filthy conditions inside the shed. "It was a very difficult crime scene," Brady said. "If they would've put the resources into testing every single thing that was in there, could they have come up with something that tied Joshua Wade to the scene? Probably they could have."

McDannel and Brady told me the loss of the bloody knife as a piece of evidence was devastating to the state's case.

"It was the only piece of physical evidence that tied [Wade] to the crime scene, and so we were trying like hell to get it in," Brady recalled.

Brady and McDannel tried unsuccessfully to get the knife admitted into evidence late into the trial but were prevented from doing so by a previous stipulation agreed to by Mary Anne Henry. Henry was apparently concerned that the knife may have been illegally seized by police from Joshua Wade's bedroom, but McDannel said it was a mystery as to why Henry would agree to giving up such a crucial piece of evidence before the trial got underway.

"I can only speculate," McDannel said. "But at that point, I think she was just running scared. She had built Jim McComas up in her mind as some bogeyman and did whatever she could to avoid having to confront him."

Defense attorney Cindy Strout had a different recollection of the knife, calling it a "meaningless" piece of evidence. The defense had its own experts test the knife and found nothing of evidentiary value.[75]

Another significant loss for the state came before testimony even began, in the form of a jury instruction that required jurors to find that Joshua Wade had "personally killed" Della Brown. Jim McComas had come up with the wording, and McDannel and Brady later argued the phrasing implied that jurors would have to rule the murder was intentional.

"That was a big mistake," McDannel said. "We tried to get the judge to go back and correct it, but he wouldn't. And it was one of those mistakes that was born out of Keri and my inexperience, and the fact that by having to go into that case without time to prepare and to take over the mess left by Mary Anne, we were just beaten down by that point."

I asked Keri Brady how she looked back on the Della Brown case, given what happened later to Mindy Schloss.

---

75 The knife had been wiped, but there remained a small amount of blood on it which was tested for DNA. The tests could not exclude Della Brown but were also not conclusive.

There was a long pause.

"This is what I think ..." Brady began. I could tell she was getting choked up. "I'm proud of doing the right thing for the right reasons ..." She let out a big sigh. "I didn't expect to get emotional about that, hold on one second." She took a moment to gain her composure. "I asked to be let into something that everyone else could see was a complete train wreck that we weren't going to win. But that wasn't even an evaluation that I made. It didn't matter to me. It was the right thing to do. And I did the very best job I could do at the time. If I was a twenty-year attorney like I am now, and I got a chance to retry that case, I would do a much better job now. But I wasn't a twenty-year attorney. So I just think when you do the right thing for the right reasons and you do your very best, you have nothing to be ashamed of. You can only be proud of that, so I am."

McDannel was equally emotional when I asked her the same question.

"I know that haunts us both to this day. I mean, I can't fault myself for a lack of effort, but of course you still carry this guilt around like, 'God why couldn't I have prevented that somehow?'"

McDannel said there wasn't just one thing that she could point to that cost prosecutors the case.

"You know, it's just this whole cascade of errors. You can't single out just one, but it was just this really long, full cascade of errors that culminated in this ridiculously weak presentation to the jury."

McDannel then quizzed me about what the jurors had told me. I shared that one juror, who didn't want me to publish her name, said she still felt guilty about acquitting Wade.

"Can you give me the number of the woman who feels guilty?" she asked. I paused, a bit taken aback by the request.

"I know this is kind of weird," she said. "But personally, it still bothers me a lot. You can probably tell from talking to me that I still have some raw emotions about this."

I promised McDannel I would e-mail the juror on her behalf.

"I would just like to, on the behalf of the Anchorage District Attorney's Office, apologize to them," McDannel explained, referring to the jurors. "I think that they've been made scapegoats for all of the horrible decisions made by that office. And every time this comes up, it pains me. I almost feel like I should reach out to them personally and say, 'I'm so sorry. I tried, I really tried. I'm so sorry, but I want you to know it's not your fault. It's not your fault. We presented a shitty case.'"

McDannel said she has struggled with her own complicity in the outcome of the case for years.

"It was an impossible situation to be put in, but still, it's hard to walk away from that, especially knowing what a monster he is and that he was going to go kill poor Mindy."

FORTY-EIGHT

Much had gone wrong in the prosecution of Della Brown's murder, but it was unclear to me what role racism had played, if any, in the outcome of the trial. I could point to a number of missteps made by the state that appeared unintentional; at the same time, after almost a year of research into these cases, it was hard to ignore the fact that Wade wasn't convicted and put away until he murdered a middle-class professional white woman.

"Do you know what apartheid is?" Desa Jacobsson asked me, as we sat in a cafe one day, sipping coffee. "Well, it's alive and well here in Alaska."

Jacobsson insisted that we drive to Bean's Cafe, a soup kitchen in Anchorage's Ship Creek neighborhood. The area surrounding the cafe and an adjacent shelter, where most of the city's homeless dwell, lacks the bustle and sophistication of downtown, just a few blocks to the west, and retains the industrial feel of the Port of Anchorage, a short distance northwest, which ranks among the most productive fishing ports in the world. On that November afternoon, the temperature was just 18 degrees Fahrenheit, and I was shocked to see a few dozen people out on the streets, unfazed by the bitter cold. Unoccupied tents and sleeping bags lined the sidewalk, where many of them had apparently spent the night.

"Look at their faces," Jacobsson said. "These are the landowners!" She exclaimed, pointing excitedly. She repeated this phrase more than once, each time becoming more agitated. "The LANDOWNERS! The LAND-OWNERS!" she said raising her voice, her outrage so palpable I thought she might jump out of my rental car. It took me a minute to realize what she meant: the faces of the men and women outside the soup kitchen appeared to belong mostly to Alaska Natives. These indigenous people of the state, whose tribes once thrived on this vast, fertile landscape, had been relegated to living on the streets, and the very thought enraged her.

Jacobsson later explained to me that the intensity of her reaction had come from a general sense of injustice, but it was also personal. She said that much like Della Brown, she had survived sexual abuse during her childhood, and as an adult had become addicted to alcohol. Thirty years ago, she quit drinking and decided to devote the rest of her life to victim advocacy. For eight years, she worked in shelters for abused women and children in rural Alaska, seeing firsthand the prevalence of alcohol dependency in Native communities and the devastating effects of fetal alcohol syndrome on a whole new generation of Alaska Natives.

The condition, which results when a mother drinks during pregnancy, besets a child with a range of physical and mental defects such as low body weight, learning disabilities, and poor coordination. Researchers have found that those afflicted with FAS are more likely to drop out of school, end up in jail, and to end up themselves, addicted to alcohol or drugs. The statistics demonstrate nothing short of an epidemic of FAS among Alaska Natives; state health records show between 1995-1998, a staggering 40 percent of children born to Native Alaskan mothers were at risk of having FAS, dramatically outpacing any other ethnic group. (Only 2.7 percent of white mothers were at risk of having children with the condition.) Health officials in Alaska have since made great progress lowering the numbers, but Jacobsson explained that for a generation of Natives, the damage had already been done.

Later, when our conversation returned to Della Brown and the other women who had been killed, Jacobsson told me that she feared all her efforts to draw attention to the unsolved cases over the years, had been ineffective.

"They have been forgotten," she said, referring to the murdered women. "And the only reason they were remembered again, briefly, was because Wade killed again, and because Mindy was white."

Alaska has a history of discrimination against its Native people, mirrored in some ways by the prejudice faced by African Americans in the U.S. before the Civil Rights Movement. In the capital city of Juneau in the 1940s, it was not uncommon to see signs that read "No Dogs, No Natives" and "We serve to white trade only." There were "white only" sections at movie theaters, and Native children were forced into schools where their languages were neither taught nor understood. The state's earliest and perhaps most important civil rights figure, Elizabeth Peratrovich, herself an Alaska Native, founded a group called the Alaska Native Sisterhood and successfully lobbied the state government to ban the discriminatory signage in Juneau. Alaska Governor Ernest Gruening signed the Anti-Discrimination Act of 1945, which was the first law of its kind in U.S. history.

"Have you heard of the Paintball Attacks of 2001?" Jacobsson asked me. I shook my head.

"When you get home, Google it," she advised, assuring me that overt acts of racism in Alaska were not just from a bygone time.

A quick internet search revealed the story: On the night of January 14, 2001, three young white men in a car cruised the streets of downtown Anchorage with paintball guns in hand, videotaping their attack. The footage showed Alaska Natives flinching and shielding their faces as the young men opened fire, erupting in laughter each time they hit one of their targets. As *The New York Times* reported, the attacks appeared to be racially motivated:

> The youths, a 19-year-old and two younger teenagers, appeared to be looking for Eskimos. "Shoot him! Shoot him!" one voice on the tape said. "You need to shoot that guy." Another voice replied: "No. He's Chinese."

Some of the victims called police, relaying the car's license plate number. Detectives traced the vehicle to a home in a suburb of Anchorage, but citing a lack of evidence, they did not arrest the three young men until two months later. The Alaska House of Representatives would condemn the attack as a hate crime. The oldest of the assailants, a nineteen-year-Old, was sentenced to six months in jail.

****

Joshua Wade appeared to be motivated by a similar disdain for Alaska Natives.

"Some of it may be racially motivated," Bubba Wade told me, speculating about additional murders his son may have committed. "For some reason, he thought Mexicans and blacks were the cream of the crop or something, and he thought Natives were scum."

Not long after Wade was convicted of killing Mindy Schloss, Wade told KTVA that the jury that acquitted him of Della Brown's murder was right to do so, explaining, "All a trial is, is a show. And whoever puts on the best act wins. And so the justice system worked." During that same

ICE AND BONE

television interview, he explained what he had done to Della
Brown in the shed:

I walked on foot and I went back and I intended to
go check [Della Brown's] pockets. And when I went
back there, there was no one there. There was a cop
coming around the corner … and I've got warrants
for my arrest and I've got drugs on me, so I ducked
in [the shed] but when I was trying to get into the
shed, I hit the lady in the head pushing the door open.
So I went in, I didn't shut the door, because I was
watching the cop. But while I was trying to watch the
cop, these two people were in the shed having sex.
They started freaking out on me. I got mad. I freaked
out. I kicked the woman in her face because that's
where most of the noise coming from. I kicked her
in her face. The guy had gotten up and tried to do a
little wrestling with me, seeing that I was a little bit
bigger than him, and he tried running while pulling
his pants up. I grabbed him by his arm which I ended
up just getting a handful of shirt and he slipped out
of his shirt and he ran. That was the red shirt that
was in all the crime scene photos. That shows how
intelligent our cops are up here. He left her behind.
And she wouldn't stop making noise. And he ran one
way, away from the direction the cop was. And he
wasn't making any noise, so I didn't go after him. So
I stayed hidden, and I ended up beating her to death.

Detectives finally had an explanation for the "mystery
suspect" Wade's attorneys had talked so much about during
the trial. The man who had left his DNA behind at the crime
scene, as well as a red T-shirt, was not a suspect as the

defense had argued, but rather, a man who had escaped the grips of a killer. Or had he? In 2014, almost fifteen years after Della Brown's murder, Wade would tell the FBI the exact same story, with one important modification. This time, the "mystery man" in the scenario didn't escape but was another victim who had apparently died at the hands of Joshua Wade.

PART FIVE:
A SERIAL KILLER
REVEALED

FORTY-NINE

Television reporter Andrea Gusty knew that viewers frequently called the newsroom at her station, the CBS affiliate in Anchorage, to pitch stories about vast conspiracies and UFOs, but when the assignment manager told her that Joshua Wade was on the line from jail, she couldn't resist taking the call. Wade had just been arrested for the murder of Mindy Schloss, and at least, Andrea reasoned, if someone was impersonating a murderer, the caller deserved credit for being timely.

"I was skeptical about whether it really was Josh," Andrea told me. "But you know, in the course of talking to him, we decided to set up a time so I could go meet him in person, in jail."

Andrea was young and ambitious, an Alaska Native who had attended the prestigious Medill School of Journalism at Northwestern University and after graduation had returned to Alaska to become KTVA's investigative reporter. Nicely coiffed, young, and brunette, Andrea approached her job with a tenacity many other reporters lacked. Andrea thought she and Wade would be separated by a pane of glass when they met face-to-face, but instead, when she arrived at the Anchorage jail, a guard escorted her to a room reserved for meetings between inmates and their attorneys. The room had a stainless steel table and chairs bolted to the floor and a window that looked out onto a hallway where she could she could see another guard who was standing watch.

Andrea was a bit thrown off by the setup. It was not what she had pictured in her mind, and she had come alone, without a photographer. She tried to hide her uneasiness when an overweight guard escorted Wade into the room and removed Wade's handcuffs. Wade sat down and then, to Andrea's surprise, the guard left her alone in the room with Wade, closing the door behind him.

"You know, that tub of lard," Wade said, referring to the guard. "It would take him a while to get back in here."

"Yep, it would," Andrea agreed, laughing nervously. She knew Wade was trying to rattle her, and she was determined not to let him have the satisfaction. She forged ahead with her questions, but Wade refused to divulge details about his cases during their first meeting. Mindy's body had not yet been found, and prosecutors had not yet charged him with her murder, so he was circumspect. Wade was in solitary confinement and had spent countless hours working on drawings of women in various poses, which he shared with Andrea, along with some court documents he had brought into the room.

"He had made threats to other inmates, which is why he was in solitary, so he wasn't happy about being alone," Andrea said. "And [he complained about] eating Cup-a-Soup, I remember that. He said he ate so much Cup-a-Soup."

Although he initially withheld information, a year later, a day after pleading guilty to Mindy's murder, Wade divulged details about his crimes during an on-camera interview with Andrea, inside the Anchorage jail. Andrea's only stipulation was that everything was on the table; she could ask him any question she liked.

When a guard escorted Wade into the room where the interview was to take place, Andrea could tell Wade had gained weight since their last visit. He had a much bulkier appearance compared to a year earlier; his skin was pale, and he had a crew cut and a goatee. Once the lighting was set up and the camera was rolling, Andrea began the hour-long interview by asking Wade why he had snapped during his sentencing in federal court.

"We saw two different sides of you yesterday," Andrea told Wade. "One was remorseful, the other was angry at the judge."

"I am a murderer. I do have a temper," Wade replied.

"Which one is the real you?"

"They are both a part of me. That's me. That is all me. I mean, you are a productive member of society. You get mad, too. You just react differently. So, this is just who I am. But I plan to better myself with how I react to my anger. Cause I'm not trying to do the rest of my life in the hole."[76]

Wade explained that he became angry when the judge called him a "coward" and portrayed him as a predator of women.

"I don't like the fact that people think I prey on women," Wade said. "I don't discriminate. I'm not going to harm a child. Certain situations have come up in my life that have resulted in these two women dying at my hands. I did not plan it. I did not hunt these people down."

Wade insisted that he broke into Mindy Schloss's house unaware that she was home.

"I didn't go in there with a gun. I didn't go in there with a mask. I went in there with a duffel bag to steal stuff and somebody was there. I did whatever I could to restrain the person. I went back to my house to get everything because the person came out of the room and saw my face. And I fought with myself right then, saying, 'Just run,' and I did not run. So in that, I did the cowardly thing because at that point, I could have ran but I didn't. And it resulted in me taking a life."

---

76 "The hole" is a reference to being in solitary confinement.

"Is there anything either [Della Brown or Mindy Schloss] could have said or done to make the outcome different? Or were you just in a blind rage?"

"I wasn't mad at any point in this case," Wade replied, referring to Mindy Schloss. "I talked to the woman, and she talked to me. The only intelligent thing the judge said was that she was the type of woman who probably would've helped me if she knew I needed help. I know that beyond a doubt."

Wade said that at one point, he asked Mindy if she had any friends in Anchorage, and she told him that she did.

"I said, 'I want you to call one of them and get them over here, and I'm going to hold them while you go to your bank and empty your bank account.' Because I was just trying to find ways to get out of the state and leave. And without hesitation she told me she would never do that to someone she cared about. She wouldn't endanger anyone she cared about. I have nothing but respect for that. Regardless of the situation, that lady treated me nice."

Wade appeared to be tearing up. "The worst thing about it all is, was when we got out there," he said, referring to the wooded area in Wasilla where Mindy's body had been found. "I was putting her under the impression that I was taking her out there to abandon her, so I could get a good head start run. I don't know if she believed that. As far as me physically torturing this woman, it never happened. I don't know what was going on in her mind, and I don't know if the ride from Anchorage to out there, that was probably torture. But when we got out there, I was going to walk her into the woods and I was going to place a gag in her mouth. And I had asked her, 'Open your mouth,' and she hesitated. This is the only time she got agitated, and she said, 'Why are you doing that?' I think that's when she realized she wasn't going to come out. I told her, 'I don't want you screaming for help while I'm trying to get back to Anchorage.' And she reiterated that she would give me money and that she would do it, without bringing anyone else into it. But if my mind was made up, she forgave me."

Wade became emotional. "That really took me aback. I just wanted to run and get away from it. I don't deserve her forgiveness. I don't. But that is the only thing that has haunted me since I've been locked up. It haunted me until I got arrested. After she said that, she listened to me and I put the gag in her mouth and I directed her into the woods. I put a bullet into the chamber of the gun as quietly as I could, because I didn't want her to hear it. I told her to stop at one point, and then I told her to kneel down. She looked at me, and I explained, 'Kneel down so I can zip tie your ankles so you don't run while I am trying to get back to Anchorage.' So she did, and the moment that she kneeled down and both knees touched the ground, I shot her in the back of the head. At that point, I went back to the car and got charcoal fluid that I found when I was walking around originally back there to find a place to do it, and I caught her body on fire."

As Wade described the sequence of events, Andrea could see the smallest amount of emotion in his eyes.

"Did you take her out there knowing that you were going to kill her?" she asked.

"Yes."

In contrast, Wade claimed Della Brown's murder was not premeditated.

"She was minding her own business. Finding pleasure outside of her abusive relationship with her boyfriend," Wade said. "I was in the wrong place at the wrong time. In that case, I was in a place I had no right to be."

"You said that you don't discriminate against women," Andrea began, before Wade interrupted her.

"What I meant is ... and I'm not trying to be a smart ass.

I'm not trying to brag, boast, or anything, I'm just saying if a situation was to come to me … can I say cuss words?"

"You can say anything," Andrea replied.

"I'm not going to hurt a kid, but other than that I don't discriminate. I am in jail because two accidents occurred. I think I have enough intelligence where if it was something intentional, I wouldn't have gotten caught. What kind of idiot goes and murders their neighbor?"

"You pled guilty to two murders," Andrea said.

"I pled guilty to one and *admitted* to one," Wade said, correcting her.

"Are there more people that you've killed that we don't know about?"

"I think everybody knows that I did a lot of bad stuff, and that's all I'm going to say."

"Did you kill anyone else?" Andrea asked.

"No comment."

****

KTVA's news director decided to cut Andrea's hour-long interview with Wade down to just a few minutes, excluding details about the killings that might have offended or disturbed the victims' families. The uncut interview was widely circulated among law enforcement, however, and viewed by both Anchorage police and the FBI.[77]

Although she found the interview chilling, Detective Perrenoud thought Wade's assertion that Mindy had offered him her forgiveness was doubtful.

"I don't believe that for one second," Detective Perrenoud told me. "I don't believe she would forgive him, I mean, why would she forgive him?" Detective Perrenoud postulated

---

[77] Even though he was already sentenced for the crime, KTVA's jailhouse interview with Wade is now considered evidence in the federal case against him.

that Wade had fabricated some of the details of Mindy's abduction and murder, including his insistence that he had no idea Mindy was home when he broke into her house.

"All of that is crap. It just didn't happen that way," Detective Perrenoud said. "He went in there knowing she was home and knowing what he was going to do to her. I don't know if he knew he was going to kill her, maybe just sexually assault her and take her stuff. But he knew she was home, there's no doubt about that."

Detective Perrenoud also found Wade's apparent display of emotion thoroughly unconvincing.

"I don't think he has any remorse at all. None."

FIFTY

During the summer of 2014, Wade struck a deal with prosecutors. He claimed he was being mistreated in prison, and in exchange for a transfer to a federal prison in Indiana, Wade admitted to three additional murders. The victims were all men and, apparently, the same victims to whom he was referring in court on the day of his sentencing: thirty-eight-year-old John Michael Martin, thirty-year-old Henry Ongtowasruk, and an unidentified man Wade said he killed the same night as Della Brown.

Wade claimed he was just fourteen years old when he killed his first victim, John Michael Martin. An unemployed schizophrenic, Martin was gunned down along a bike trail, killed with a single gunshot to the back of his head, and his unexplained murder had baffled Anchorage police for more than two decades. On May 11, 1994, Martin came to the Village Inn restaurant on Northern Lights Boulevard, ordered coffee and a meal, then left to walk home, just after two o'clock in the morning. Douglass Foster, who managed the restaurant and who coincidentally had once employed Wade's wife Lisa Andrews, described Martin as a frequent customer and a "nice guy" with "hair down to his ears and parted in the middle." Foster told police that no one followed Martin out of the restaurant, and that he left alone. Less than an hour later, a passing motorist who happened to be an off-duty paramedic, found Martin's body about a quarter-mile from the Village Inn.

Wade's older sister, Mandy Huson, told me that in 2014 Wade had explained to her in further detail the circumstances that led him to kill Martin. According to the story, Bubba Wade was withholding food from his fourteen-year-old son, and the younger Wade was out on the streets in the middle of the night, looking for something to eat.

"This guy would apparently help people," Mandy said of Martin. "I think the guy was like, 'Hey come with me,' and Josh said that he got the creeps from him. I think he thought the guy was just a creep or a pervert or something. At some point, he ended up behind the guy … and he shot him."

Despite being a man of very little means, Martin was a generous person. In his obituary, Martin's family said:

> John had a generous heart and would give the shirt off his back to anyone in a less fortunate situation. He loved camping, hiking, fishing, and loved to share his love for the outdoors with friends and family. His abhorrence of violence on personal and societal levels was in direct contrast to the manner in which he was killed, by a random act of violence when a trigger-happy gunman took his life.

Five years after killing Martin, Wade claimed, he took the life of Henry Ongtowasruk. A maintenance worker at the Alaska Budget Motel in Fairview had discovered the thirty-year-old man's strangled and brutalized body in room 221 of the motel. Like Martin, Ongtowasruk was mentally ill and received financial support from the state. In an interview with radio station KNOM, Ongtowasruk's mother, Arlene Soxie, expressed her shock to hear that Wade had confessed to killing her son during a botched robbery.

"It was like he died all over again," Soxie told KNOM's

Matthew Smith. Soxie was angry to learn that Wade had used his confession as a bargaining chip to get out of Alaska, and she was disappointed that Wade would apparently not face charges for her son's murder, given that Wade was already serving a life sentence.

"It seems like the law is for the people who have committed the crime and not for the family members who are left suffering," Soxie told the radio station.

****

Agent Jolene Goeden was given the task of hearing Wade's confession to the additional murders. During their interview, Wade had explained to Agent Goeden in detail why he killed a third man, on the same night he had killed Della Brown.

"He said he went into the shed to avoid police," Agent Goeden recalled. "And when he got into the shed, a fight ensued because he pushed his way into the shed." Agent Goeden said Wade claimed the man was having sex with Della Brown and that upon interrupting their intercourse, Wade began to fight with them.

"During the fight, Della is hit to the point where he thinks she may have died. So then, he goes after the guy in order to kill him, to cover up what he had done to Della."

Wade went on to claim to Agent Goeden that he had knocked the man unconscious, placed him in the trunk of a car, and taken him to a location in Wasilla, near the same spot Wade had killed Mindy Schloss. There, Wade claimed, he shot and killed the man and disposed of his body.

Wade called KTVA, and in a recorded phone interview, explained that at some point during the drive to Wasilla, the man had regained consciousness and began "thumping around" in the trunk. Wade claimed that he had pulled over the car and "stomped" on the man's head to quiet him; he killed him once they reached Wasilla.

"I found a spot, took the guy out, took his clothes off, and shot him in the head two times with a shotgun and pretty much took everything from the shoulders up," he told KTVA.

Wade divulged the location of the alleged murder, but the FBI did a thorough search of the area and did not find evidence of a homicide. Investigators also examined dozens of reports of missing people but never were able to identify a possible victim.

Despite admitting to the carnage, Wade said that he didn't view himself as a serial killer.

"Absolutely not," Wade said. "People need to quit reading books."[78]

More than a few people agreed with Wade's assessment of himself, that he was *not* a serial killer and conjectured that he was making up stories about the additional killings simply to manipulate law enforcement.

Sheila Toomey, a veteran reporter for the *Anchorage Daily News* who is now retired, told me there was reason to doubt Wade's most recent claims.

"Was he a serial killer? I don't think so. Obviously, he's a sociopath. But serial killers are crazy psychopaths. He didn't think things through, you know?"

Toomey spent decades on the court beat in Anchorage and had covered extensively the case of bona fide serial killer Robert Hansen; she also was well acquainted with Joshua Wade. In fact, it was her front page article about the killings of six women in 2000 that was used by the FBI to illicit a reaction, and ultimately, a confession from Wade in the Della Brown case. Toomey told me she didn't think Wade fit the same profile as Hansen. I asked her if she thought Wade

---

78 Wade made this comment to KTVA during a phone interview broadcast on June 20, 2014.

had committed any of the additional killings to which he had had confessed, and she said she thought it was probably just braggadocio. Then she paused. "I can't be sure. On the other hand, what he did with Mindy's body suggests more of a depravity," she said.

"Every time we came across something about Mr. Wade saying he murdered someone, we would try to track that down," Assistant U.S. Attorney Steven Skrocki said. "He made statements about 'I killed this person or that person,' and there's no way for us to verify it. He has a degree of wanting to be self-important, a high degree of needing attention, and a very high degree of insecurity, which folds into the need for attention. He's also quite manipulative."

"Do you think he's a serial killer?" I asked Skrocki.

"Define serial killer," he countered.

"I would say someone who's killed multiple victims. Someone who borders on psychopathic, has no remorse, picks random victims who are vulnerable and does it for the thrill of killing," I offered.

"He's opportunistic, in my opinion."

"What do you mean by that?" I asked.

"That if the circumstances are available, and they warrant it, then he's capable of killing people. Is he a serial killer as compared to the Zodiac Killer or Israel Keyes? He's not of that caliber. If he's angry enough, needs enough, then he would take a life. Would he do it as a pattern or a lifestyle choice? I don't see that."

Israel Keyes was a serial killer whose murderous rampage ended in Anchorage, after committing a series of killings across the United States. Keyes kidnapped his last known victim, eighteen-year-old Samantha Koenig, in 2012 from *Common Grounds*, one of the dozens of shack-like espresso stands in Anchorage, where she worked as a barista. Haunting surveillance footage showed the abduction as Keyes escorted the teen girl from her workplace to his pickup truck. He later sexually assaulted her, strangled her, and eventually dumped her dismembered body in Matanuska Lake, thirty miles northeast of Anchorage. In all, Keyes confessed to murdering eleven people. He committed suicide in his jail cell in December of 2012.

Agent Goeden, who worked the Israel Keyes case and interviewed both Keyes and Wade about their crimes, told me that Keyes was more cold and calculating.

"Keyes was very methodical, very planned out," Agent Goeden said. "He didn't do anything without thinking and planning, and that's how he got away with it for so many years. Wade is very spontaneous. Anger is a big thing for him, and he'll react. That isn't Keyes. Keyes might become really angry, but he's not going to act out. He's going to wait."

"So Keyes is clearly a psychopath," I said. "Do you think Wade is also on that spectrum somewhere?"

"I think he is," she affirmed. "He's definitely antisocial, which is a whole part of that. He's definitely, definitely there. But [Keyes and Wade] are very different. Wade made a lot of mistakes, even back to the Della Brown case. Unfortunately, he was found not guilty in that case, but he made a number of mistakes, where Keyes wouldn't have. The other thing I noticed with Wade, there's still an element of emotion with him. Of humanness, I guess. I didn't see that with Keyes."

"You think Wade has more humanity in him?" I asked.

"Granted, I'm well aware that some of that can be manipulative with Wade, but he showed a lot of emotion at his sentencing. He was apologizing, and whether there was any true remorse I don't know, but there was a lot of emotion there. And that was never the case with Keyes. Even in talking with Wade regarding the additional three homicides, there was also emotion tied to that. So when I say kind of a 'humanness' that's what I mean."

"Is Wade a serial killer?" I asked.

"By definition he's a serial killer," she replied.

"So he definitely killed five people, in your mind?"

"He's definitely responsible for the deaths of four to five people," Goeden replied, explaining that they've never been able to identify the male victim who was allegedly in the shed with Della Brown. "Wade had information that was specific to one homicide that he would not have had any other way, and he could have just admitted to one and not three additional homicides. So I walked away from that pretty confident he was responsible."

FIFTY-ONE

Wade's father, Greg "Bubba" Wade, eventually moved to Bremerton, Washington, across the Puget Sound from Seattle. A professional cartoonist, Bubba maintained an active presence online as the purveyor of an internet business called "Bubba's Toone Tees and Gifts." The website's logo featured a headshot of Bubba himself at the center of a series of rainbow-colored circles with bubble lettering, evoking the "Looney Toons" cartoons. In the photograph, Bubba has long, white hair and an equally long, white beard. He is sporting round, John Lennon-style glasses, and a cigar is dangling from his mouth.

The comic strip artwork on T-shirts and other products feature Bubba's original designs and depict a number of characters, including versions of himself, often seen riding a Harley-Davidson motorcycle and wearing a top hat decorated with the stars and stripes of the American flag. His line of products also include caricatures of politicians: former Alaskan Governor and vice presidential candidate Sarah Palin holding a shotgun; disgraced former Illinois Governor Rod Blagojevich in prison clothes; and President Obama, featured in the most negative of terms. An ongoing series called "The Adventures of Curious 'O' and 'Ranger Joe'" depict President Obama and Vice President Joe Biden, who, according to the website, were "wandering the world on bended knee, kissing the asses of terrorists, thieves, and others we've fought, bled for and freed." On one T-shirt,

President Obama appears as the devil himself, with red horns coming out of his ears and "Beelzebub" written over his head, along with the numbers "666."

On his YouTube page, Bubba posted a montage of photos from his son's murder trial with the song "Bridge" by Queensryche playing in the background. The last verse in the song ends with the following lyrics:

You say, "Son, let's forget the past.

I want another chance, gonna make it last."

You're begging me for a brand new start,

Trying to mend a bridge that's been blown apart,

But you know you never built it, Dad.

Bubba replied to my e-mail requesting an interview, saying, "I'll agree. ... However, I want a hard copy of whatever it is you print or publish." I agreed, and I booked a flight to Seattle for the following week. As soon as I arrived, I called Bubba, and he suggested that we meet the following day, at a dive bar in Bremerton called Brother Don's.

I arrived early at the bar and it was mostly empty. I found a table at the back, where I figured we would have some privacy, and I ordered a Diet Coke. Fifteen minutes later, hearing a commotion, I glanced up and saw an overweight man approaching in a motorized wheelchair, plowing past empty tables and chairs. A small brown dog was riding on his lap.

"Are you Mr. Wade?" I asked.

"Yeah," he replied, avoiding the usual pleasantries.

"And what's your dog's name?" I asked.

"This is Frodo," he said, stroking the small terrier mix.

Bubba had on a striped gray and white conductor's cap; his beard was white with small flecks of brown, and he stroked it occasionally as we talked. At 400 pounds, however, his most striking feature was his size. He often shifted back and forth in his wheelchair during our conversation and winced in pain, explaining that his back and hips were "shot." Bubba said that after his son's conviction, he had spiraled down into a deep depression and, at his worst point, had reached a weight of 600 pounds.

"I was suffocating. To save my life, they gave me a tracheotomy," Bubba said.

"What caused the weight gain?" I asked.

"I was literally eating my depression. Just eating it," he replied. As he said this, Frodo climbed up on his chest and started licking his face.

"I've been trying to stay healthy. I was going to the gym all the time, but then I had people harassing me about my dog," Wade said. He suddenly became emotional and started to sob. Once he had composed himself, I explained that I was looking into the unsolved cases of the women who were murdered around the time of Della Brown's death.

"Some dad I was," Bubba remarked. "My son came to me about midnight when this stuff happened and told me he killed someone. But he told me he killed some guy, and it was someone who ratted on him or some bullshit like that."

"You mean the night Della Brown was killed?"

"Right. Well, I didn't believe it for one thing. I was kinda drunk. Anyways … um … I thought he was just lying, but I told him that if he did anything he better make sure that person …" Bubba paused. "If they're still alive, he should go back and call an ambulance and make sure that somebody comes out there to help them. Or you better make sure that nobody can ever tell that you were there. Right? Well, apparently, they didn't even find DNA in my car or

anything. And I will always feel horrible for that, because
another person lost their life."

Bubba explained that he and his ex-wife, Catherine,
had divorced in 1987 after ten years of marriage, when Josh
was seven years old. Bubba moved to Anchorage in 1991,
leaving his ex-wife and two children, Josh and Mandy, in
Seattle. Josh had severe behavioral problems, and in 1993
Bubba's ex-wife called him to say that their son, who was
thirteen at the time, was coming to live in Alaska.

"It was either me or she was going to give him to a home
or something." Bubba's voice wavered. "I wanted him to be
with me, and I did the best I could. But you can't support
someone on a bouncer's wages, working evenings and stuff
like that. And you know, I couldn't leave him alone. Like, I
went for a welding job and he snuck out of my apartment,
and I'd wake up and he'd be gone. So I ended up going back
to selling drugs. Because I thought at least I'd be around,
you know? But that ends up not being true either, because
then I'm out having to run around to sell drugs."

Bubba admitted to his vast failings as a parent but said he
was shocked to learn how he had been portrayed by his son's
attorneys during the Mindy Schloss case. Defense attorney
Gilbert Levy had painted a bleak and tragic picture of Josh's
childhood during the sentencing hearing in federal court and
placed much of the blame at the elder Wade's feet.

"Josh was always extremely close to his father, and at
age five Josh's father abandoned him," Levy told the court.
"Josh would wait at the front door, at the window, for his
father to appear. He'd fall asleep waiting for his father, but
his father never came."

Before their parents' divorce, Levy said, Josh and
his sister had witnessed terrible acts of domestic violence
committed by their father.

"Josh and his sister were forced to watch Mr. Wade stick

a gun in their mother's face, stick a gun in her mouth," Levy claimed.

Levy said Bubba was a neglectful parent and a drug dealer who not only tolerated but "may have encouraged his twelve-year-old son's use of drugs."

"Greg Wade's method of discipline with his son was to deprive him of food," Levy said. "Josh was forced to scavenge in the garbage for his meals. On many occasions at age twelve, thirteen, and fourteen, Josh was forced to live on the streets."

Bubba claimed defense attorneys had told him not to attend any of his son's court proceedings, which is why he seldom showed up to the hearings.

"Now I know why, because of all the things they were going to say. They were being all nicey-nice and buddy-buddy when they wanted to interview me for the trial and I was very honest with them. And they turned everything I said around, and they rearranged it to fit their own needs."

Bubba admitted to me, however, many of the allegations were true, although he claimed that Levy had taken the facts out of context.

"I'd tell Josh, 'Get up and clean the house,' and he'd say, 'Fuck that, I'm not going to do it,'" Bubba recalled. "Then I'd say, 'Then I'm not going to feed you.' How long do you think that would last? You know what I mean? But for them to say Josh had to fend for himself, to dig through the garbage, that's just horseshit."

"Did he ever live on the streets?" I asked.

"The times he was on the streets, it was by his choice," Bubba said. "He was always allowed to come home. It was his choice not to be there. Because when he was gone, I was trying to get him to come home. I love my son."

I asked Bubba if he had put a gun into his ex-wife's mouth as his children watched.

"That's true. They saw me," he replied, matter-of-factly. Bubba explained that at the time, he had discovered that Catherine was having an affair, so he had asked her to pick him up from work. When she arrived, Josh and Mandy, who were just six and eight years old at the time, were in the backseat of the car.

"I ended up sticking a gun in her mouth and making her drive me out to where this guy lived at. I went out there and beat the hell out of him in his own bed. Somebody dared to screw around with my wife knowing who the hell I am? But yeah, they saw me stick the gun in her mouth."

Bubba denied he had ever encouraged his son's use of drugs but said by the age of sixteen, Josh was stealing from his stash.

"He took things from me and went out and made money from it or generated an income for himself. That's how Josh thinks: he's going to take from other people and he just does whatever he wants with the proceeds. The same thing he did with that Schloss lady, you know, he went out and bought fucking bandanas and some bullshit rap CDs with her money, you know?"[79]

Bubba's large, round face narrowed and streams of tears rolled down his cheeks.

"I would do anything to …" His voice trailed off and he began to sob. Frodo, the small terrier perched on his lap, again leaped onto his chest and began gently licking his tears.

"It must be painful," I offered, not sure what to say. We sat for a few moments, not speaking, and as Bubba cried, Elvis Presley's "Jailhouse Rock" played softly in the background.

****

---

79 In the backpack turned over to police by Christina Greaser, police found receipts for various items such as CDs and bandanas, apparently purchased by Wade with Mindy's cash.

Aware that Josh had attempted suicide at age ten by drowning himself in a bathtub, Bubba said he always worried that Josh would try to hurt himself again. When Josh reached his early teens, however, Bubba began to notice that Josh was focusing his violent tendencies on others, rather than himself.

"I found out he had done some home invasions and cut people up with a machete. He threatened a friend of mine in front of me one time, and I grabbed him by his neck, and I'm a pretty strong guy, and I had him by his neck against the wall, and I told him never to speak to someone like that again."

Bubba also recalled that as a teen, Josh was obsessed with "Faces of Death," a 1978 film that depicted various ways to die. The film, which was banned in several countries, included actual footage of gruesome acts of violence. Josh also would draw cartoons that Bubba interpreted as fantasies Josh had about murdering him.

"He would draw rabbits and stuff like that, being violent. Like one of the rabbits would be a heavy rabbit with long hair that he'd murdered. I think the reason he never tried to actually do something to me is that he was afraid I'd wake up and I'd finish him," Bubba said, chuckling.

During the Della Brown murder trial, several witnesses testified that Bubba had told his son to hide the rock Josh had used to kill Della Brown. I asked Bubba what exactly he had told his son.

"I didn't know what [the weapon] was. I told him to get rid … I told him if there was anything to prove that you were there … to get rid of it."

Given that his son had confessed to him that he had committed a murder, I asked Bubba why he didn't testify.

"They tried to get me to testify, and I was more concerned about my drug business and all that other shit and what it was going to do to me. So I went in and pled the Fifth so I didn't have to testify.[80] And that's something else that keeps me up at night. Had I testified, the chances are he would have been convicted, and then Mindy Schloss never would have happened."

"What do you think about these admissions he's made recently?" I asked, referring to the murders of the three men to which Wade had confessed.

"You know what? I'm more suspicious about other women [victims] than other men," Bubba replied.

"Why is that?" I asked.

"Both of these women look a lot like his mother," Bubba said, postulating that his son had an unexplained fixation on maternal figures.

"You mean Della Brown and Mindy Schloss?"

"Yeah," Bubba replied. "His mom is half Mexican, and both of these women had dark curly hair just like his mother does. I mean, they're not exact replicas, but they ... you know what I'm saying? He didn't kill some big fat guy. Why'd he kill two women?" Bubba claimed that Lisa Andrews, whom Josh had married in jail, was not only close in age to Josh's mother, Catherine, but that she also resembled her.

"And these guys he fuckin' killed, it sounds more like an anger thing," Bubba said.

"Do you see any kind of remorse in your son?" I asked.

"Nope. The only thing I see from him is regret that he got caught."

"Do you have any contact with him anymore?"

"I've written to him, and he won't respond. I thought if there was any way I could get to see him ... but ... I'm sorry man." Bubba shifted forward in his chair and winced in pain, explaining that his hips hurt. "I'd like to have some

---

80 "Pleading the Fifth" is a reference to the Fifth Amendment of the U.S. Constitution, which protects an individual from self-incrimination.

kind of relationship with him and find something of my son in there."

"Do you think he's a serial killer?" I asked.

"Absolutely. He's the prime suspect for one … because he looks so meek to a lot of people. He's like the wolf that's in the sheep's clothing." Bubba paused. "I mean, I could see that I could have been the same way."

"Really?" I responded, taken aback.

"Oh yeah."

"Why do you think that?"

"I don't know, because sometimes I wonder if it's something you inherit." Bubba's voice wavered. "Because I know that there's … a specific coldness about myself. The way I could react to people. But I always believed there's a higher power in life, and the punishment for that is going to be far worse than whatever thing I'm going to get away with here. Josh doesn't have that trigger. I don't think he believes in anything. What Josh has done, it's completely senseless. He shot that poor woman in the back of her head. She would have done nothing to hurt him. You know? Over a fucking credit card."

Bubba paused, seeming to be deep in thought. "He had another friend of his, a black kid who was supposed to have killed himself. Now I wonder if he had something to do with that, too."

Bubba told me he had given up drug dealing, and was now focused on his artwork. Even though he was struggling financially, he said, "I'm trying to be a better person. I wish you could get a do-over in this life. I'd sure change a lot of things. If I put the effort into my family that I put into a lot of other stupid shit, things might have turned out differently for everybody."

Bubba thanked me and later told me that our conversation had been therapeutic. He was also adamant that I donate some of the book proceeds to a victims' charity, and was pleased when I said I planned to do so.

"I just want to see something good to come from it," Bubba said. "I don't know what's going on with this current shit. Like I said, I've got suspicions that there would be more women that Josh killed."

FIFTY-TWO

The contemporary understanding of the term *serial killer* can be traced to the work of FBI Special Agent Robert K. Ressler, who is credited with coining the term. During his career, Ressler conducted face-to-face interviews with Jeffrey Dahmer, Ted Bundy and John Wayne Gacy, studied the backgrounds of dozens of such killers for his research, and developed a list of characteristics he used to distinguish an everyday murderer from those certifiable few he felt stood in a class of their own.

Writer Harold Schechter summarized Ressler's work and listed several main qualities shared by serial killers in his book, *The Serial Killer Files.* While Joshua Wade did not fit the profile of the cold, unfeeling psychopath like Israel Keyes did, Wade had many of the qualities on Schechter's list.

"[Most serial killers] are single white men," Schechter wrote, who "tend to be smart, with a mean IQ of 'bright normal'… [and] despite their intelligence, they do poorly in school, have spotty employment records, and generally end up as unskilled workers."

Despite his uncontrollable temper, Joshua Wade had been described as intelligent by almost all of the law enforcement sources I had interviewed. Wade also had an impressive talent for art, but he was not a strong student and had worked a number of jobs that involved hard labor.

"They come from deeply troubled families," Schechter

went on to write. "Typically, they have been abandoned at an early age by their fathers and grow up in broken homes dominated by their mothers."

By all accounts, Wade's family was deeply troubled. He had, indeed, been abandoned by his father at a young age and had grown up in a household in which his mother was the main authority figure.

"There is a long history of psychiatric problems, criminal behavior, and alcoholism in their families," Schechter observed. "They manifest psychiatric problems at an early age and often spend time in institutions as children." Schechter explained that most serial killers also felt suicidal as teenagers.

Wade had grown up in a criminal environment; his father was a drug dealer, and the younger Wade had brushes with the law that began during his adolescence. Wade's attorney during the federal proceedings, Gilbert Levy, said Wade was "deeply troubled" as a child and had attempted suicide at age ten, after which he spent three months in a psychiatric hospital in Washington.

"When he got out of the hospital, he never received any counseling or any kind of ongoing treatment," Levy said in his statement to the court.

Just after moving to Alaska at age thirteen, Wade was admitted to a psychiatric hospital again, this time for "mutilating himself," Levy explained. "There were two or three other drug treatment hospitalizations and mental health hospitalizations that followed that. In each case, the caretakers recommended Josh for long-term care. Instead, Josh went back to the custody of his father, the drug dealer, Greg Wade."

Schechter also posited that most serial killers had suffered "significant abuse," most often sexual in nature. Joshua Wade says between the ages of five and seven he was repeatedly raped by a group of neighborhood boys, while his mother was at work.

"[The abuse] was never reported to the police. Josh never got any help. He never got any therapy. He never got any treatment for what happened to him, and his trust was taken away as a very young child," Levy said.

Wade spoke about the abuse during his interview with Andrea Gusty, recalling, "I didn't want to talk about it. I figured if I could just bury it, at seven or eight years old, you know, I'm thinking if I can just bury it, it will just go away eventually."

"Such brutal mistreatment instills [most serial killers] with profound feelings of humiliation and helplessness," Schechter concluded.

Serial killers, Schechter wrote, also "display a precocious and abiding interest in deviant sexuality and are obsessed with fetishism, voyeurism, and violent pornography."

In addition to his drawings, which suggested an interest in violent sexuality, Wade also had a history of voyeurism. "He would prowl into people's houses while they were sleeping," Bubba Wade recalled. In 1996 when Joshua Wade was just sixteen years old, a woman named Rosemary Clark reported to Anchorage police that someone appeared to be spying on her in her room at the Royal Suites Lodge. Upon seeing a small camera dangling outside her window, Clark slid the window shut, trapping the camera inside her room, and she promptly called the front desk. A hotel employee, in turn, had called police. When police arrived at the hotel, an officer observed the remote camera still hanging by a cord that led to the room directly above Clark's, where Greg "Bubba" Wade had been staying with his son. When confronted, the teenaged Wade claimed the camera was a thermometer but later admitted he had lowered the camera from above because he had "heard strange sounds coming from downstairs."[81]

That same year, Wade also faced accusations that he had molested a six-year-old girl. The girl's mother had hired the teenaged Wade to babysit at the behest of Bubba Wade, who lived across the street and who told her his son needed to earn some money. Wade babysat the girl twice, and after the second time the girl told her mother Wade had touched her inappropriately. Prosecutors outlined the girl's accusations in a sentencing memorandum filed during the Della Brown murder trial. The girl is referred to by the initials E.M.:

Wade came into the bedroom after she went to bed. E.M. stated that she pretended to be asleep. Wade nudged her, and when she did not appear to awaken, E.M. felt him touch his tongue to hers. E.M. demonstrated for Officer Logan how she was positioned in the bed and how her mouth was partially open. After Wade touched her tongue, she moved about and closed her mouth, still pretending to be asleep. She waited for Wade to leave the room, but he did not. E.M. [later] awoke to feeling Wade's hand pressing on her right hip. The blankets had been pulled off of her, and her nightgown had been pulled up to reveal her nipples. E.M. reported that Wade's hand was pressing down on her hip. His thumb was positioned toward her back, his fingers were curved around and down toward her vagina. According to E.M., Wade's fingers touched her vagina but did not penetrate her. E.M. heard someone at the door. Wade did too; he got up and left the room.

When the girl's mother arrived home from work at 2:30

---

81 This quote is taken from a sentencing memorandum filed during the Della Brown murder trial.

a.m., Wade asked her if the girl ever had nightmares or if she ever talked in her sleep, claiming that the six-year-old had yelled his name during the night. The woman found the question and comment strange, and the next day, when Wade came by the house, a sad expression came over the girl's face. After Wade left, the girl's mother asked her what was wrong.

"Is Josh coming back to babysit me?" the girl asked.

"No," her mother replied. "Why?"

"Because I felt another tongue," the girl replied. After hearing her daughter's full account of what had happened, the woman confronted Bubba with her daughter's allegations and later called the police. Bubba told me he had pressured the woman not to press charges.

"I intimidated her into not reporting it ... thinking that he didn't do it. And now I feel so fucking bad."

"Because now you think he did it?" I asked Bubba.

"Yeah," he replied.

Included in the police report was an illustration Joshua Wade had drawn while babysitting the girl. The drawing, which he had left behind, showed a man holding a mallet in one hand and a gun in the other. Apparently repulsed by Wade's presence and what he had done to her, the six-year-old had scribbled out much of the drawing and written the word "NO" repeatedly on the page:

****

In his character study of serial killers, Harold Schechter referred to an ongoing "resentment toward [the killers'] distant, absent or abusive fathers," which contributed to "trouble with male authority figures." Since his incarceration, Wade had expressed disdain for his father, and in his interview with Andrea Gusty, he seemed to erase Bubba from the family portrait altogether, listing only his sister, mother, and stepfather as members of his immediate family. Wade's ongoing problem with male authority figures was well-established throughout his life, and most obviously evidenced by his frequent outbursts in court, his ire frequently aimed squarely at the ultimate male authority figure in the room.

Schechter also cited a "powerful hostility toward women" exhibited by most serial killers, which came as a result of being "dominated by their mothers." Wade's hostility toward women was evident, but it was unclear whether he had been dominated by his mother. Wade's mother, Catherine Davi, had largely been absent from his adult life. She was remarried and had other children and, as of 2015, still lived in suburban Seattle. I tracked her down online and sent her a Facebook message explaining who I was and that I was working on a book about several cases that involved her son. I apologized for the intrusion and asked if she would be willing to talk to me. Her response was as curt as it was clear: "NOT EVEN INTERESTED!!!!"

****

There was only one other person, aside from Wade himself, who could provide the insight I was seeking: Wade's older sister, Mandy Huson. Mandy was reticent to talk with me at first, but after months of exchanging e-mail and Facebook messages, she finally agreed to an interview. We spoke on the phone during one of her twenty-four-hour shifts at an adult family home in the Seattle area, where she worked as a caretaker. Part of her apprehension in talking to me, she explained, involved her fear that I would portray her as someone who didn't support her brother.

"No matter what, I love my brother and that is never going to change. I don't agree with the decisions that he's made in his life, but he is my brother and I do remember good things about him. I don't see him as a monster."

Mandy, a thoughtful and intelligent person, did not describe their mother as a domineering figure, rather as a divorced alcoholic struggling to raise her children.

"There was a time when my mom was a good mom. I have fond memories of her being really creative during holidays with my brother and me, really memorable stuff. But then everything changed."

Mandy described a tumultuous childhood and a fractured

home life in which both she and her brother had suffered greatly. Things had not started out that way, however. Bubba and Catherine Wade were devout Mormons living in San Diego when Mandy was born on August 4, 1978. Two years later, the family moved to Great Falls, Montana, where Bubba was employed as a security officer at Malmstrom Air Force Base. Shortly after arriving in Great Falls, on March 18, 1980, Catherine gave birth to Joshua. The family did not stay in Montana for long, soon returning to San Diego where Bubba got a job as an officer for the San Diego Humane Society.

"Though I love animals, I just did not see a life writing people up for pet infractions or felony pet offenses over the next twenty years," Bubba recalled in an essay he wrote, outlining his occupational and personal history. Bubba decided to relocate the family again, this time to Silverdale, Washington, where he found a job as a security officer. Bubba was subsequently fired from that job, eventually finding employment as a bouncer at a nightclub called Chugwaters.

Mandy told me that by this time her parents were no longer involved with the Mormon church. Surrounded by the culture of drugs and alcohol, Bubba began to deal drugs and to have multiple affairs with women he encountered at the nightclub.

"That's when he just changed. He turned into a different person completely," Mandy recalled of her father. Mandy said her mother also had been unfaithful and had slept with a man with whom she worked at a wood mill, and that she had become pregnant with the man's baby.

"When my dad found out, right in front of my brother and me, he put a gun to her head and kicked her in the stomach," Mandy recalled. Catherine returned to San Diego with Josh and Mandy, moved in with her in-laws, and carried the baby to term. Apparently unable to financially care for another child, she gave the girl up for adoption.

"I watched my mom be pregnant, go the hospital, and then not come home with a baby," Mandy said. "It was extremely traumatizing for both me and Josh. She told us that she was putting the baby up for adoption, and it was really hard."

The best friend of Bubba's sister adopted the girl, but Mandy said she and Josh were expecting to welcome a new member to their family and were both devastated by their separation from their half-sister.

"I remember as kids, Josh and I were crying and hugging and staring out the window and looking at her baby picture. It was terrible."

"You know, I've got this photo of Josh and me when we were little," Mandy reflected. "You look at that picture and you look at both of us and it looks like we have got the weight of the world on our shoulders. It's a really sad picture."

Mandy later e-mailed me the photo, which showed her, at age five, sitting quietly in the grass, wearing a hooded sweatshirt. Josh, who was three, was sitting next to her, wearing a plaid button-down shirt, his arms crossed over his knees. Neither child is looking at the camera but rather staring off into the distance, their faces each reflecting a silent anguish that seemed far beyond their years.[82]

"Just the look in our eyes. We were so young. Life just looked rough. It looked hard in that picture. It just goes to show the kind of childhood that we had, and it's unfortunate, because our childhood was taken away from us. We didn't have a childhood," Mandy said, choking up. "It was unfair, how we were raised."

---

82 The childhood photo Mandy Huson referred to appears in the photo insert in this book.

****

After a decade of marriage, Bubba and Catherine divorced in 1987, and in 1991, Bubba relocated to Alaska, where he found work as a deckhand and cook aboard a commercial fishing boat. Faced with the prospect of single motherhood, Mandy recalled, her mother, who had an alcohol problem, essentially gave up trying to raise her children.

"She partied a lot after we got back from California, and she pretty much just … she couldn't control either one of us," Mandy said. "So she was kind of just out doing her own thing. She put us in a lot of really bad situations."

Mandy recalled going to dance clubs at the age of twelve and running away from home on numerous occasions. It was during this same period that Wade had been repeatedly abused and raped by a group of neighborhood boys. Wade had defended his mother during his interview with Andrea Gusty, claiming that the abuse had happened "while she was out working a man's job to support her family."

Mandy said her mother remains in contact with Josh, and that she struggles with feelings of guilt about what he has done.

"I think she feels responsible. I think she wonders if there was something she could have done to help him. She blames herself for not being a good mom, and of course it's devastating for her. Her son is a murderer."

Reflecting on Josh's childhood, Mandy then added, "I know that my mom had reached out for help, and she didn't know what to do. I remember my mom begging a social worker to help her because she didn't know what to do with him."

"Because he was so out of control?" I asked.

"Yeah, and he really needed help. And it's unfortunate that Josh is where he is, because if he had received some help sooner, or at any point, maybe none of this would have turned out like it has."

Mandy recalled a few good memories of her brother during our conversation, such as playing with him in the mud and laughing when they were young. She also recalled physical fights with him growing up—the usual kind of tussling siblings did—but remembered that once he had come after her with a knife. I asked Mandy when she noticed something was psychologically wrong with her brother.

"Josh was always troubled. He wasn't right. He needed help. He's always had anger problems. I don't know. Like I said, we had a hard life. He just dealt with it totally differently."

Mandy has never been in trouble with the law, is a married mother of three, and has spent her professional life caring for the elderly. I asked her how she accounted for the vast difference between herself and her brother, given they had grown up in the same environment.

"You know, I wonder the same thing," she replied. "For a long time it really messed with my head, because I thought, gosh, if he's capable of that am I capable of that?"

"I guess what I'm asking is if you think it is something innate," I said. "Was it something that was always inside of him, or was it something that was formed by his environment?"

"I think it was both," Mandy said. "I think a lot of it had to do with our childhood, and I think as far as the environment, I think that just made the whole situation worse."

PART SIX:
REASONABLE
SPECULATION

FIFTY-THREE

It is still a mystery to this day who killed three of the six women who were named in that front page article in the *Anchorage Daily News* on September 28, 2000. The families of Vera Hapoff, Annie Mann, and Michelle Foster Butler have spent years wondering who would have so cruelly taken them from this world, leaving no trace as to why.

Police had always considered Wade a suspect in some of the women's deaths, although investigators had never made public their specific suspicions, nor said for certain to which cases they had reason to connect Wade. Fifteen years later, Anchorage police were not forthcoming with updates on the cases or with even the most basic information. After repeated phone calls and e-mails over a series of weeks, the head of the department's homicide unit, Sergeant Slawomir Markiewicz, finally agreed to meet with me.

Known to everyone by his nickname "Slav," Markiewicz was a twenty-five-year veteran of the police force, handsome and affable, a Polish immigrant who came to the U.S. in the 1980s and whose English retained the slightest Polish accent. I had written down dozens of questions to ask him, but once in a conference room at the Anchorage police station, Markiewicz politely explained that he couldn't say much if anything about the unsolved cases because they were still technically "open investigations."

"As we sit here today, do you have any reason to believe Wade is responsible for the murders of Vera Hapoff, Annie

Mann, or Michelle Foster Butler?" I asked.

"Well ... uh ... I ... we don't have any evidence," Sergeant Markiewicz replied, letting out a long sigh. "And if we did ... I wouldn't talk about it until the case is solved. So it's really difficult."

Markiewicz said he had not personally worked on any of the unsolved cases but added the detectives who did never found evidence to connect Wade to the women's murders.

"That doesn't mean he didn't to do it," Markiewicz said. "Just at that time, that there was no evidence, and there wasn't enough to charge anyone."

The body of twenty-six-year-old Vera Hapoff had been discovered in Ship Creek in June of 1999, and at first, police thought her death was a simple drowning. However, when an autopsy revealed injuries that may have indicated an assault, homicide detectives were assigned to the case.

"There were some injuries on her that were ... they thought, maybe not because she had drowned. But she was lodged in the dam, so there could have been some injuries from that," Sergeant Markiewicz explained.

Annie Mann, forty-five, was found murdered on August 8, 1999, behind a building on Post Road. Markiewicz refused to say how Mann had been killed and a description on the Anchorage Crime Stoppers website provided few details:

Mann was a Native woman, 5-foot-1 and 100 pounds, wearing green pants, a purple jacket and a gray T-shirt with the word "Hawaii" on the front.

While Sergeant Markiewicz would not tell me of which killings Wade had initially been suspected, I found buried deep in thousands of pages of court documents a lab order requesting a comparison of DNA. The "Request for Laboratory Services" was dated October 24, 2000, and stated that a sample of spermatozoa had been recovered from Mann's body during an autopsy. Lab technicians were to compare the sample to the known DNA profile of Joshua Wade. Detective Mark Huelskoetter, who submitted the report, wrote:

> Joshua Wade was arrested in connection with a homicide in which information was obtained that he may be involved in more than one murder, possibly including this case.

In addition to Della Brown's murder, Mann's killing would account for two of the three homicides to which Wade had referred on the Beckett/Troxel police wire:

> **Wade:** There's only three on here, man. They ain't got shit on me! Motherfuckers trying to put extra shit on me!

Later in the recording, however, Wade admitted to keeping newspaper clippings about some of the women, and he made clear the identity of the third woman, Michelle Foster Butler, the only victim who was African American:

> **Wade:** I got plenty of newspaper clippings. I got this bitch's newspaper clippings and this bitch's newspapers.
>
> **Beckett:** What?
>
> **Wade:** No, not that bitch.
>
> **Beckett:** All those bitches? You did all those bitches?

Wade: These bitches and those bitch.

Beckett: Those are all you, right there? Man, what's up with you and Native women?

Wade: She was black, man.

Michelle Foster Butler was a graceful woman with an ebullient personality, magnetic smile, and she always looked her best. She applied this same careful attention to her daughter and two sons.

"She always dressed me in pink and did my hair," Jelila Abdul Bassit recalled with fondness. Jelila, who was just fourteen when her mother was killed, excelled at basketball, and as the only girl in a family of boys, she wanted to be like her dad and brothers.

"I would come home with grass stains from playing sports, and she tried her best to keep me a little girl. Everybody who knew my mom loved her. She was the cool mom in the neighborhood. All my friends always wanted to spend time at our house."

Michelle Foster Butler's husband, Claude Butler, was a local sports legend who had gone on to play Division I basketball at the University of New Orleans in the 1980s. Known to local sports fans by his nickname, "Muff" Butler, he later returned to Anchorage where he coached basketball and ran a janitorial business. When I reached Butler and expressed an interest in his wife's case, he agreed to meet me at a local coffee house. Butler, a towering man both in stature and personality, was candid and amiable, and I was surprised when he told me he had spent a considerable time in jail for dealing drugs. He was behind bars, in fact, when his wife was killed, and months later, Butler said, he had an encounter with Wade inside the Cook Inlet Pretrial Facility.

"I was in the holding cell, and Joshua Wade came up to

my cell and said to me, 'Man, I didn't kill your wife.'"

Butler said Wade's denial did not come as a shock; Butler had heard rumors that Wade had confessed to his wife's murder from friends with whom he worked.

"One of the guys knew Josh Wade," Butler said. "And we were talking one day, and he said, 'Man, I think Josh Wade killed your wife.' And I said, 'Why do you say that?' And he said, 'Cause I knew Josh in jail, and he had told me he killed someone.'"

"So how did you respond when Wade said this to you?" I asked.

"I said, 'That's not what I heard.' You know, cause I had a lot of family in jail at that time. And they knew Josh Wade, and he thought something was going to happen to him.'"

"Did you believe him?" I asked.

"I didn't know. I didn't know he had done all these other murders at the time."

Michelle Foster Butler was found stabbed to death just after midnight on September 26, 1999, on East 10th Avenue, in Fairview, a neighborhood southeast of downtown Anchorage. She had been stabbed at least ten times and, unlike the other murdered women, Michelle was not heavily intoxicated at the time of her death. She had defensive wounds that indicated she had tried to fight off her attacker. Family members said the thirty-eight-year-old mother of three was likely walking home from a nearby grocery store called Carrs, a trip she made frequently, although police never recovered a purse, wallet, or any purchased items from the scene. According to Claude, Michelle was bipolar and occasionally wandered off, which was partially why her family didn't immediately report her missing and why her body went unidentified for two days. Claude was in jail and unable to keep tabs on his wife and to remind her to take her meds; it also was homecoming weekend, which meant the couple's teenaged daughter, Jelila, was spending the weekend at a friend's. Their youngest child, six-year-old Jelil, was being cared for by other family members and the couple's oldest son, Rahim, twenty, had recently left Alaska to attend college in Oregon.

On Monday, two days after the murder, Jelila went to the Fairview Rec Center, as was her usual routine, where her mother would come to pick up her and her little brother after school. By five o'clock in the afternoon, her mother still hadn't arrived, and at about this same time, a friend of Jelila's ran into the gym in a hysterical state. Thinking the girl was having boy trouble, Jelila followed.

"What's wrong?" Jelila asked the girl, prepared to console her friend. At first, the girl was crying too hard to respond, but finally she was able to get out the words, "Your mom."

"What about her?" Jelila asked, taken aback.

"She's been stabbed," the girl replied, sobbing.

Jelila panicked. "Well, let's go to the hospital," she stammered.

"She's dead!" the girl wailed.

Frantic, Jelila found her little brother, who was at the rec center playing basketball, took him by the hand and headed to a friend's house around the corner, where there were adults who she thought may know what had happened. There, she was shown a brief article from that morning's *Anchorage Daily News*, which had described a homicide:

> Police described the victim as having short hair pulled back in a short ponytail and tied with a blue-green band. She had a mole on the lid of her left eye and wore distinctive nail polish: green with yellow and black designs on her fingers and black with white marks on her toes. And she wore a red San Francisco 49ers sweatshirt over a plaid T-shirt, black stretch pants and black flip-flop sandals with yellow thongs.

As soon as she read the description, Jelila knew that her mother was dead. Her mom always had her nails painted in various colors and had just had them done with yellow and black designs. Jelila was overwhelmed by shock and grief, but with her father behind bars and a six-year-old brother to care for, at fourteen she felt the premature weight of adulthood suddenly on her shoulders.

"I planned her funeral and even chose what she wore in the casket," Jelila told me. "I literally did everything. I did everything but pay for the service."

Jelila also had to break the news to her older brother and console her younger brother, for whom she felt an overwhelming maternal responsibility.

"He was like the kid I never had," Jelila recalled. "And he was angry. Extremely angry. He had good days when everything would be okay, but when something went wrong, if he got trouble or something, he would just shut down completely."

Jelila's younger brother, Jelil Abdul Bassit, who was just six years old when his mother was killed, became a star basketball player at the University of Oregon.[83] His success in Division I basketball and in the national spotlight is tempered by the constant reminder of his mother's untimely death.

"It still affects me to this day," Jelil told a reporter at *The Oregonian* newspaper. "It affected the whole family. I grew up fast."[84]

"They are strong kids," Claude Butler told me of his three children. "But it's hard to grow up without a mother. It's painful, every anniversary. Her birthday, the day she got

83 Claude Butler and Michelle Foster Butler converted to Islam before marrying and gave Islamic last names to their children but never legally changed their own last names.

84 This quote is from an article written by Tyson Alger which appeared in *The Oregonian* on February 21, 2015.

killed. We always connect on those days. But you know, I told my kids, this is something that you'll never get over but you have to learn how to deal with it."

Over the years, there have been a few leads in Michelle's case, but none has panned out. Early on, police suspected a man whom officers had stopped the night of Michelle's murder; he was driving through Fairview, and when officers pulled him over for speeding, they noticed he was covered in a fair amount of blood. The man denied having anything to do with a homicide and claimed he had just been injured and robbed. Police confiscated his car and after testing the blood for traces of Michelle's DNA, the man was cleared as a suspect. Then in 2004, prompted by an anonymous tip, police announced they were investigating three unnamed men as suspects in Michelle's murder, who were apparently involved in drug activity in Fairview. Despite the lead, police never made any arrests.

Although he expressed frustration with the Anchorage Police Department, Claude Butler has resigned himself to the possibility he will never know why his wife died.

"She was my girl, and we were married for nineteen years. Sometimes I beat myself up, you know, if I was there it wouldn't have happened. But that's not true, not true. Cause when it's your time to go, it's your time, no matter what. I'm Muslim, and I believe it didn't matter if I was in jail or outa jail … it was written already that that's when she was gonna die."

Jelila, on the other hand, has questions she would still like answered. Her mother's tragic death coupled with her father's frequent incarcerations for selling drugs, had prompted her to pursue a collegiate degree in criminal justice. When we spoke in the fall of 2015, she was working as a family services specialist in Las Vegas, helping children in abusive situations. Jelila told me she had learned to live with the loss of her mother but had also accepted that it was a wound from which she may never fully heal.

"You know, she's gone. She's not coming back. What happened … or how it happened … or why it happened … is small compared to the fact that she's not here. There might not be a good explanation, but I'd still like to know why it happened."

Jelila told me she is nagged by suspicions that her mother may have died at the hands of Joshua Wade.

"It just so happens that one of my friends who I grew up with, when I told him about Joshua Wade he was like, 'You don't remember him? He used to hang out in Fairview,' which was the neighborhood where my mother was killed. He said that [Wade] used to hang around there because he was always trying to fit in with certain kids."

Jelila said another friend had told her that she attended a vocational high school with Wade. The friend, who was seventeen and pregnant at the time, had apparently been threatened by Wade during a gym class.

"And he got mad at her over a game that they were playing and threatened her with a pole or something. He actually threatened to kill her."

In January of 2015, Jelila decided to write to Wade at the federal prison where he was being held in Pennsylvania. In her letter, she said that although it had been fifteen years since her mother's death, her family still had no closure. She asked Wade if he had killed her mother and assured him she wasn't reaching out because she wanted him to be punished even more.

"I mean, you can't punish a man who's already spending his life in prison. He's got to deal with a higher power when it comes his time. But if I knew it was [Wade], if he could just admit that, I'm sure that would help us in some kind of way."

She is still waiting for a response.

FIFTY-FOUR

In March of 2015, Joshua Wade wrote to me from his prison cell at a maximum security federal penitentiary in Waymart, Pennsylvania. He was responding to a number of letters I had written to him inquiring about the unsolved cases of Vera Hapoff, Annie Mann, and Michelle Foster Butler. He did not return my first few letters but was apparently motivated to respond when I had raised questions about his childhood and statements his father had made to me during our interview in Seattle. At the top of the letter Wade wrote the following disclaimer:

> *Nothing in this letter is for public viewing and or publishing. I am attempting to reserve my right to privacy. So, have the decency to respect this.*

Without divulging details from his letter, I feel obliged to share that Wade proposed a legal arrangement requiring me to sign a contract—which he said he would have drawn up by his attorneys—promising to tell only the truth and not to misrepresent the events of his childhood. In return, he promised to disclose "other crimes" he had committed. I responded to his letter, saying I was, indeed, committed to the truth, but that I had no intention of signing any such contract:

Please understand that as a journalist, I cannot enter into any kind of legal agreement with those I write about. This is a standard ethical practice and it exists to protect the integrity of the writing, and my integrity as well. I can, however, assure you that I am not out to lie or to misrepresent you or your childhood, or any of your acts. You have my word that I am committed to telling the truth.

Wade clearly wanted control of the narrative. For that reason, I doubted I would hear from him again. He had confessed to the murders of the three men only in an attempt to gain a transfer out of Alaska. This time, what did he have to gain?

In 2011, furious that he had not immediately received the transfer out of Alaska he had sought, Wade had meticulously handwritten more than a dozen pages of legal motions, alleging that prosecutors had gone back on their promise:

My whole purpose for bringing a murder charge to state court instead of remaining solely in federal custody was due to verbal assurances that I would not serve a day of my 99 year sentence in Alaska.

Claiming that "years in the media spotlight" had made him a target of the "gossip committees," Wade said he wished to be incarcerated in a place "where [he'd] just be a number."

"I'll never be just that in the Alaska system," Wade asserted. Wade claimed he never would have agreed to pleading guilty to Mindy Schloss's murder had he expected to serve the rest of his life in solitary confinement within Alaska.

"I would rather be sentenced to lethal injection than be kept in Alaska," he wrote.

Even if Wade had received such "verbal assurances" from prosecutors as he claimed, nothing was ever put in writing and the federal government had no legal obligation to move him from the Spring Creek Correctional facility in Seward, Alaska, where he was being held in segregation and under maximum security. However, in June of 2014, after confessing to the murders of three men, Wade finally got his wish and was transferred to a federal penitentiary in Terre Haute, Indiana.

Wade's wish to live among other inmates in the general population, however, would not be realized. Classified as "an escape risk, or as one of the most assaultive, predatory, riotous or seriously disruptive prisoners," Wade was kept in solitary confinement, permitted only one hour per day to exit his eighty-square-foot cell to exercise.[85]

The feds had reason, they claimed, to keep other inmates out of Wade's reach. Robert Palmquist, the warden of the federal detention center in Seattle, where Wade had served time in 2008 and 2009, cited Wade's history of violent outbursts:

Inmate Wade continues to display a poor attitude and difficulty controlling his temper. He frequently erupts with rage during phone calls, yelling so loudly that his conversation is unavoidably overheard by staff and other inmates. Recently, inmate Wade continued to display inappropriate behavior when during a telephonic court hearing he held the telephone receiver over the toilet in his cell, when unnecessarily flushing the toilet.

Prison officials also said they had placed Wade in the

85 This quote is from a ruling issued by Superior Court Judge Patrick J. McKay on November 15, 2011.

SHU—Special Housing Unit—for the protection of other inmates, citing two prior assaults. The first occurred in August of 2008 at the federal detention center in Seattle. An incident report submitted by prison guards recounted a dispute between Wade and another inmate named Shaun Raffie that ended with Wade choking and threatening to kill him. According to an inmate who had witnessed the altercation, the dispute had something to do with Wade's murder case:

> Josh had inmate Raffie up against the wall in a one-arm choke hold with his left hand while his right hand was balled in a fist. Josh yelled at Raffie, "Go to sleep! Go to sleep!" Josh told Raffie stuff about his case, and he was scared Shaun would repeat it.

At first, Wade denied that he had choked Raffie but eventually admitted to the assault, saying, "I was very stressed and just lost it. I am looking at a lot of charges and having girl trouble. I will not do anything else, and I'm sorry for what I did."

The second alleged assault was sexual in nature, and the victim was an inmate referred to in court documents as B.F.S., a petite Native Alaskan man who suffered from Fetal Alcohol Syndrome. The condition caused a host of physical and mental impairments for B.F.S., rendering him vulnerable to attacks by other inmates. In a civil complaint filed on behalf of B.F.S. against the Bureau of Prisons for failing to adequately protect him from such attacks and sexual advances, B.F.S. was described as "[having] low intelligence and easily manipulated by other inmates through the use of fear or trickery."

On May 30, 2009, Wade allegedly invited B.F.S. into his cell, and then forced B.F.S. to perform oral sex, and threatened to kill him if he refused. After the assault, Wade allegedly told B.F.S. to keep quiet about what had happened, or "[B.F.S.] would never see his wife or children again." Despite this, B.F.S. later passed a note to a prison guard, recounting what had happened.

When confronted by a prison official, Wade denied the assault and demanded to speak to his attorney.

"I don't force men to suck my dick," Wade told the officer. "That's nasty."[86]

****

Just days after Wade wrote his letter to me, he was transferred to a high security prison in Beaumont, Texas. Months went by, and I didn't hear anything from Wade. Making sure to exhaust all options, I wrote to the warden in Beaumont to officially request an interview with Wade, explaining that I was a journalist writing a book about a series of crimes in Anchorage. On November 19, 2015, I received a letter denying the request "for reasons of institution security and the inmate's safety."

Wade's older sister, Mandy, told me she hadn't heard from him in more than a year but said she knew that he remained in solitary confinement.

"It's got to make you insane," Mandy said. "To be by yourself for that long, for ten years. That's got to make you crazy."

Mandy said she was not surprised to learn that her brother had recently admitted to three additional murders. In fact, she confessed that as a teenager Josh told her that he had murdered a clerk at a convenience store.

---

86 The quotes from both Wade and B.F.S. appear in an incident report filed by prison officials.

"Of course he was a teenager so I was thinking, *whatever*, you know, *you liar. Yeah right, Josh. Whatever.* But knowing what I know now, I'm like, oh my God, he was telling the truth."

Wade's description of the murder of a convenience store clerk did not jibe with any of the recent killings to which he had confessed, prompting Mandy to wonder if it was just one more murder her brother had committed, which had eluded police.

Mandy stressed to me again that she still loves and supports her brother. At the same time, she remains convinced that he has, indeed, killed others.

"In my heart, I really believe that there are more victims," she said.

"Why do you think that?" I asked.

"I just think he was never caught. I don't know, I mean, to find out that he killed three more people, you know, I don't think that's it. He's still hiding stuff."

EPILOGUE

Although Joshua Wade has spent almost a decade behind bars, his evil acts continue to have repercussions in many people's lives. The FBI is confident Wade has killed at least five people and we can speculate about at least a few other unsolved crimes, but the true number of his victims reaches into the dozens. That's because murder is never just a solitary act; the consequences for the victim's loved ones often play out in the most unfortunate and tragic of ways for years following the crime.

Most of these additional victims are people Wade never even knew. Della Brown's grandchildren, for example, are now growing up without their grandmother. Della's siblings, who were just getting to know her, will never have the chance to develop full and satisfying relationships with their sister. Gerri Yett now faces the prospect of retiring and growing old without her best friend and companion, Mindy Schloss. Robert Conway and Kathy Hodges continue on in life without the friendship and affection of a woman they both deeply loved. The families of John Michael Martin and Henry Ongtowasruk are left to make sense of their unresolved murders, destined to never fully understand how two such harmless men fell prey to a violent predator. The children of Michelle Foster-Butler—if she is, indeed, another of Wade's victims—are each, in their own way, continuing to cope with the loss of their mother, a wound inflicted upon them at the most vulnerable of ages, and one they have carried into adulthood.

Wade's own family also continues to suffer. His sister Mandy struggles to reconcile the love she feels for her brother with the unfathomable cruelty of his crimes. Wade's father, although far from a sympathetic character, lives with a torturous sense of guilt and regret.

For those closest to the victims, the void created by their sudden and unexpected absence is profound. No one truly overcomes such a loss. When a murder happens, those left behind are forced to find the courage to go on living, to find a source of strength somewhere from deep within. They struggle to trudge through the sorrow and to rise again. Sometimes, the darkness is too much to overcome.

Before my first meeting with Daisy Piggott, I had been warned by Desa Jacobsson and by three of Daisy's children that she was in a fragile state. The guilt Daisy felt for abandoning her daughter as a girl had proved debilitating and ultimately, insurmountable. She still felt responsible somehow for all of the turmoil in her daughter's life, and she continued to blame herself for Della's death. The feeling had so overwhelmed Daisy that during the summer of 2014, a few months prior to our meeting, she attempted suicide. Gloria Durham, one of Daisy's daughters, told me that Daisy had downed a bottle of antidepressants, an entire bottle of Tylenol, and two fifths of whiskey.

"When I got [to the hospital] she was hooked up to every machine possible," Gloria recalled. "I would talk to her, and tears would come out. I don't know if she heard anything I said."

Much to her family's relief, Daisy recovered. About five months later, on a day in November, we spoke on the phone, and she told me that some days were better than others. At times, she felt like talking, and on other occasions, she felt like shutting out the world.

"Today is a good day," she said. "Why don't you come over now?"

I drove from the bed-and-breakfast in downtown Anchorage where I was staying to the trailer park where Daisy lived, on the eastern side of town. It was a bitterly cold and snowy day, and when I arrived, Daisy came to the door and quickly ushered me inside. She introduced her husband, Kenneth, who was in the living room reading the newspaper, and who, she explained, had recently suffered a stroke. Daisy and I entered the den, where sunlight streamed through yellow and red curtains, creating a soft, golden glow in the room.

"I hope you don't mind if I smoke," Daisy said, sitting down and lighting the first of several cigarettes.

Daisy is a diminutive woman, and her voice has the pitch and timbre of a child's. She has thinning gray hair (she explained she suffered from alopecia) and wore moccasin-type boots lined with fur, black pants, and a blue sweatshirt with wolves embroidered on the front. During our conversation, she was at times animated and at other moments in despair. She readily admitted that she was battling depression, and a couple of times she wept openly.

"For the first two or three years, I couldn't say, 'He killed Della.' Because at that point, I didn't want to accept that he did. So you go through a lot of stages. Now I can say he's a murderer. He killed my daughter. My first born."

Daisy admitted that on a day in June, she had experienced an emotional breakdown. She said the ordeal had given her insight into what Della must have felt just prior to her death.

"She was in an abusive relationship. I think it was her way of self-medicating. I can see it because I'm ..." Daisy paused and then began to cry. "I almost killed myself. I almost succeeded. So I know how powerful depression is."

Depression, fueled by guilt, had driven Daisy to her

lowest point. She couldn't seem to talk herself out of being responsible for all of Della's misfortunes.

"I know logically it isn't my fault," Daisy said, tears streaming down her face. "Even if I was here in Alaska, [Della's murder] could have happened. But you can't convince me. I know you can't go back. You can't make it all right, and I tried. I tried so hard."

At Della's funeral, Daisy had connected with Della's daughter Nora, who was adopted more than thirty years prior by a couple in the village of Shishmaref, Alaska. Nora's adoptive parents had made the 600-mile drive south so that Nora could attend her biological mother's funeral. Since then, Daisy had stayed in touch with Nora and even made a trip to Shishmaref to become acquainted with Nora's three boys. Daisy got up from her chair, disappeared into a back room, and returned with photos of her three great grandsons.

"We are a family now," she said proudly, showing me the snapshots of the boys. "So not everything was bad that came out of it. There were lots of struggles, sure, but those little bitty ones, that's what you live for."

I asked Daisy how Della's son was doing. She explained that Robert, who was eighteen when his mother was killed, had been battling drug and alcohol addictions.

"He's had his problems, but he's starting to mend," she said. A stern look came over Daisy's face.

"Unfortunately, the perp never has just one victim. He has a *whole slew* of victims," she said. "It's like a tidal wave. One little drop, there's the body," Daisy said, descending an index finger in the center of an imaginary circle. "But then, you're affecting the friends, family members, in this case, a whole community," she said, holding out both of her palms.

Daisy said that one of her sisters, who is a devout Christian, had been urging her to forgive Joshua Wade.

"At that time, I was seeing a psychologist. And I was

breaking down, crying all the time, making all kinds of noise with my sobbing. And I asked my psychologist, 'Am I now crazy? Have I finally met crazy? Am I getting lost?' And that was scary. What I realized is that I don't have to forgive. All I have to do is remember to breathe. And if I want to, down the road, I will. But in my heart, no, I can't. Not now, and I may not ever. But that's my choice. It's something I have to live with."

Daisy's daughter Gloria had told me she and her siblings worried that Daisy might attempt suicide again. Daisy said she was getting a handle on her depression and grief, and she was in a better place. As for whether Wade should have been given the death penalty, Daisy said she was never ambivalent.

"Death was too easy. This way, he has to live, and he's quite young. He has to wake up to whatever size his cell is and remember why he's there." Raising her voice and speaking more deliberately, Daisy added, "I like where he is. Because he's paying for it every day of his life, until he dies. And he'll never get out of prison, ever."

As we finished our conversation, I asked Daisy why she agreed to talk to me. She said that talking about Della was cathartic.

"This is kind of a healing," she explained. "You don't realize that's what I'm doing right now, but it is. Also, my daughter doesn't have a voice. So I will always be her voice. And I didn't want Wade to have the last word."

"What do you want the last word to be?" I asked.

"That he didn't get away with it. And this is my way of saying she lives *here*," Daisy said, bringing her right hand to the center of her chest. She pinned her shoulders back and let out a long sigh.

"Now," Daisy said. "Can you drive me down the street to get some cigarettes?"

"Sure," I replied.

It was snowing as we left the trailer, and the afternoon sun was just slipping from view. Daisy shifted her face toward the day's last light, as a flock of migrating birds crossed the sky in a V-formation, instinct guiding them toward a warmer horizon, their wings beating madly against the wind.

ACKNOWLEDGMENTS

I am indebted to a host of people for their help throughout the process of researching, writing and editing this book. First, I would like to thank the families and friends of the victims. When asked to recall the most painful moments of their pasts, they demonstrated a courage and resilience for which I have the deepest respect. Desa Jacobsson convinced me that this was a story worth telling, and her constant encouragement was a godsend.

I would like to express my thanks to Matt Kreamer for his careful judgment and insight editing the manuscript, and for his enduring friendship. I am also grateful to Andrea Ferak for her edits, and to Steve Jackson and Michael Cordova for bringing me on board at WildBlue Press, and for their confidence in me and in this book. I also would like to thank my dear friend Stacey Toyoaki for her sound legal advice.

I am indebted to the other journalists, both from print and TV, who covered various aspects of these cases, and who provided a vital context to this narrative. I am particularly grateful to reporters from the *Anchorage Daily News* and KTVA.

Angela Bell in the Public Affairs Office at the F.B.I. helped me tremendously in setting up interviews with the case agents, and Special Agent Jolene Goeden was more than generous with her time and in providing me much of the case evidence and background.

I am grateful to Kelley Robinson at the Anchorage

courthouse, who always received my numerous requests for more files and transcripts with a smile. Pam Perrenoud, who now works in the D.C. area for the F.B.I., was generous with her insights and patient with my repeated questions.

While in Alaska, Jonathan White and Anne Ducey White, and their lovely daughters Julia, Rachael and Carleigh, made sure I had my regular fill of the most excellent coffee in the state, (*SteamDot Coffee*), treated me to a standout performance of *the Nutcracker,* and were kind enough to share their Thanksgiving Day table. Their friendship was a welcome refuge during those dark weeks of winter I spent in Anchorage.

My dear friend and partner-in-crime Julia Madden patiently trudged through various drafts of this manuscript, adding insights and improvements, as did my brother and confidant, Matthew Francis. Pat Umberger, Diane Dwyer, Kathy Hendricks and Henry Lee also deserve my thanks. Others likely are unaware of their contributions: Karen Inderlied, who in ninth grade gave me a book of Langston Hughes poems, helped me realize that I was a writer; Ellen Geisler extended not only her vast knowledge of literature, but her friendship to me during one of the most difficult periods of my life; Poet Connie Hales taught me to value the power and sound of each word I put to the page; and Mary Karr, who taught my first collegiate writing workshop at Syracuse University, showed me that writing was a way to make sense of an often cruel world, a lesson I have taken with me into every true crime story about which I have written.

Finally, my partner, Antoine, was unwavering in his love and support during the writing of this book, as were my two beloved dogs, Gracie and Cooper, who often slept at my feet as I typed these words.

Use this link to sign up for advance notice
of new books from Monte Francis.
http://wildbluepress.com/AdvanceNotice

Word-of-mouth is critical to an author's long-term success.
If you appreciated this book please leave a review on the
Amazon sales page:
http://wbp.bz/iceandbonereviews

WILDBLUE
P R E S S

AVAILABLE NOW FROM WILDBLUE
PRESS
SMOOTH TALKER
Trail of Death

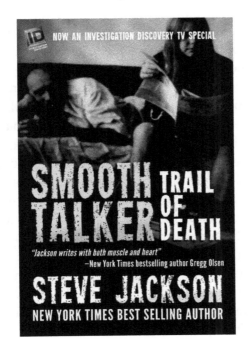

Smooth Talker by Steve Jackson
http://wbp.bz/smoothtalker
www.WildBluePress.com

SMOOTH TALKER: Trail of Death
by STEVE JACKSON

In July 1974, Anita Andrews, the owner and bartender at Fagiani's Bar in Napa, California was found one morning in her bar raped, beaten, strangled and murdered. She'd befriended a stranger that night, but no one knew if he did it, and he'd disappeared. A month later, young Michele Wallace, was driving down a road in the mountains near Crested Butte, Colorado, when she gave two stranded motorists, Chuck Matthews and a man named Roy, a ride. Dropping Matthews off at a bar, she agreed to take "Roy" to his truck. She was never seen alive again. The trail for her killer grew cold. Fourteen years later, Charlotte Sauerwin, engaged to be married soon, met a smooth-talking man at a Laundromat in Livingston, Parish, Louisiana. The next evening, her body was found in the woods; she'd been raped and her throat slashed. But like the other two women above, her killer had simply disappeared. In fact, not until the early 1990s, when a Gunnison County sheriff's investigator Kathy Young started looking into the still-unsolved Wallace Case, would a single name eventually be linked to the murder of all three women. That name was Roy Melanson, a serial rapist considered to be a prime suspect in the rape and murder of several other women as well. Smooth Talker is the story of Melanson, his depredations and the intrepid police work that went into bringing him to justice.

Read More About SMOOTH TALKER At:
http://wbp.bz/smoothtalker
www.WildBluePress.com

WILDBLUE
P R E S S

FAILURE OF JUSTICE: THE TRUE
STORY OF AMERICA'S LARGEST
WRONGFUL CONVICTION CASE

Failure of Justice by John Ferak
http://wbp.bz/failureofjustice
www.WildBluePress.com

Feb. 5, 1985 marked one of the coldest nights on record that winter in small-town rural Nebraska. That chilly evening, tenants in one downtown three-story apartment building hunkered down for a night of restful sleep. The next day, they were horrified to see several police cars lined along North Sixth Street. A demented, dangerous predator had bound, raped and suffocated an older widow who lived in unit 4.

The local Beatrice police force made a gallant effort to identify the killer rapist who had been preying upon vulnerable older women since two summers ago. A specially trained FBI profiler, Peter Klismet Jr. was flown into Nebraska to determine the killer's traits. After all, victim Helen Wilson was one of her tight-knit town's nicest ladies. She enjoyed bingo. She babysat the children at her Methodist church. Who want to harm her, everyone wondered?

At the time of the revolting murder, Gage County hog farmer Burt Searcey was three years removed from the Beatrice police force. He quickly became obsessed with solving the gruesome murder after the sickening news was broadcast on the local radio. Years later, as a county sheriff's deputy, Searcey arrested six lost souls for the terrorizing rape and murder. All six of the codefendants went convicted and sentenced to prison in 1990.

Then in 2008, the Nebraska Attorney General's Office faced a conundrum. One of the accused, Joseph White was fighting for a chance to allow DNA testing. Would the DNA tests cement his guilt or lead to a shocking new revelation: Helen Wilson's twisted rapist and killer was still out there somewhere, waiting to be identified?

Read More About FAILURE OF JUSTICE At:
http://wbp.bz/failureofjustice
www.WildBluePress.com

More True Crime You'll Love
From WildBlue Press.

Learn more at: http://wbp.bz/tc

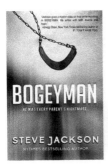 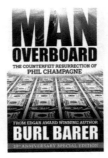 

  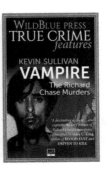

www.WildBluePress.com

More Mysteries/Thrillers You'll Love From WildBlue Press.

Learn more at: http://wbp.bz/cf

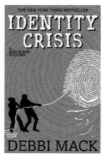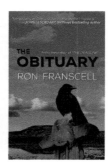

www.WildBluePress.com

Go to WildBluePress.com to sign up for our newsletter!

By subscribing to our newsletter you'll get *advance notice* of all new releases as well as notifications of all special offers. And you'll be registered for our monthly chance to win a **FREE collection of our eBooks and/or audio books** to some lucky fan who has posted an honest review of our one of our books/eBooks/audio books on Amazon, Itunes and GoodReads.

Let Someone Else Do The Reading.
Enjoy One Of Our Audiobooks

Learn more at: http://wbp.bz/audio

**Please feel free to check out more True CRIME books
by our friends at**

www.RJPARKERPUBLISHING.com

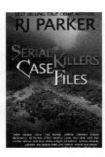

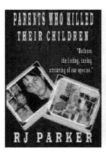

Lightning Source UK Ltd.
Milton Keynes UK
UKHW02f2045280618
324951UK00017B/495/P